Natural Law

Ethics, Metaphy
Work of Germain Grisez

Natural Law and Moral Inquiry

Ethics, Metaphysics, and Politics in the Work of Germain Grisez

EDITED BY

Robert P. George

GEORGETOWN UNIVERSITY PRESS / WASHINGTON, D.C.

Georgetown University Press, Washington, D.C.
© 1998 by Georgetown University Press. All rights reserved.
Printed in the United States of America

10 9 8 7 6 5 4 3 2 1   1998

THIS VOLUME IS PRINTED ON ACID-FREE OFFSET BOOK PAPER

Library of Congress Cataloging-in-Publication Data

Natural law and moral inquiry : ethics, metaphysics, and politics in
  the work of Germain Grisez / edited by Robert P. George ; with a
  response by Germain Grisez and Joseph M. Boyle, Jr.
      p. cm.
    1. Grisez, Germain Gabriel, 1929–   . 2. Christian ethics—
  Catholic authors. 3. Christian ethics—History—20th century.
  4. Catholic Church—Doctrines—History—20th century. I. George,
  Robert P.
  BJ1249.N39   1998
  241′.042′092—dc21
  ISBN 0-87840-673-5 (cloth)
  ISBN 0-87840-674-3 (pbk.)   97-37975

Contents

Introduction

For more than thirty years, Germain Grisez's writings have generated intense controversy among Catholic moral philosophers and theologians. Grisez's theory of practical reasoning and morality has won the allegiance of a number of influential Catholic moralists, such as John Finnis, William E. May, and Gerard Bradley. At the same time, it has drawn criticism from natural law theorists committed to neo-scholastic methods, such as Ralph McInerny and Henry Veatch, on the one hand, and from proportionalist critics of traditional approaches to Catholic moral theology, such as Richard McCormick, Charles Curran, and Edward Vacek, on the other.

Neo-scholastic philosophers object to Grisez's claim that the most basic principles of practical reason and moral judgment cannot be inferred from metaphysical or other speculative premises. In their view, this claim compromises Grisez's commitment to "objectivism" in ethics and renders his theory of practical reasoning unacceptably "Kantian" or even "Humean." At the same time, proportionalist philosophers and theologians—some of whom accept (in substance) Grisez's theory of first practical principles—argue that Grisez's view of moral reasoning rests on an implausible theory of human action and, as a result, fails to escape the "legalism" of which Grisez has rightly been critical in his writings on neo-scholastic natural law theory.

Even Grisez's most vigorous critics, however, acknowledge the significance of his philosophical achievement and the centrality of his thinking to the contemporary debate among Catholic moralists. Furthermore, over the past decade or so Grisez's thought, as mediated through Finnis's writings on natural law as well as through Grisez's collaborative writings with Finnis and Joseph M. Boyle, Jr., has attracted attention from notable philosophers outside the Catholic academy. Many secular thinkers have evinced interest in the question whether Grisez and his collaborators have managed to devise a viable nonintuitionist alternative to the consequentialist and contractarian theories that have dominated secular moral philosophy for several generations.

The essays presented in this volume, together with the Reply by Grisez and Boyle, will, then, be of interest to people of widely divergent backgrounds, interests, and philosophical and theological commitments. They represent a spectrum of viewpoints, ranging from William May's sympathetic exposition and defense of Grisez's teaching on natural and Christian moral principles and norms, to Benedict Ashley's sharply critical treatment of the scriptural basis of Grisez's work in moral theology. Ralph McInerny carefully defends the neo-scholastic account of the relationship of practical and theoretical reasoning which Grisez and his supporters reject. Edward Vacek offers a thoughtful proportionalist critique of Grisez's famous argument for the immorality of contraception.

From a more sympathetic perspective, Gerard Bradley criticizes Grisez's claim that capital punishment is necessarily "direct," and hence wrongful, killing; and Kevin Flannery proposes some revisions of Grisez's important "retorsive" argument in defense of metaphysical free choice. Patrick Lee, taking Grisez's powerful case against body-soul substance dualism as his point of departure, presents a highly original argument for the unity of the human agent from a "third-person" perspective. If sound, Lee's argument defeats the familiar Humean claim that the person is not a substance, but merely a set of experiences united by psychological factors such as memory. John Finnis argues that Grisez's understanding of the common good of political society as instrumental, rather than intrinsic, is not so alien to the thought of St. Thomas Aquinas as Grisez and his critics have supposed. Finnis's work has profound implications not merely for scholars interested in the authentic interpretation of Aquinas, but for anyone concerned properly to understand the nature of the political common good.

The volume closes with an Afterword by Russell Shaw on Grisez's pioneering role in the renewal of Catholic moral theology in the wake of the Second Vatican Council. Shaw, who has collaborated with Grisez to make his work in moral philosophy and theology accessible to nonprofessionals, deploys his estimable talents as a journalistic writer to give readers a vivid sense of the personality of Germain Grisez.

Robert P. George

Acknowledgments

The editor is grateful to David R. Oakley and Gregory Sullivan for valuable editorial assistance, and to the Homeland Foundation for generous financial support.

PART ONE

Ethics

Germain Grisez on Moral Principles and Moral Norms: Natural and Christian

WILLIAM E. MAY
Michael J. McGivney Professor of Moral Theology
John Paul II Institute for Studies on Marriage and Family

Here I propose to examine the thought of Germain Grisez on two important issues. The first is of critical importance in natural law theory and concerns the movement from the first principles of natural law to specific moral norms. The second is a matter heatedly debated among Catholic moral theologians today, namely, the specificity of Christian morality and, in particular, whether or not there are any moral norms specific to Christian morality in addition to moral norms pertaining to natural law. The two issues, as will be seen, are closely related. My thesis is that Grisez has made a significant contribution to understanding both issues. I also hold, as I hope to show, that the teaching of Pope John Paul II in his encyclical *Veritatis splendor* is relevant to both these topics and lends support to Grisez's thought.

THE MOVEMENT FROM NATURAL LAW PRINCIPLES TO SPECIFIC MORAL NORMS

The Teaching of St. Thomas

To provide a context for Grisez's understanding of the movement from natural law principles to specific moral norms, I will first summarize the position of St. Thomas with respect to it.

In several important texts (*Summa Theologiae*, I–II, q.100.a.1, a.3, and a.11) St. Thomas maintains that there are three interrelated "grades" or "levels" of natural law "precepts." The first "grade" consists of "certain naturally known principles" (q.100.a.1),[1] the "first or common" precepts of natural law (q.100.a.3),[2] its "most certain . . . precepts" (q.100.a.11).[3] "No 'edition' of these precepts is necessary save insofar as they are, as it were, inscribed in natural reason as self-evidently known" (q.100.a.3)[4]; indeed, these "most certain [precepts] are so evident that they need no 'edition'" (q.100.a.11).[5]

The second "grade" of natural law precepts embraces specific moral norms concerned with matters that "are so manifest in human actions that they can immediately, with but little consideration, be approved of or repudiated in the light of those common and first principles" (q.100.a.1).[6] These precepts are concerned with actions "which of itself the natural reason of every person immediately judges must be done or not done" (q.100.a.1).[7] St. Thomas affirms that the moral precepts of the Decalogue belong to this second grade of natural law precepts. These precepts "are those which can immediately, with little consideration, be known from the common principles," and the "first and common precepts are contained in them just as principles are contained in their proximate conclusions" (q.100.a.3).[8] Although these precepts are "more determined" (*magis determinata*) than the first and common principles of natural law, nonetheless "anyone, even an ordinary person, can easily see" their truth (*rationem*). However, "because it happens that human judgment with respect to very few things of this kind can be overturned, precepts of this kind require 'edition'," and that is why God has made them known by promulgating the Decalogue (q.100.a.11).[9]

The third grade of natural law precepts is made up of moral precepts concerning actions "for whose judgment much consideration of different circumstances is required, and to do this with care is not for everyone, but for the wise." These precepts concern matters "which are judged necessary for observance by the more discriminating consideration of reason by those who are wise" (q.100.a.1).[10] These precepts are not included in the precepts of the Decalogue precisely because they are precepts "which are found to be in accordance with reason through the careful inquiry of the wise." They are contained in the precepts of the Decalogue "as conclusions are contained in their principles" (q.100.a.3).[11] These are precepts "whose meaning is not evident to everyone but only to the wise, and these are moral precepts added over and above the Decalogue" (q.100.a.11).[12]

As these texts clearly show, St. Thomas held that the first and common precepts of natural law—principles naturally known to everyone—serve as truths in light of which the truth of the specific moral norms found in the Decalogue can be shown, and that even the most ordinary individual is able to grasp the truth of the Decalogue's moral precepts by relating them to the first and common principles, although he grants that it is possible (particularly because of the reality of original sin and its consequences) for their truth to be obscured. For this reason God has deigned to make them known through divine revelation. St. Thomas further holds that the truth of more particular moral precepts (e.g., such norms as "Rise up before the hoary head" and "honor the person of the old," q.100.a.1)[13] can be shown in the light of the precepts of the Decalogue, which serve as premises for such more determinate moral norms.

But what are the *first and common principles* (q.100.a.1) of natural law, its *naturally known principles* (cf. q.100.a.3), its *most certain moral precepts* (q.100.a.11)?

In q.100.a.1, St. Thomas says that he had previously discussed these first and common principles, and editors of the *Summa theologiae* uniformly refer readers to St. Thomas's discussion in I–II.q.94.a.2 of the "precepts" or "principles" of natural law. In that article Thomas affirmed that the very first precept of natural law is the following: *good is to be done and pursued, and evil avoided (bonum est faciendum et prosequendum, et malum vitandum)*. He also said that on this precept are based all the other precepts of natural law, and further, that human practical reason "naturally grasps as good, and consequently to be pursued by action, all those things toward which man has a natural inclination, and that it grasps their contraries as evil and thus to be avoided."[14] Thomas identified certain forms of human flourishing—life itself, the union of male and female and the education of children, life in society with others and knowledge of the truth, especially the truth about God—as goods toward which man is naturally inclined and which, consequently, practical reason naturally apprehends as the goods to be pursued and their opposites as the evils to be avoided.

But do the first and common principles of natural law discussed in I–II.q.94.a.2, provide the sort of premises needed to show the truth of the specific moral norms or precepts of the Decalogue? It is not immediately evident that they do. Moreover, in q.95.a.2, Thomas said that the specific moral precept, "one ought not to kill," (*non esse occidendum*) is a conclusion that can be derived from the proposition (principle) that "evil is to be done to no one" (*nulli esse malum faciendum*) but this principle had not been identified by him in q.94.a.2 as one of the natural law's primary precepts. Even more significantly, in answering the first objection of q.100.a.3—concerning whether *all* the moral precepts of the Old Law could be reduced to the ten precepts of the Decalogue—St. Thomas said that the "first and principal precepts of the law" (*prima et principalia legis praecepta*)," namely, "you shall love the Lord your God" (*diliges Dominum Deum tuum*) and "you shall love your neighbor" (*diliges proximum tuum*), are the "first and common precepts of natural law" (*prima et communia praecepta legis naturalis*) and that "all the precepts of the decalogue are referred to these two as conclusions to their common principles" (*omnia praecepta decalogi ad illa duo referuntur sicut conclusiones ad principia communia*) (q.100.a.3.ad1). And in q.100.a.3, when speaking of the "most certain moral precepts" (*praecepta moralia . . . certissima*) of natural law, he gave as examples of these the "commandments regarding love of God and neighbor and others of this kind" (*mandata de dilectione Dei et proximi, et alia huiusmodi*). Finally, in answering the first objection to q.94.a.4, he said that the Golden Rule, or the precept "whereby one is commanded to do to another what he would have done to himself" (*quo quisque iubetur alii facere quod sibi vult fieri*) is also one of the first and common precepts or principles of natural law. It is highly important, it seems to me, to note that St. Thomas at least twice in these texts (q.100.a.3.ad1 and q.100.a.11) identifies the commands (precepts) to love God and neighbor as first and common precepts of natural law, as its most certain *moral precepts,* and as the principles to which the specific moral precepts of the Decalogue are to be referred as conclusions are referred to their common principles. In fact, he explicitly states that love of God and love of neighbor "are, as it were, the ends of the precepts" (*sunt quasi fines praeceptorum*) (q.100.a.11).

Thus, according to St. Thomas, the movement from the first principles of natural law to specific moral norms such as those found in the precepts of the Decalogue is roughly as follows: The highest *moral* principles of natural law are to love God and neighbor. But in addition to these highest moral principles, there are other first and common moral principles (*principia prima et communia*) of natural law, for St. Thomas explicitly says, after identifying the commands to love God and neighbor as the most certain moral principles of natural law, that there are "other commandments of this kind" (*alia mandata huiusmodi*; q.100.a.11), and in other texts, as we have seen, he names such moral principles as the Golden Rule (q.94.a.4.ad1) and the principle that "evil is to be done to no one" (*nulli esse malum faciendum:* q.95.a.2). Evidently, in the mind of St. Thomas, one can "immediately, with little consideration" (*subito, cum modica consideratione:* q.100.a.1; cf.q.100.a.3) grasp the truth of such specific moral norms as those found in the precepts of the Decalogue by appealing to these moral principles. Indeed, he believed that any man, even the most ordinary person (*popularis*) can easily grasp the truth of these specific moral precepts in light of these moral principles, of which the most important are the principles that we are to love God and neighbor.

The foregoing helps us see that St. Thomas included two sorts of universally true propositions of practical reason among the *prima et communia principia legis naturae*. The first sort—the sort of propositions explicitly taken up in *Summa theologiae* I–II.q.94.a.2—are principles of practical reasoning. These principles direct us to do and pursue the good and avoid its contrary, and they articulate the general determinations of human good by identifying some of the goods that are to be done and pursued (human life itself, the handing on and education of human life, knowledge of the truth, especially about God, life in fellowship with others—and, as St. Thomas himself explicitly says, there are other goods of this kind [*cetera huiusmodi;* q.94.a.2]). The other sort of *prima et communia principia legis naturae* concerns our way of pursuing these goods: we are to do so by acting fairly (the Golden Rule), by refusing to do evil to anyone, and above all by loving God and neighbor. This second sort of *prima et communia praecepta legis naturae* embraces the first principles of morality, that is, principles enabling us to distinguish between alternatives of choice that are morally good and alternatives of choice that are morally bad. And among these St. Thomas regards the principles directing us to love God and neighbor as the highest. In the light of these first moral principles, according to Thomas, we can grasp the truth of specific moral norms, norms such as those contained in the precepts of the Decalogue. Although St. Thomas himself never explicitly distinguishes between these two sorts of *prima et communia praecepta legis naturae*—principles of practical reasoning and principles of morality—the texts cited show that this kind of distinction seems warranted.

This is evidently the way in which St. Thomas sees the movement from the first moral principles of natural law to specific moral norms. Nonetheless, his thought on this matter is not rigorously ordered or very clear—undoubtedly, because he was writing in an age of faith, when his readers uniformly held, from their understanding of Scripture as proclaimed by the Church, that the highest moral norms are those of love of God and love of neighbor and that the Ten Commandments simply articulate the requirements of this love.

Still the problem, as an issue of natural law theory, remains: precisely how does one move from the *first* principles of natural law to such specific moral norms as those forbidding adultery or the intentional killing of innocent human persons? I now wish to examine Grisez's thought on this matter.

The Thought of Germain Grisez

First Principles of Practical Reasoning

Grisez clearly distinguishes between the first principles of practical reasoning and the first principles of morality. According to him, "practical reasoning has two phases: one concerned with what might be done [the principles of practical reasoning belong to this phase], the other with what ought to be done [the principles of morality belong to this phase]" (CMP, p. 178).[15] All people, whether good or bad, use the principles of the first phase of practical reasoning in considering what they might do.

With St. Thomas, Grisez identifies the first principle of practical reasoning (the first phase of practical reasoning) as the principle that "*the good is to be done and pursued: the bad is to be avoided (S.t. I–II.q.94.a.2).*" He continues by saying, "this is a directive for action, not a description of good and evil. 'Good' here means not only what is morally good but whatever can be understood as intelligibly worthwhile, while 'bad' refers to whatever can be understood as a privation of intelligible goods" (CMP, pp. 178–179). This first principle of practical reasoning "articulates the intrinsic, necessary relationship between human goods and appropriate actions bearing upon them (see *S.t.* I–II.q.94.a.2; cf. q.90.a.1; q.99.a.1; II–II.q.47.a.6)" (CMP, p. 180).[16]

Grisez maintains that this first principle of practical reasoning is specified—given its general determinations—by identifying the basic forms of human flourishing which are the goods that are to be pursued and done. St. Thomas had provided an illustrative, not taxative, list of such goods in *Summa theologiae* I–II.q.94.a.2. Grisez argues that there are eight such basic goods, which, when grasped by human practical reason, serve as principles of practical reasoning or starting points for considering what might be done.[17] Grisez's position on basic human goods has been the subject of much discussion (and misrepresentation). It is not however, of central concern in this paper.[18] I will turn, then, to his position on the first principle of morality and its specifications or "modes of responsibility."

The First Principle of Morality and Its Specification or "Modes of Responsibility"

The first principle of practical reasoning and its determinations are principles concerned with what might be done, that is, with intelligent, rational human behavior. These principles are used by all human persons, the morally bad as well as the morally upright. They do not enable us to determine which possibilities of human choice are morally good or morally bad; rather, as Grisez says, "they generate the field of possibilities in which choices are necessary" (CMP, p. 183).

St. Thomas, as we have seen, formulates the first principle of morality as the twofold command to love God and neighbor—the precepts of charity. However, as Grisez shows (CMP, pp. 183–184), Vatican Council II offered another basic formulation of the first principle of morality. In *Gaudium et spes*, this council affirmed that "the norm of human activity is this: that in accord with the divine plan and will, it should harmonize with the genuine good of the human race, and allow men as individuals and as members of society to pursue their total vocation and fulfill it" (*Gaudium et spes*, n. 35; cited by Grisez in CMP, p. 184).

It needs to be emphasized that Grisez (and his coworkers John Finnis and Joseph Boyle) in no way denigrate these ways of formulating the first principle of morality. Referring to the Thomistic formula (rooted in Scripture), namely, that we are to love God above all things and our neighbor as ourselves, they note that "for Jews and Christians, God is the supreme good and source of all goods." Thus "loving him requires the cherishing of all goods . . . [including] the basic human goods. . . . And loving one's neighbor as oneself at least excludes egoism and means accepting the fulfillment of others as part of one's own responsibility."[19] One loves one's neighbors by willing that the goods of human existence flourish in them. Grisez (and Finnis and Boyle) keenly recognize that Scripture's love commandments, which St. Thomas had identified as the "prima et principalia legis praecepta" (S.t., I–II.q.100.a.3.ad1), authentically express the basic or first principle of morality in religious language.

Grisez, moreover, says that "the functions of a first principle of morality are indicated by the formulations proposed by St. Thomas and Vatican II. It must provide the basis of guiding choices toward overall human fulfillment. As a single principle, it will give unity and direction to a morally good life. At the same time, it must not exclude ways of living which might contribute to a complete human community" (CMP, p. 184). Nonetheless, Grisez believes that these ways of formulating the first principle of morality "are not entirely satisfactory for purposes of ethical reflection and moral theology. To serve as a standard for practical judgment, a formulation must refer to the many basic human goods which generate the need for choice and moral guidance" (CMP, p. 184). It should do so because the function of the first principle of morality is to provide us with a criterion for distinguishing which alternatives of choice are morally good and which are morally bad. It is formulated more clearly and fully, Grisez maintains, when it is more closely related to the first principles of practical reasoning. When it is, it articulates "the integral directiveness of the first principles of practical reasoning, when they are working together harmoniously in full concert."[20]

Grisez thus holds that the basic principle of morality is better formulated as follows: "*In voluntarily acting for human goods and avoiding what is opposed to them, one ought to choose and otherwise will those and only those possibilities whose willing is compatible with a will toward integral human fulfillment*" (CMP, p. 184).

Formulating the first principle of morality in this way makes it clear that the fundamental attitude of one who wills to be a *morally good* person is that of a person who is eager to embrace, revere, and honor the real goods perfective of human persons and the persons in whom these goods are meant to flourish.[21] We are directed to these goods by the first principles of practical reasoning. A person about to choose in a morally good way is open to *all* the real goods perfective of human persons and listens to *all* the appeals they make through the principles of practical reasoning. A morally upright person is one whose practical reason is "unfettered" inasmuch as one is responsive to the "integral directiveness of all the first principles of practical reasoning."

It is essential to recognize that the "integral human fulfillment" to which we are directed by the first principle of morality is *not* itself a basic human good alongside of or in addition to the basic human goods already identified. Integral human fulfillment, while in no way individualistic self-fulfillment, is not "some sort of supergood transcending all other categories of goodness,"[22] or "some gigantic synthesis of goods in a vast state of affairs, such as might be projected as the goal of a worldwide billion-year plan."[23] Unlike basic human goods it is not a *reason* for acting, but an ideal whose attractiveness depends on *all* the goods that appeal to persons as reasons for acting. This ideal guides human persons by directing them "to avoid unnecessary limitation and so maintain openness to further goods" (CMP, p. 186). By doing so, the ideal of integral human fulfillment, while not itself a specific human good, constitutes the "object" of a good will and as such it "rectifies" the will. The will of a person committed to choosing and acting in accord with the requirements of integral human fulfillment is the will of a person inwardly disposed to choose well, to choose in accord with unfettered or "right" reason. It is the ideal of a community of all persons richly fulfilled in all goods, whose realization a virtuous or morally upright person wills.[24]

Note that Grisez's thought (and that of his colleagues Finnis and Boyle) is in perfect accord with St. Thomas's thought with regard to "unfettered" or "rectified" human practical reason. For St. Thomas the moral virtues inwardly dispose persons rightly toward the "ends" of human existence—toward the basic human *goods* perfective of them as individuals and as members of a community (see S.t., I–II.q.58.a.5, cf. q.58.a.3.ad2). For Grisez (Finnis and Boyle), the ideal of integral human fulfillment, proposed by the first principle of morality, is the "object" of unfettered or rectified human reason. It thus provides the criterion in terms of which moral virtues are intelligible, because moral virtues are dimensions of a person who is integrated with moral truth, that is, they are characteristics of a person committed to choose in accord with the requirements of integral human fulfillment.

Just as the first principle of practical reasoning—the good is to be done and pursued and the bad is to be avoided—is given its general determinations by identifying the basic forms of human flourishing as the goods that are to be pursued and done, so too, Grisez believes, can the first principle of morality be given its general determinations by identifying ways of choosing that, in fact, fail to honor and respect "integral human fulfillment," that is, the whole range of real goods perfective of human persons. It is necessary to provide these general specifications of the first principle of morality because by itself it is "too general to provide practical guidance." Its specifications, Grisez proposes, "must have a clear bearing on possible choices, so that the relationship—positive or negative—between the choices and integral human fulfillment will be clear" (CMP, p. 189).

St. Thomas included moral principles of this kind among the *prima et communia principia legis naturae*, for example, the Golden Rule (see S.t. I–II.q.94.a.4.ad1) and the normative principle "nulli esse malum faciendum" (q.95.a.2). Yet he surely did not attempt to provide a systematic, coherent identification of moral principles of this kind.

Grisez holds that the primary specifications of the first principle of morality "are intermediate principles which stand midway between the first principle and the completely specific norms which direct choices [e.g., one ought not intentionally to kill innocent human persons; one ought not to commit adultery, i.e., choose to have intercourse with someone other than his or her spouse]" (CMP, p. 189). He calls these intermediate moral principles " 'modes of responsibility,' because they shape willing in view of the moral responsibility inherent in it. The modes of responsibility," he continues, "specify—'pin down'—the primary moral principle by excluding as immoral actions which involve willing in certain specific ways inconsistent with a will toward integral human fulfillment" (CMP, p. 189).

In his earlier writings, that is, from 1964 through 1978,[25] Grisez sought to formulate these intermediary moral principles or "modes of responsibility" in both affirmative and negative propositions. But in his more mature writings on moral theology he formulates all these modes negatively, and he clearly explains why: "The modes of responsibility take the form of negative propositions. This does not mean that morality itself is negative; the principles of practical reason in general are affirmative, and the first principle of morality calls for openness to integral human fulfillment." But, and he emphasizes this: "*each mode of responsibility simply excludes a particular way in which a person can limit himself or herself to a quite partial and inadequate fulfillment.* Their negative form precludes conflict among them. Their demands cannot be incompatible, for one can always simultaneously *not make* any number of possible choices" (CMP, p. 191).

Grisez then proceeds to formulate these modes of responsibility in a very systematic way. He does so in particular by searching Scripture (CMP, pp. 206–231) and the writings of St. Thomas. He concludes that there are eight such modes of responsibility. Two of them (his seventh and eighth modes) exclude two different ways of intentionally choosing to do evil, and the eighth mode is certainly suggested by St. Paul's teaching in Romans 3:8 and by St. Thomas when he identified the proposition "nulli esse malum faciendum," as one of the primary principles of morality. But persons can choose immorally not only by intentionally willing (choosing) that evil *be* but also in other ways: by culpably ignoring, slighting, or neglecting human goods, by acting purely out of emotional desires unregulated by reason, by choosing in ways that unfairly and arbitrarily limit any person's participation in these goods (a way of choosing obviously excluded by the Golden Rule). Grisez's way of formulating the eight modes of responsibility is perhaps, with respect to some of them, a bit awkward, but their nature and function is clear.[26] They are more determinate, definite, than the first principle of morality, yet more general than moral norms regarding specific kinds of human acts. Each excludes a definite unreasonable way of willing, a particular way of choosing and acting which is incompatible with a will toward integral human fulfillment (cf. CMP, p. 205).

These modes of responsibility serve as premises for showing the truth of *specific moral norms,* norms such as those requiring us to keep our promises, never to choose intentionally to kill innocent human persons, never to choose freely to commit adultery, and so on. I shall show how they do so by presenting Grisez's teaching on the movement from the modes of responsibility to specific moral norms.

From Modes of Responsibility to Specific Moral Norms

The modes of responsibility are normative principles specifying or "pinning down" the requirements of the first principle of morality. But they are not specific moral norms; that is, they are not normative propositions of practical reason identifying specific sorts of human acts as morally good or morally bad sorts of acts. Examples of specific moral norms are the precepts of the Decalogue (as these have been understood in the Christian tradition) such as the norms prohibiting the intentional killing of innocent human persons, engaging in adultery, or stealing. Other examples of specific moral norms are those requiring us to keep our promises and to feed the hungry.

The central question is this: how are such specific moral norms derived from first moral principles and shown to be true in their light? As we have seen, St. Thomas held that one can easily, with little consideration, move from the primary moral precepts of the natural law to grasp the truth of the specific moral norms found in the Decalogue. But his thought on this issue seems undeveloped and it is not presented in a rigorous and coherent manner. Grisez's great contribution, in my opinion, is the rigor and coherence of his thought on this matter.

Grisez observes that all the modes of responsibility exclude unreasonable choices and acts and all embody the same first principle of morality (see CMP, pp. 251, 267). Nonetheless they differ in important ways: they exclude different unreasonable grounds of choice and action; and some demand appropriate acts, others forbid unreasonable ones, and some do both (see CMP, pp. 253, 267).

The movement from these modes of responsibility to specific moral norms is described by Grisez as follows:

> Since specific moral norms refer to kinds of actions and apply to them moral determinants, one obviously needs something common to kinds of action and to moral principles as the middle term of the reasoning by which a specific moral norm is drawn from a mode of responsibility. What is common

to both are relationships of the will to basic human goods. The modes of responsibility indicate the moral exclusion of certain relationships, and various kinds of action are morally significant insofar as they involve such relationships. . . . Thus, a specific, negative moral norm can be derived as follows. First one considers how the voluntariness involved in a certain kind of action is related to basic human goods. Next one considers the moral determination which the modes of responsibility indicate for this relationship. From these two premises one deduces the negative moral determination of that kind of action. . . . A specific, affirmative moral norm logically depends on the affirmative first principle of morality, which directs the choice of those and only those possibilities whose willing is compatible with a will toward integral human fulfillment. Thus, a certain kind of act is morally good if it offers a way of voluntarily serving a human good and involves no voluntariness excluded by any of the modes of responsibility. Not all morally good acts are obligatory—for example, feeding the hungry is good yet not obligatory. The reason is that an act of this kind can have an alternative itself morally good. However, whenever a morally good kind of act is such that its alternative is excluded by one or more modes of responsibility, then that sort of act is obligatory (CMP, p. 255, bold emphases omitted).

As an example of a specific kind of action excluded by a negative moral norm whose truth can be shown in this way, Grisez considers "beating a man to teach him a lesson, with a definite risk to life." This kind of action "is a kind of act which involves a will hostile to the good of life. 'To teach a lesson' in the sense intended here brings this kind of act under the seventh mode of responsibility, for one is acting out of hostility and accepts the destruction of a basic human good [that of life]. Therefore, this kind of act is wrong" (CMP, p. 255), and the relevant specific moral norm is that "one ought not to beat a man to teach him a lesson, with a definite risk to life."

As an example of an affirmative obligatory moral norm, Grisez considers promise keeping. He writes:

Promise keeping is a kind of act that bears upon the good of interpersonal harmony. One sets up expectations in others by making a promise, and one fulfills or disappoints these expectations by keeping or breaking it. . . . Among the various modes of responsibility, the fifth [Grisez's way of stating the Golden Rule] will certainly be relevant to making and keeping promises. If one allows the keeping and breaking of promises to be determined by one's own convenience, one violates this mode. By contrast, one who keeps promises is plainly not doing so because of differences in feelings toward different people. Therefore, keeping promises is obligatory; breaking them is wrong (CMP, pp. 255–256).

In summary, we can say that specific moral norms are discovered by considering proposed human acts (possibilities of choice) and seeing how such acts relate a person's will to basic human goods, and then determining whether they entail the willingness to violate one or more modes of responsibility. If they entail such willingness, they are unreasonable kinds of human acts and are excluded by a specific moral norm. If they do not entail such willingness, they are morally good kinds of acts and morally permissible. They are morally obligatory in virtue of an affirmative moral norm, if the alternatives to the morally good kinds of acts are excluded by one or more modes of responsibility.

Most specific moral norms (e.g., promise keeping) admit of exceptions. In other words, they are not *absolute*. The reason why they are not is that most specific norms are open to further specification in light of the same moral principles (the basic human goods and the modes of responsibility) from which they were derived. Thus, while one is obligated to keep one's promises in light of the good of interpersonal harmony and the fifth mode of responsibility, which excludes arbitrary partiality (the Golden Rule), promises and the interpersonal cooperation that they foster frequently concern goods other than interpersonal harmony. When keeping a promise would require one to violate the seventh or eighth modes of responsibility, which require one not to damage, destroy, or impede an instance of a basic human good, then one ought to break the promise and by doing so one does not violate the fifth mode which generated it (cf. CMP, pp. 256–257). Thus specific moral norms of this kind are not absolute.

But some specific moral norms, for instance, the specific moral norm forbidding one intentionally to kill an innocent human person, a specific kind of human act excluded by the seventh and eighth modes of responsibility, are absolute or without exceptions. The reason is that no further specification of the act excluded by the norm can prevent it from violating the relevant mode or modes of responsibility and the first principle of morality itself. In short, any moral norm which so specifies an object of human choice so that no further condition or circumstance could so modify it that it no longer violated a relevant mode of responsibility and, therefore, the first principle of morality, is absolute. In choosing such a moral object one cannot be acting in accord with the ideal of integral human fulfillment (cf. CMP, pp. 257–258, 267).

This, in short, is the movement from moral principles to specific moral norms that Grisez's understanding of the first principles of natural law and its specifications clarifies.

The Relevance of Pope John Paul II's Veritatis Splendor

In *Veritatis splendor,*[27] Pope John Paul II, reflecting on our Lord's response to the rich young man who asked him, "Teacher, what good must I do to have eternal life" (Matt 19:16), stresses that Jesus wished to "draw the young man's attention to the *'centrality' of the Decalogue* with regard to every other precept inasmuch as it is the interpretation of what the words 'I am the Lord your God' mean for man." Continuing, John Paul II says:

> We cannot fail to notice which commandments of the Law the Lord recalls to the young man. They are some of the commandments belonging to the so-called "second tablet" of the Decalogue, the summary (cf. Rom 13:8–10) and foundation of which is the *commandment of love of neighbor:* "You shall love your neighbor as yourself" (Matt 19:19; cf. Mk 12:31). In this command-ment we find a precise expression of the *singular dignity of the human person,* "the only creature that God has wanted for its own sake" (n. 13).

Here John Paul II, like St. Thomas (whom he frequently cites) is affirming that the precepts of the "second tablet" of the Decalogue—the precepts concerned with human acts affecting our neighbor—are derived from the commandment to love our neighbor as ourselves. Then, in a very illuminating passage, he says:

> The different commandments of the Decalogue are really only so many reflections of the one commandment about the good of the person, at the level of the many different goods which characterize his identity as a spiri-tual and bodily being in relationship with God, with his neighbor, and with the material world. ... The commandments of which Jesus reminds the young man are meant to safeguard the *good* of the person, the image of God, by protecting his *goods.* "You shall not murder; You shall not commit adultery; You shall not steal; You shall not bear false witness" are moral rules formulated in terms of prohibitions. These negative precepts express with singular force the ever urgent need to protect human life, the commu-nion of persons in marriage, private property, truthfulness, and people's good name (n. 13; cf. nn. 50–52, 67, 99).

This text is illuminating because in it John Paul II, in order to show more clearly why the acts proscribed by the negative precepts of the Decalogue are incompatible with love of neighbor, explicitly relates these precepts and the acts proscribed by them to human *goods,* and thus lends support to Grisez's understanding of the first principle of morality and its modes of responsibility. Grisez, as will be recalled, agrees that formulat-ing the first principle of morality in terms of the commands to love God and neighbor is a valid way of formulating this principle in *religious language,* particularly to readers of the Bible. But he holds that this way of formulating the first principle of morality is not entirely satisfactory for purposes of ethical reflection and moral theology because this formulation fails to refer to the many basic human goods which generate the need for choice and moral judgment (CMP, p. 184). Note that in this passage (and similar passages) in *Veritatis splendor,* John Paul II also finds it necessary, in order to show more clearly how specific moral norms are related to the love commandment, to refer to the *goods* of human persons. He is, in effect, so it seems to me, asserting that the first principle of morality requires us to choose and otherwise will those and only those alternatives of choice that are in accord with a will open to and respectful of the *goods* of human persons, the goods constitutive of integral human fulfillment. He is, in short, proposing something quite analogous to Grisez's formulation of the first principle of morality. He does not, it is true, seek to "pin down" this principle by specifying generic ways of choosing that are not in accord with it. But he nonetheless realizes the need, one that Grisez takes up with rigor, to relate possible human acts to the goods of human persons and the way in which willingness to engage in them relates the person choosing to those goods and to the persons in whom they are meant to flourish.

CHRISTIAN MORAL PRINCIPLES AND THE MOVEMENT TO SPECIFICALLY CHRISTIAN MORAL NORMS

Introduction

At the beginning of this paper, I noted the heated debate among Catholic moral theologians regarding the question of a specifically Christian morality and of specific Christian moral norms.[28] Here I wish to summarize Grisez's position on this matter and comment on its significance.

The principles proper to the Christian moral life and the specific moral norms which these principles engender, Grisez affirms, "presuppose and build on the principles of common human morality . . . but what they add can only be known with the light of faith" (CMP, p. 471). The first principle of common human morality directs us toward integral human fulfillment. But from experience we realize that this ideal is in fact not attainable by our own efforts. We experience defeat and, ultimately, the defeat of death. In the light of faith we know that because of sin and its effect on human existence, the ideal of integral human fulfillment is in fact realizable only in union with Jesus the Lord, who has come to redeem us from sin and make it possible for us to be, in truth, children of God and members of the divine family, sharing in the divine nature as Jesus shares in our human nature.

Through faith we know that Jesus is the only mediator between God and sinful humankind, that his gospel provides a unique reason for repentance and hope that the ideal of integral human fulfillment is realizable if we unite ourselves with his redemptive work (cf. CMP, pp. 552). The choice central to the Christian life is the choice made in baptism, to accept in living faith the revelation communicated to humankind by Christ and his Church and to commit oneself to a life of union with Jesus. This act of living faith is a human choice, the sort of choice rightly called a commitment. It is the fundamental option of the Christian, whereby he or she turns away from sin, is reconciled to God through Jesus, becomes one with Jesus in the covenant community of the Church, which Jesus established and in which he is really present. As Grisez puts it, "by their fundamental option of faith Christians are united with Jesus in a communion they celebrate in the Eucharist. Their common vocation is to follow Jesus by fulfilling his commandments, particularly his command to love others as he has loved them" (CMP, p. 551).

Christian Love: The Existential Principle of Christian Morality

The act of living faith, whereby we accept the revelation communicated to us by Jesus and enter into communion with him, is simultaneously a free human act and entirely God's free gift to us of divine life. He gives us this life when he pours his divinizing love into our hearts, and his love abides in us so long as we abide in it. As such, Christian love, which enables us to share in the divine nature as Jesus shares in human nature, is not a human act but a divine gift (CMP, p. 599f), although it is related to human acts. It is the existential principle of the Christian moral life, because the Christian moral life is proper to those who have become, through union with Jesus and the infusion of divine love into their hearts, members of the divine family, called to be perfect as the heavenly Father is perfect.

Christian Love Transforms the First Principle of Morality into a More Definite Form

The divine love abiding in our hearts and making us truly God's children and members of the divine family is a disposition to perfect fulfillment in divine life. Thus it demands moral goodness, the requirements of which are partly but not completely expressed by the commands to love God and neighbor, which, remember, is the first principle of morality formulated in religious language. The twofold commands: love of God and love of neighbor partially express the requirements of Christian love because Christians, like all people, are obliged to shape their lives in accordance with the moral requirements of the Old Law and of the natural law (cf. CMP, pp. 603–604).

The love commands do not, however, fully express the demands of divine love. After all Jesus gave his disciples a *new* command: "As the Father has loved me, so I have loved you; abide in my love" (John 15:9). Christian love, Grisez emphasizes, "disposes both to divine and human goodness—that is, to the perfect accomplishment of the divine-human communion which God is building up upon Jesus. . . . The hope which springs from Christian love will only be satisfied when the fulfillment of all things in Jesus is accomplished, when Jesus hands over the kingdom to the Father, and God is all in all (see 1 Cor 15:20–28; Eph 1:7–20, 22–23; Col 1:18–20)" (CMP, p. 605).

Continuing, Grisez writes:

> The first principle of all human morality is: In voluntarily acting for human goods and avoiding what is opposed to them, one ought to choose and otherwise will those and only those possibilities whose willing is compatible with a will toward integral human fulfillment. . . . Such fulfillment is more than an ideal; it is being accomplished in the fulfillment of all things in Jesus. . . . Thus, Christian love transforms the first principle of morality into a more definite norm: One ought to will those and only those possibilities which contribute to the integral human fulfillment being realized in the fulfillment of all things in Jesus (CMP, p. 605, bold type omitted).

Here it is important to recall that we become Christians, members of Jesus' body and members of the divine family—God's very own children—when, moved by God's love, we make the fundamental option of the Christian, to accept the revelation communicated to us by Jesus and to participate in his redemptive act. The first principle of Christian morality as expressed here simply articulates the requirements of this fundamental option: to integrate *everything we subsequently freely choose to do into this basic Christian commitment.* As followers of Jesus our task as Christians, St. Paul tells us, is to fill up in our own flesh "what is lacking in the sufferings of Christ, for the sake of his body, the Church" (Col 1:24). Christians are *to be* Christ in the world in which they live. Because of this vocation entrusted to them, the divinizing love of God inwardly transforms the first principle of morality into the more definite principle that Grisez, rooting his thought in the teaching of the New Testament (cf. texts cited by Grisez in CMP, pp. 605–606), has formulated here.

Christian Love Transforms the Modes of Responsibility into Modes of Christian Response

Just as the requirements of the first principle of common human morality or the natural law are spelled out, "pinned down," by the modes of responsibility, so too are the requirements of the first principle of Christian morality spelled out, "pinned down" by the "modes of Christian response."

Grisez proposes that the Beatitudes of our Lord's Sermon on the Mount "express, in language suited to the audience, the modes of Christian response, which transform the modes of responsibility" (CMP, p. 628). By doing so Grisez, in my opinion, is simply developing in a more systematic way the Catholic tradition. Indeed, as St. Augustine so aptly said, "If a person will devoutly and calmly consider the sermon which our Lord Jesus Christ spoke on the mount, I think he will find in it, as measured by the highest norms of morality, the *perfect pattern (magna carta) of the Christian life.*"[29] And St. Thomas also said that the Lord's Sermon on the Mount "contains completely the information needed for the Christian life."[30]

Grisez notes that the Beatitudes of the Sermon on the Mount express principles of Christian moral life as "blessings." They do so, he writes,

> because these modes of Christian response transform the modes of responsibility. The latter limit the inclinations of one's flesh; the former rejoice in the inclinations of a mind led by the Spirit (see Rom 7:22–8:9). The latter forbid what does not conform to a will toward the ideal of integral human fulfillment; the former commend what is characteristic of a will, enlivened by charity, hoping confidently for the reality of the fulfillment of all things in Jesus. Still, the modes of Christian response are like the modes of responsibility in proposing eight distinct conditions met by a person whose life is oriented toward true human fulfillment (CMP, pp. 628–629).

The Beatitudes are internal dispositions, inclining Christians to do what is pleasing to the Father and to carry out their task of participating in Christ's redemptive work. Thus, the Beatitudes are intimately related to distinctively Christian virtues, and as rooted in God's gift of life and love, they can be rightly regarded as related to the "gifts" of the Holy Spirit.

Reflection on the Beatitudes helps us understand that they propose norms of Christian life more specific than the commandment to love as Jesus does—the first principle of Christian morality. Yet they are not so specific as definite norms of Christian life, that is, norms identifying specific human choices and acts that one, as a Christian, is called on to do here and now in carrying on the redemptive work of Christ.

Considering the Beatitudes in this framework, Grisez believes that the modes of Christian response can be formulated as follows:

1. *To expect and accept all good, including the good fruits of one's work, as God's gift*—for the "poor in spirit" understand that their achievements are only a share, given freely and generously by God, in his fullness. The virtuous disposition is humility; the vice is pride. The corresponding gift of the Spirit is fear of the Lord.

2. *To accept one's limited role in the Body of Christ and fulfill it*—for the "meek" understand that submissiveness to God's will involves no loss or delay to their personal fulfillment. The virtuous disposition is "Christian dedication," while lukewarmness and minimalism are opposed to it. The corresponding gift of the Holy Spirit is piety or godliness, an attitude of filial reverence and dutifulness toward God.

3. *To put aside or avoid everything which is not necessary or useful in the fulfillment of one's personal vocation*—for those who "mourn" (not only contrite sinners but all those who turn from transient goods to fulfillment in Jesus) understand that to be disposed to goodness itself frees one from the pursuit of particular, finite goods for their own sake. The virtuous disposition is detachment; worldliness and anxiety are opposed dispositions. The corresponding gift of the Spirit is knowledge, by which one discerns what belongs to faith and judges everything by its light.

4. *To endure fearlessly whatever is necessary or useful for the fulfillment of one's personal vocation*—for those who "hunger and thirst for righteousness" understand that they have nothing whatsoever to fear. The virtuous disposition is the faithfulness and heroism characteristic of the martyr, though required of all Christians, while weakness of faith and faintheartedness in the face of non-Christian standards are among the Christian vices. The corresponding gift of the Spirit is fortitude.

5. *To be merciful according to the universal and perfect measure of mercy which God has revealed in Jesus*—for those who "are merciful" understand that they are to be as disinterested and selfless as God is. The virtuous disposition is mercy, compassion, service to others on the model of Jesus, while the opposed vice is a legalistic attitude toward others. The corresponding gift of the Spirit is counsel. . . .

6. *To strive to conform one's whole self to living faith, and purge anything which does not meet this standard*—for the "pure of heart" understand that in this life

charity requires continuous conversion. The virtuous disposition is single-minded devotion to God, including a sense of sin and continuing conversion, while the Christian vice is reflected in mediocrity and insincerity. The corresponding gift of the Spirit is understanding.

7. *To respond to evil with good, not with resistance, much less with destructive action*—for "peacemakers" understand that the effort to live according to divine love must be universally conciliatory. The virtuous disposition is the conciliatoriness which seeks the redemption of enemies; one opposed disposition is the tendency to shun evil instead of carrying on a redemptive ministry to those enslaved by it. The corresponding gift of the Spirit is wisdom, the power of putting in order as peacemakers do.

8. *To do no evil that good might come of it, but suffer evil together with Jesus in cooperation with God's redeeming love*—for "those persecuted for righteousness' sake" understand that one must undergo evil in order to bring the evildoer in touch with perfect goodness. The virtuous disposition is self-oblation, the Christian vice the fragile rectitude of the person who does not wish to sin but seeks fulfillment in this world. Since there are only seven gifts, Augustine assigns none here; however, one might say there is a corresponding gift, unique to each Christian and disposing him or her to offer God the unique gift of himself or herself (CMP, pp. 654–655).

Christian Modes of Response and Specific Christian Moral Norms

Specific moral norms pertaining to the natural law or common human morality are generated by the modes of responsibility, as we have seen, and the truth of these specific moral norms can be shown in the light of these modes of responsibility. Christian love requires that Christians shape their lives in accord with these specific norms of common human morality.

But there are specific Christian moral norms, known only in the light of faith. These are generated by the Beatitudes, or the "modes of Christian response" (cf. CMP, p. 611). To take one example: The second mode of Christian response, based on the second Beatitude that calls the meek "blessed," inwardly disposes one to accept one's limited role in the Body of Christ and fulfill it. But to do this, one should, as Grisez says, "find, accept and faithfully carry out one's personal vocation" (CMP, p. 609). This is a specific Christian moral norm, known only in the light of faith and discernible only by seeking to conform one's Christian life in accord with the blessings promised by the Beatitudes, the *magna carta* of the Christian life.

The modes of Christian response, Grisez emphasizes, "take into account what must be done if one is to live an upright life and realize human goods in the fallen human condition. They direct men and women to commit themselves to a definite kind of action—that begun by Jesus" (CMP, p. 662). All Christian vocations, since they are ways of cooperating with Jesus' redemptive work, embody the modes of Christian response; but since each individual Christian has his or her own unique role to play in the drama of salvation, each Christian life is unique and embodies these modes of Christian response in a unique way. The affirmative responsibilities of the Christian life follow from the commitments which constitute one's personal vocation and are discerned in the light of these commitments and the modes of Christian response (CMP, pp. 661–666).

The whole point is that the Christian moral life is a life in conformity with Christ's. Obviously, Christians must avoid mortal sin, since this is utterly incompatible with life in Christ. But they must also weed out of their lives deliberate venial sins and imperfections. Their call is to holiness, to sanctity. And they respond to this call by discerning their unique personal vocations, the indispensable roles they have in carrying on the redemptive work of Jesus and with, in and through him, choosing and doing only what is pleasing to his Father, only what will contribute to the fulfillment of all things in Jesus. To do this, they need guidance for the specific choices and acts of their lives. This guidance is provided by the specific Christian moral norms, mostly affirmative in nature, which they are called upon to discern by examining their lives in the light of the first principle of Christian morality—to love as Jesus loves—and its modes of response or the Beatitudes.

The Relevance of John Paul II's Veritatis splendor to Specific Christian Morality

In my opinion, *Veritatis splendor* supports much that Grisez has to say about the specificity of Christian morality.[31]

First of all, the Christian morality set forth in this encyclical is, like that of Grisez's, Christocentric. According to John Paul II, "*Jesus brings God's commandments to fulfillment. . . . Jesus himself is the living 'fulfillment' of the Law* inasmuch as he fulfils its authentic meaning by the total gift of himself: *he himself becomes a living and personal Law,* who invites people to follow him; through the Spirit, he gives the grace to share in his own life and love and provides the strength to bear witness to that love in personal choices and actions (cf John 13:34–35)."

Moreover, like Grisez, John Paul II identifies the fundamental option or choice of the Christian as the act of living faith, for he affirms:

There is no doubt that Christian moral teaching, even in its Biblical roots, acknowledges the specific importance of a fundamental choice which qualifies the moral life and engages freedom on a radical level before God. It is a question of the decision of faith, of the *obedience of faith* (cf. Rom 16:26) "by which man makes a total and free self-commitment to God," offering "the full submission of intellect and will to God as he reveals." This faith, which works through love (cf. Gal 5:6), comes from the core of man, from his "heart" (cf. Rom 10:10), whence it is called to bear fruit in works (cf. Matt 12:33–35; Luke 6:43–45; Rom 8:5–10; Gal 5:22) (n. 66; internal citation from Vatican Council II, Dogmatic Constitution on Divine Revelation, *Dei Verbum*, n. 5).

John Paul II observes that the "Beatitudes are not specifically concerned with particular rules of behavior" (n. 16). That is, they are not *specific moral norms*. However, he goes on to say that "they speak of basic attitudes and dispositions in life. . . . [They] are above all *promises,* from which there also indirectly flow *normative indications* for the moral life" (n. 16). This text is most important, for in it the Pope seems to attribute to the Beatitudes a function similar to that attributed to them by Grisez. The Beatitudes, while not being specific moral norms, are nonetheless dispositions characteristic of one who follows Jesus, and they give rise to *normative indications* or specific moral norms of Christian life.

Moreover, in speaking of the Beatitudes, John Paul II affirms that "in their originality and profundity they are a sort of *self-portrait of Christ,* and for this very reason are *invitations to discipleship and to communion of life with Christ*" (n. 16). He likewise insists that the vocation to perfect love is addressed to *everyone,* and that each person has a unique vocation to fulfill. He sees the perfection of the Christian life in a following of Christ, a *sequela Christi.* Indeed, "*Following Christ is thus the essential and primordial foundation of Christian morality.* . . . [But] this is not a matter only of disposing oneself to hear a teaching and obediently accepting a commandment. More radically, it involves *holding fast to the very person of Jesus,* partaking of his life and destiny, sharing in his free and loving obedience to the will of the Father" (n. 19). He insists that the *new* commandment of Jesus, that "you love one another as I have loved you" (John 15:12), "requires imitation of Jesus and of his love" (n. 20), and that "*following Christ* . . . touches man at the very depths of his being. . . . [It] means *becoming conformed to him* who became a servant even to giving himself on the Cross (cf. Phil 2:5–8)" (n. 21).

All that John Paul II says here is central to the Christian morality set forth by Grisez. The Pope, as we have seen, says that the Beatitudes are, as it were, a "self-portrait of Christ" (n. 16). Grisez, in effect, says the same, for according to him the Beatitudes or modes of Christian response "are ways of acting characteristic of a person whose will, enlivened by charity, is directed in hope toward the fulfillment of everything in Jesus" (CMP, p. 653), and prior to saying this he had already shown that the Beatitudes or modes of Christian response are fully exemplified in Jesus' life (cf. CMP, pp. 609–611), a life culminating in Jesus' gift of himself on the Cross. Remarkably, here too the teaching of John Paul II in *Veritatis splendor* supports the position taken by Grisez, for the Pope is at great pains to show, in the final chapter of this Encyclical, that *"the Crucified Christ reveals the authentic meaning of freedom: he lives it fully in the total gift of himself* and calls his disciples to share in his freedom" (n. 85; cf. the whole of chapter three of *Veritatis splendor*). It is precisely Grisez's teaching that Christian morality, shaped inwardly by the modes of Christian response, is a morality requiring the sincere gift of self, demanding selfless commitment to participate in Christ's redemptive work, even unto death.

CONCLUSION

As this paper demonstrates, Grisez has made genuine contributions first, to the development of natural law theory and, second, to the question of whether there can be a specific Christian morality and specific Christian moral norms. With respect to the first, he has greatly clarified the movement from the first principles of morality to specific moral norms. St. Thomas himself recognized the need to proceed from first principles of morality to specific moral norms and indicated the generic nature of this movement: the first principles of morality serve as the premises in whose light the truth of more specific moral norms can be shown. He did not, however, clearly identify these "premises" or specify the way in which the truth of specific moral norms can be established. Nor, so far as I know, have any of St. Thomas's successors attempted to do this. Grisez, on the other hand, has provided a rigorous and coherent account of this movement.

With respect to the specificity of Christian morality and the question of specific Christian moral norms, Grisez, rooting his thought in Scripture, has shown that Christian morality is more than a question of internal dispositions and attitudes—although it definitely entails such attitudes. As a thoroughly christocentric morality made possible only because human persons, through God's gift of love, have been inwardly transformed into new creatures, that is, into living members of the divine family,

Christian morality requires—and empowers—Jesus' followers to commit themselves to participate in his redemptive work. It requires—and enables—Christians to shape their lives and actions in accord with the fundamental Christian moral principle that they are to love others even as Christ loves them—with a redemptive, healing love—and in accord with its modes of specification—the Beatitudes or *magna carta* of the Christian moral life. The Beatitudes are the internal dispositions characteristic of those who seek to participate in Christ's redemptive work, the moral principles in whose light they can choose, ever more deeply, to conform their lives to Christ and to integrate all their choices and actions into their fundamental option of living faith.

NOTES

1. The Latin text reads: "... omne iudicum rationis practicae procedit ex *quibusdam principiis naturaliter cognitis. . . .*"

2. The relevant Latin text reads: "illa quae sunt *prima et communia* continentur in eis [i.e., praeceptis decalogi] sicut principia in conclusionibus proximis."

3. The pertinent Latin text reads: "... *praecepta moralia* ex ipso dictamine naturalis rationis efficaciam habent, etiam si nunquam in lege statuantur. Horum autem triplex est gradus. Nam quaedam sunt *certissima . . .*"

4. The full text reads: "Inter praecepta . . . decalogi non computantur duo genera praeceptorum: illa scilicet quae sunt prima et communia, *quorum non oportet aliam editionem esse nisi quod sunt scripta in ratione naturali quasi per se nota. . . .*"

5. Here the Latin reads: "quaedam sunt *certissima, et adeo manifesta quod editione non indigent.*"

6. Here the Latin reads: "Quaedam enim sunt in humanis actibus adeo explicita quod statim, cum modica consideratione, possunt approbari vel reprobari per illa communia et prima principia."

7. The Latin text follows: "Quaedam enim sunt quae statim per se ratio naturalis cuiuslibet hominis diiudicat esse facienda vel non facienda."

8. Here the Latin text reads: "praecepta decalogi . . . sunt illa quae statim ex principiis communibus primis cognosci possunt modica consideratione . . . illa quae sunt prima et communia continentur in eis sicut principia in conclusionibus proximis."

9. Here the Latin reads: "Quaedam vero sunt magis determinata, quorum rationem statim quilibet, etiam popularis, potest de facili videre; et tamen quia in paucioribus circa huiusmodi contingit iudicium humanum perverti, huiusmodi editione indigent; et haec sunt praecepta decalogi."

10. "Quaedam vero sunt ad quorum iudicium requiritur multa consideratio diversarum circumstantiarum, quas considerare diligenter non est cuiuslibet,

sed sapientum. . . . Quaedam vero sunt quae subtiliori consideratione rationis a sapientibus iudicantur esse observanda."

11. The full relevant text reads: "Inter praecepta ergo decalogi non computantur . . . illa quae per diligentem inquisitionem sapientum inveniuntur rationi convenire . . . illa vero quae per sapientes cognoscuntur continentur in eis [i.e., in praeceptis decalogi] . . . sicut conclusiones in principiis."

12. "Quaedam vero sunt quorum ratio non est adeo cuilibet manifesta, sed solum sapientibus; et ista sunt praecepta moralia superaddita decalogo."

13. "Coram cano capite consurge, et honora personam senis."

14. ". . . omnia illa ad quae homo habet naturalem inclinationem, ratio naturaliter apprehendit ut bona, et per consequens ut opere prosequenda, et contraria eorum ut mala et vitanda."

15. *Christian Moral Principles*, Vol. 1 of Grisez's *The Way of the Lord Jesus* (Chicago: Franciscan Herald Press, 1983).

16. Grisez's understanding of the first principle of practical reasoning and his interpretation of St. Thomas have been the subject of criticism by some contemporary writers.

Grisez insists that the first principle of practical reasoning, *good is to be done and pursued, and evil is to be avoided*, is *not* of itself a *moral principle*. It is not the first principle of *morality*, but the first principle of *practical reasoning*. He has consistently set forth this understanding of the first principle of natural law, beginning briefly in his first book, *Contraception and Natural Law* (Bruce: Milwaukee, 1964), and arguing for it more extensively in his essay, "The First Principle of Practical Reason: A Commentary on the *Summa Theologiae*, 1–2, Question 94, Article 2," *Natural Law Forum* [now *American Journal of Jurisprudence*] 10 (1965) 168–201 (abridged version in *Modern Studies in Philosophy: Aquinas: A Collection of Critical Essays*, ed. Anthony Kenny. Garden City, NY: Doubleday, 1969, pp. 340–382). He has likewise insisted that this is the way St. Thomas understood the first principle of natural law.

Grisez's interpretation of this principle has been vigorously criticized by a number of authors, who maintain that this principle is the first principle of *morality* and that St. Thomas understood it in this sense. Among the principal critics of Grisez's interpretation are Ralph McInerny, "The Principles of Natural Law," *American Journal of Jurisprudence* 25 (1980): 1–15 (substantially reprinted as the third chapter of McInerny's *Ethica Thomistica: The Moral Philosophy of Thomas Aquinas* [Washington, D.C.: The Catholic University of America Press, 1982]); Henry Veatch, "Review of *Natural Law and Natural Rights* by John Finnis," *American Journal of Jurisprudence* 26 (1981): 247–259; Vernon Bourke, "Review of *Natural Law and Natural Rights* by John Finnis," *American Journal of Jurisprudence* 26 (1981): 247–259; Russell Hittinger, *A Critique of the New Natural Law Theory* (Notre Dame, IN: University of Notre Dame Press, 1987); Hittinger, "The Recovery of Natural Law and the 'Common Morality,' " *This World*, No. 18 (Summer, 1987): 62–74. These authors also maintain that Grisez has divorced natural law from its metaphysical and anthropological roots by insisting that the principles of natural law are not derived from knowledge of human nature.

Grisez (and Finnis) have responded to these critics in several important articles. Chief among these are Germain Grisez and John Finnis, "The Basic

Principles of Natural Law: A Reply to Ralph McInerny," *American Journal of Jurisprudence* 26 (1981): 21–31; Germain Grisez, "A Critique of Russell Hittinger's Book, *A Critique of the New Natural Law Theory,*" *New Scholasticism* 62 (1988): 62–74; John Finnis, "Natural Law and the Is-Ought Question: An Invitation to Professor Veatch," *Catholic Lawyer* 26 (1980–81): 265–277.

It is, in my opinion, important to note here that McInerny took note of the "Reply to Ralph McInerny" in his book *Ethica Thomistica*. Chapter Three of that work includes, as noted already, the material from his article in the *American Journal of Jurisprudence*. In a "Bibliographic Note" appended to his book, McInerny refers to the Grisez-Finnis "Reply." He then says: "Alas, this book was already in proof before I became aware of their response and thus I am unable to give it the attention it deserves here. The two authors now seem reluctant to be assessed in terms of fidelity to St. Thomas. That of course was the angle from which I read them" (p. 128). McInerny here clearly leaves his readers with the impression that Grisez and Finnis concede that McInerny's interpretation of St. Thomas's understanding of natural law is correct and that they simply do not wish to be judged on Thomistic grounds. This, unfortunately, is a very erroneous impression, for in their "Reply" Grisez and Finnis take great pains to show that on a key matter, namely, the underivability of the first principles of practical reasoning and on the nature of the first principle of natural law as a principle of practical reasoning and not, as such, a principle of *morality*, they, and *not* McInerny, are being faithful to St. Thomas. In short, on this point McInerny unfortunately gives his readers the wrong impression. He ought not to have added the two final sentences to his "Bibliographic Note."

An excellent study of Grisez's thought, comparing it extensively with the teaching of St. Thomas on natural law, is that of Aurelio Ansaldo, *El Primer Principio del Obrar Moral y Las Normas Morales Específicas en el Pensamiento de G. Grisez y J. Finnis* (Rome: Pontificia Universita Lateranense, 1990). Ansaldo's patient study supports both Grisez's interpretation of the first principle of natural law and his interpretation of St. Thomas on this issue.

17.   The eight basic goods identified by Grisez are life itself, including health and the handing on of life; knowledge of truth and appreciation of beauty; satisfaction in playful activities and skillful performances; self-integration (harmony among aspects of the self); practical reasonableness and authenticity (harmony among moral reflection, free choices, and their execution); justice and friendship (harmony among human persons); religion (harmony between humankind and God); and marriage. For the first seven of these goods see CMP, pp. 115–139; for marriage as a basic good see *Living a Christian Life* (hereafter LCL), Vol. 2 of his *The Way of the Lord Jesus* (Quincy, IL: Franciscan Press, 1993), pp. 555–569.

Grisez calls four of the basic human goods (self-integration; authenticity; justice and friendship; and religion—the goods whose common theme is harmony) "reflexive" or "existential." He calls them "reflexive" because choice is included in their very definition, and "existential" because they fulfill persons insofar as persons make free choices and are capable of moral good and evil (cf. CMP, pp. 123–124, 135–136; "Practical Principles" 107–108). He emphasizes that, since these goods are realized primarily in and through choices and since choice has a communal dimension, these goods cannot be perfectly realized in an imperfect community and that, given the imperfect character of this world, perfect peace cannot be fully realized in it (cf. CMP, p. 132). Moreover, since these goods depend upon choice for their realization and because choice is within human power, they pertain essentially to the goodness of the person precisely as a moral being who is called "good" without qualification if and only if he or she is morally good (cf. CMP, pp. 128–130, 132). Although they pertain essentially to the goodness of the person precisely as a moral being, i.e., as unqualifiedly good, they do not, of themselves, have *moral* value insofar as one can participate in them immorally by compromising moral principles (e.g., one can participate in the good of friendship by cooperating with others in immoral activities). Nevertheless, precisely because they pertain essentially to the moral order and the moral goodness of the person (who has dominion over his or her choices), interest in them takes priority whenever they are at stake. Interest in these goods requires us to establish priorities in living out our lives and in ordering our interests in the basic goods (cf. CMP, pp. 128–130). One of these reflexive, existential goods is that of religion, or of harmony between humankind and God (or some more-than-human source of meaning and value). Interest in this good holds priority in the establishment of a plan of life and makes clear "the duty to seek religious truth, embrace what appears to be true, and to live by it" ("Practical Principles" 142).

Since choice is not included in the meaning of the other basic goods, Grisez calls these goods "substantive" goods, i.e., goods which fulfill persons not as agents through deliberation and choice, but as intelligent, animate beings (CMP, pp. 124–125, 136–138). These goods, in other words, fulfill or perfect dimensions of the human person other than those fulfilled by the existential goods. The realization or instantiation of these goods is contingent both on effective action and, at times, good fortune; effective action is not always possible for persons of good will, nor is good fortune under their dominion. Persons, therefore, can be *morally good*, by *rightly* choosing to realize the reflexive goods pertaining to the moral order and perfecting persons as moral agents, yet remain "unfulfilled" (cf. CMP, p. 132).

Marriage, which Grisez now insists is a distinct basic good of human persons, was omitted from his writings prior to 1993:

> because of the supposition that in respect to the marital communion itself marriage could be reduced to the reflexive good of friendship and in respect to having and raising children to the substantive good of life and other basic goods. The reduction of the good(s) of marriage to other basic goods, however, is unsatisfactory for three reasons. First, in marrying, people seem to intend only one many-faceted good rather than several distinct goods. Second, since the good of anything is the fullness of its being, and since basic goods of diverse sorts are irreducible to one another, either there is one basic human good proper to marriage or marriage is not one reality; but recent Church teaching, which resolves the tensions in the tradition, presents an integrated view of marriage; therefore marriage is one reality having a basic good proper to it. Third, while marital friendship and fidelity might be reducible to the reflexive good of friendship, the core of the good of marital communion is the good which Augustine calls the *"sacramentum"*

(Thomas argues that, if the goods of marriage are considered in themselves, this good is the most essential, since marriage cannot exist without it: *In Sent.*, 4, d. 31, q. 1, a. 3 [*S.t.*, sup., q. 49, a. 3]). Now, this good, the couple's one flesh unity itself, is not reducible to the existential good of friendship, for, while the couple's consent gives rise to the marital bond, it transcends the moral order; unlike a friendship, a marriage is indissoluble (LCL, p. 568, n. 43).

It is most important, in my opinion, to recognize that Grisez has come to acknowledge marriage as a distinct human good, irreducible to other human goods, precisely in light of the development of magisterial teaching on marriage from Pope Pius XI through Pope John Paul II. The development of the Catholic tradition on marriage, which Grisez briefly but accurately sets forth in LCL, pp. 555–567, *prior* to his conclusion that marriage is a basic human good, is exceptionally instructive. Grisez shows that, although Scripture itself suggests that the marital communion is an intrinsic human good, that is good *in itself*, the *theological* tradition rooted in the thought of St. Augustine, who strongly defended the goodness of marriage against its detractors, nonetheless regarded marriage not as something intrinsically good but rather as something instrumentally good, that is, as instrumental to the continuation of the human race through procreation (even St. Thomas was not fully successful in rectifying this understanding, although elements for its rectification are found in him). Grisez shows that, beginning with Pius XI and continuing through Pius XII, Vatican Council II, Paul VI, and John Paul II, the magisterium has ever more clearly presented marriage as *intrinsically* and not merely as instrumentally good, that is, as a basic good of human persons.

In these pages of LCL Grisez also provides an excellent explanation of why the recent magisterium has eschewed the "primary-secondary" terminology regarding the ends of marriage. He correctly points out that in *Gaudium et spes* Vatican Council II in no way equated the having and raising of children (the procreative *end* of marriage) with conjugal love as *ends of marriage*, a claim erroneously made by many contemporary theologians. Rather, it uniformly taught that the having and raising of children is the *intrinsic end* to which marriage and marital love are intrinsically ordered and that marital love, which the Council *never* identified as an *end* of marriage, was uniformly presented as the vivifying source of the whole communion of marriage and family life. Noting that in recent magisterial teaching, including the revised 1983 *Code of Canon Law*, the having and raising of children (procreation) is not called the *primary* end of marriage, Grisez goes on to propose that the reason why this terminology is eschewed is by no means based on a demotion of the place of having and raising children in marriage or on an effort to "equiparate" procreation and conjugal love, but simply to avoid the implication that the having and raising of children is an end *extrinsic* to marriage and that marriage itself is merely an instrumental good for the achievement of this extrinsic end. Grisez's analysis, in my judgment, is in perfect agreement with the very valuable and helpful commentaries on the Council's teaching provided by such scholars as Marcellinus Zalba, S.J., "De dignitate matrimonii et familiae fovenda (ad cap. 1 partis II Const. de Ecclesia in mundo commentarium)," *Periodica de re morali, canonica, liturgica* 55 (1966) 381–429, Francisco Gil Hellin,

"El Lugar Propio del Amor Conyugal en la Estructura del Matrimonio segun la *Gaudium et spes*," *Annales Valentinos* 6.11 (1980) 1–35, and Ramon Garcia de Haro, *Marriage and Family in the Documents of the Magisterium,* trans. William E. May (San Francisco: Ignatius, 1993), pp. 234–256.

When Grisez first proposed, in the preliminary drafts of LCL, that marriage is a basic good, I was skeptical, principally because Grisez had himself insisted (and still insists) that the basic goods of human persons perdure into the eschaton, into the heavenly kingdom; and I wondered how the good of marriage so endures in light of such Gospel passages as "the children of this age marry and are given in marriage, but those judged worthy of a place in the age to come and of resurrection from the dead do not" (Luke 20:34–35). However, in revising his drafts for publication Grisez has, I believe, adequately responded to this criticism, showing in what sense this basic human good participates in heavenly communion, effectively utilizing passages from Pius XII and John Paul II to support his interpretation (cf. LCL, pp. 605–610).

18. Benedict Ashley, O.P., argues that since Grisez includes choice in the definition or meaning of four of the basic human goods, they *cannot* be considered, as Grisez insists, *ultimate ends* of human choices and actions. Since choice is included in their meaning, Ashley contends, they can only be regarded as *means* and not as fundamental *goods* or *ends* of human action (see Ashley's "What Is the End of the Human Person? The Vision of God and Integral Health Fulfillment," in *Moral Truth and Moral Tradition,* ed. Luke Gormally [Dublin: Four Courts Press, 1994], pp. 68–96, at p. 85). His point is that the *goods* perfective of human persons are not matters of free choice; they are *givens* because we are *naturally* inclined to them and because they are intrinsically perfective of us.

In my judgment Ashley here shows that he has not rightly understood Grisez's thought. Grisez, in calling four of the basic goods "reflexive" or "existential," and in maintaining that choice enters into their very meaning, is *not* claiming, as Ashley thinks, that we are free to choose the goods of human existence. Grisez holds that we are naturally inclined to these goods because they are intrinsically perfective of dimensions of our existence. He is simply saying that the reality which *is* good and which intrinsically fulfills human persons requires human choice as a condition for its realization. But friendship (harmony with others) and religion (harmony with God) and the other reflexive goods are *goods* perfective of human persons whether or not human persons choose to realize them or not. Choice is necessary only because it enters into the very meaning of these goods as actualized. Their *being* depends on human choice, but their being *good* does not. Ashley has simply confused matters here.

19. John Finnis, Joseph Boyle, and Germain Grisez, *Nuclear Deterrence, Morality and Reality* (New York and Oxford: Oxford University Press, 1987), p. 284.

20. Germain Grisez, Joseph Boyle, and John Finnis, "Practical Principles, Moral Truth, and Ultimate Ends," *American Journal of Jurisprudence* 32 (1987):128.

21. Some contend, mistakenly, that Grisez is more concerned with love of human *goods* than with love of human *persons,* and make it one of the major shortcomings of his moral theory.

Some critics, for example, Russell Hittinger (cf. his *A Critique of the New Natural Law Theory* [Notre Dame, IN: University of Notre Dame Press, 1987], pp. 29–35) have faulted Grisez's formulation of the first moral principle for shifting attention from human *persons* to human *goods*. According to such critics, we are morally obligated primarily to love *persons*, not *goods*.

This objection, as Grisez himself has noted, ignores both what he has written on this matter and the account that he gives of the relationship between human persons and the goods perfective, that is, fulfilling, of them (cf. Grisez, "A Critique of Russell Hittinger's Book, *A Critique of the New Natural Law Theory*," *The New Scholasticism* 62 [1988]: 438–465, at 448–450). In speaking of the good of procreation or of human life in its transmission in his very first book, Grisez had written:

> The good which is an object of the parents' effort is strictly speaking only what the parents can attain—not the child in his totality as a person but rather the child only insofar as his being and perfection depend upon the action of his parents. We easily become confused about this point because we assume that the relevant value is *what* is loved, and obviously the child as a whole is loved. However, persons are not among human goods as if they were values to be desired. Instead, they actualize and receive the human goods into personal existence. We love persons, including ourselves, when we will relevant values to the person, when we will that the person *have* the goods (*Contraception and the Natural Law* [Milwaukee: Bruce, 1964], p. 78).

In an appended note (ibid., p. 104, n. 5) Grisez, explicitly referring to St. Thomas, *Summa theologiae* 1, q. 60, a. 3; 1–2, q. 2, a. 7, ad 2; q. 66, a. 6, ad 2, makes his own St. Thomas's distinction between the love of concupiscence and the love of friendship; the goods are loved with the former, whereas persons are loved with the latter, and both are involved in every act of love. [On this question readers may fruitfully consult David Gallagher, "Person and Ethics in Thomas Aquinas," *Acta Philosophica* 4 (1995) 51–73.]

Grisez, Finnis, and Boyle clearly respond to this criticism in "Practical Principles, Moral Truth, and Ultimate Ends." They write:

> The basic goods of the diverse categories provide diverse reasons for choices which fulfill persons in diverse ways. ... Are we saying that the basic reasons for acting simply are persons—individual and in communion? Yes and no. Yes, in the sense that in acting one *primarily loves persons* (emphasis added), oneself and others with whom one is somehow in community and who one hopes will benefit from one's actions. In acting *for the basic goods*, one's hope simply is to foster them *in and for persons*. In the fullest sense, one loves (and such love includes feeling) the whole person, including both the person's given reality (here love is not practical but is contentment or joy) and whatever still may be hoped for as that person's fulfillment. But no, because the already existing reality of persons simply does not depend upon human action. So, the reasons for acting are more limited—the basic goods. These are not the whole reality of any individual or community, but those intelligible aspects of the fulfillment of persons (as individuals and in communion) to which human actions can contribute (p. 115).

22. "Practical Principles, Moral Truth, and Ultimate Ends," p. 128.

23. *Nuclear Deterrence, Morality and Reality*, p. 283.

24. See "Practical Principles, Moral Truth, and Ultimate Ends," 127–132.

25. These earlier writings include *Contraception and the Natural Law* (Milwaukee: Bruce, 1964); *Abortion: The Myths, the Realities, and the Arguments* (New York/Cleveland: Corpus, 1970); the first two editions of *Beyond the New Morality: The Responsibilities of Freedom* (with Russell Shaw) (Notre Dame, IN: University of Notre Dame Press, 1974, 1980); and *Life and Death with Liberty and Justice: A Contribution to the Euthanasia Debate* (with Joseph Boyle) (Notre Dame, IN: University of Notre Dame Press, 1978), and a number of important articles.

26. Grisez's eight modes of responsibility, along with brief explanations, are the following:

1. One should not be deterred by felt inertia from acting for intelligible goods. This happens when one refrains from doing something worthwhile out of laziness, conquerable depression, or the like. . . .

2. One should not be pressed by enthusiasm or impatience to act individualistically for intelligible goods. This happens when one acts by oneself, although knowing that by cooperation with others the good would be more perfectly attained insofar as others could share in it. . . .

3. One should not choose to satisfy an emotional desire except as part of one's pursuit and/or attainment of an intelligible good other than the satisfaction of the desire itself. Violations occur when people act for no good reason, on account of impulse, craving, routine, or the continued lure of goals which no longer make sense. . . .

4. One should not choose to act out of an emotional aversion except as part of one's avoidance of some intelligible evil other than the inner tension experienced in enduring that aversion. This happens when one is deterred from reasonable action by feelings of repugnance, fear of pain, anxiety, and so forth. . . .

5. One should not, in response to different feelings toward different persons, willingly proceed with a preference for anyone unless that preference is required by intelligible goods themselves. This mode is violated when one's treatment of others is marked by partiality toward some (including partiality toward oneself) [Grisez's way of formulating the Golden Rule]. . . .

6. One should not choose on the basis of emotions which bear upon empirical aspects of intelligible goods (or bads) in a way which interferes with a more perfect sharing in the good or avoidance of the bad. This happens when people act for the conscious experience of a good rather than its fuller reality. . . .

7. One should not be moved by hostility to freely accept or choose the destruction, damaging, or impeding of any intelligible human good. Violations occur when negative feelings cause people to act destructively (including self-destructively).

8. One should not be moved by a stronger desire for one instance of an intelligible good to act for it by choosing to destroy, damage, or impede some other instance of an intelligible good. This happens when one deliberately acts to bring about something bad, either for the sake of a good or to prevent something else bad . . . (CMP; pp. 225–226).

27. It is essential to note here that John Paul II stated explicitly in *Veritatis splendor* that "the Church's Magisterium does not intend to impose on the faithful any particular theological system, still less a philosophical one" (n. 29). Rather, in writing *Veritatis splendor* he was exercising his duty "to state that some trends in theological thinking and certain philosophical affirmations are incompatible with divine truth" (ibid.).

Obviously, then, John Paul II is not endorsing the moral theory of Germain Grisez, nor is that my claim. My claim is simply that the way in which John Paul II relates the specific precepts of the second table of the Decalogue to the commandment to love our neighbor as ourselves seems to lend support to Grisez's way of deriving specific moral norms from first principles insofar as John Paul II explicitly links observance of these precepts to a respect and love for the *goods* perfective of human persons. His point, like Grisez's, is that we can love our neighbors by being willing to let the goods of human existence flourish in them and by being absolutely unwilling intentionally to damage, destroy, or impede these goods in them.

28. Many influential Catholic moral theologians today—among them Josef Fuchs, Bruno Schueller, Louis Janssens, and Richard McCormick—maintain that Christian morality can add no specific normative content—that is, no specifically Christian moral norms—to the general human norms which belong to natural law. While acknowledging that Christian faith provides the Christian with motives and intentions not accessible to non-Christians, they see no need for affirming the existence of norms identifying specific sorts of human choices and actions that are uniquely Christian. This position is reflected in the essays by Fuchs, Schueller, and McCormick found in *Readings in Moral Theology No. 2: The Distinctiveness of Christian Ethics*, ed. Charles E. Curran and Richard A. McCormick, S.J. (New York: Paulist, 1980). For this position see also Schueller's essay, "Christianity and the New Man: The Moral Dimension—Specificity of Christian Ethics," in *Theology and Discovery: Essays in Honor of Karl Rahner, S.J.*, ed. William J. Kelly, S.J. (Milwaukee: Marquette University Press, 1980), pp. 307–328.

Theologians who adopt this position at times invoke the authority of St. Thomas to support it, referring to the text in which St. Thomas affirms that the new law of love adds no new directives for external actions above and beyond the directives for external actions provided by the moral norms of the natural law (see St. Thomas Aquinas, *Summa theologiae* 1–2, q. 108, a. 2). Although St. Thomas did indeed say this, appeal to this text does not resolve the question even on Thomistic grounds. For St. Thomas also taught very vigorously that there are *specific* Christian moral virtues, divinely given to those united to Christ through the outpouring of God's love, and that these virtues are the principles from which specifically Christian ways of acting proceed (see *Summa theologiae* 1–2, q. 51, a. 4; q. 63, a. 3). The fact is that the question, as posed by theologians today, simply was not asked during the time of St. Thomas.

Other contemporary theologians, for instance, Hans Urs von Balthasar, vigorously maintain that there is greater specificity to Christian morality than that acknowledged by the theologians already mentioned. Balthasar clearly affirms the primacy of Jesus in the Christian life; Christ is the "concrete norm" of the Christian life and on his lips the "Golden Rule" goes beyond mere human fraternity and includes the interpersonal exchange of the divine life. Nonetheless, Balthasar passes over in silence the question of whether or not there are specifically Christian moral norms of conduct. See his "Nine Theses in Christian Ethics," in the volume edited by Curran and McCormick, pp. 190–206.

Vincent McNamara provides an interesting discussion of this issue in his book *Faith and Ethics: Recent Roman Catholicism* (Washington: Georgetown University Press, 1985). Unfortunately, McNamara does not consider the position set forth by Grisez. He has summarized the substance of his work in an article, "Moral Life, Christian," in *The New Dictionary of Theology*, ed. Joseph Komonchak et al. (Wilmington, DE: Michael Glazier, 1987), pp. 676–688.

Servais Pinckaers, O.P., offers a beautiful presentation of the distinctiveness of Christian ethics in his magnificent presentation of the teaching of St. Paul, St. Augustine, and St. Thomas in *The Sources of Christian Ethics*, trans. Sister Mary Thomas Noble, O.P. (Washington: The Catholic University of America Press, 1995), pp. 95–1990. His perspective, however, is quite different from that of Grisez; I would say that their approaches to this issue are complementary and not contradictory. Pinckaers does not consider the question of specific Christian norms very helpful; in fact, he dislikes talk of specific Christian norms. But he does so because he, like Grisez, is totally opposed to a legalistic understanding of morality and he fears that talk of specific "norms" puts too much emphasis on "obligations," or "duties," and easily leads to legalism. Grisez, of course, repudiates this way of understanding moral norms, which he regards (as does Pope John Paul II in *Veritatis splendor*) as *truths* meant to guide human choices and actions.

29. Cf. St. Augustine, *The Lord's Sermon on the Mount*, I.1; trans. John J. Jepson, S.S., in *Ancient Christian Writers*, N. 15 (Westminster, MD: The Newman Press, 1948), p. 11.

30. St. Thomas Aquinas, *Summa theologiae* 1–2, q. 108, a. 3: "Sermo quem Dominus in Monte proposuit (Matt 5) totam informationem Christianae vitae continet."

31. Unfortunately, Grisez's thought regarding the specificity of Christian morality has been simply ignored by contemporary Catholic moral theologians. I know of no significant commentaries or critiques of his thought on this matter. It appears that Grisez's creative effort to articulate Christian moral principles has evoked, on the part of most influential Catholic theologians, the response feared by Benedict Ashley, O.P. Ashley, one of the very few theologians in the English-speaking world even to reflect on Grisez's articulation of Christian morality, who expressed the fear that his highly creative presentation of Christian moral principles was likely to provoke, on the part of Catholic theologians, either "angry replies or the hostile 'silent treatment' " ("Christian Moral Principles: A Review Discussion," *Thomist* 48 [1984] 450). The silent treatment is what it has been given. Ashley, whose critique of Grisez's understanding of human goods has been taken up in note 18, offers some "reservations" about his understanding of specific Christian morality in this review article. His reservations, however, do not deal explicitly with Grisez's way of deriving specific Christian moral norms from his modes of Christian response.

The Scriptural Basis of Grisez's Revision of Moral Theology

BENEDICT M. ASHLEY, O.P.
Aquinas Institute of Theology
St. Louis, MO

I

In the first pages of his remarkable *The Way of the Lord Jesus*,[1] Germain Grisez joins the consensus of most current moral theologians, whether "conservative" or "progressive" that the moral theology of pre-Vatican II manuals was excessively legalistic and in need of serious revision. Thus he commends both a leading progressive, Josef Fuchs, S.J. and an influential conservative Carlo Caffarra, for their acknowledgments of this need in the light of the Council.[2] Accomplishing such a revision is the aim of both wings working today in moral theology.

But Grisez sharply criticizes the methodology of the revision proposed by the self-designated "mainstream revisionists":

> Insofar as the requirement to assent to Catholic teaching is denied, the minimum set by the new moral theology is much lower than that set by classical moral theology. But the new remains as legalistic as the old. It provides no account in Christian terms of why one should seek human fulfillment in this life, what the specifically Christian way of life is, and how living as a Christian in this life is intrinsically related to fulfillment in everlasting life.[3]

In this "new moral theology" Grisez opposes not only its dissent from sacred tradition as embodied in the documents of the living magisterium of the Church, but also its odd interpretation of Vatican II statements, for example, that "the study of sacred Scripture . . . ought to be the soul of all theology"; and "Special attention needs to be given to the development of moral theology. Its scientific exposition should be more thoroughly nourished by scriptural teaching."[4] The prevailing revisionist view seems to be that, as even St. Thomas Aquinas admitted, the moral precepts of Christian life are for the most part materially identical with the natural law, and differ principally only in their supernatural motivation; therefore, in view of the modern historical-critical approach to the Bible, the classical "argument from Scripture" is largely irrelevant to current moral theology, whose arguments must be principally based on purely rational, philosophical, psychological, or social data.

Grisez, on the other hand, holds that there is a specifically Christian ethics.[5] No doubt this is one reason his work is so strikingly entitled *The Way of the Lord Jesus*. As a Thomist, I heartily agree, since in saying that revealed moral law and natural moral law are materially identical, Aquinas surely did not intend to contradict his fundamental principle that matter and form are proportionate to each other. Hence the formal difference of natural and revealed ethics also implies the respective modification of their otherwise materially identical contents. For example, as Aquinas explicitly points out, although the infused virtue of abstinence has the same material object as the natural virtue, namely, moderation as regards food, the formal difference resulting from the differing supernatural and natural ends to be achieved establishes a different *mean for each:* in one case the amount of food that best serves earthly health; in the other, the amount that best prepares for eternal life in heaven.[6] Thus for actual moral judgment—and that is what moral theology is all about— the Christian can arrive at decisions of conscience quite other than those dictated by reason, although not contradictory to it.

Grisez, therefore, has no patience with those who attempt to revise moral theology by dissenting from the magisterium, or for those who seek to cut it free from its concrete biblical foundations. Hence, like the rest of us moral theologians who agree with him, he finds himself in an interdisciplinary dilemma. What moral theologian today can claim competence in the highly complex and controverted field of biblical scholarship? On the other hand, has the training and orientation of biblical scholars made them competent to construct a systematic ethics or to apply it to current ethical problems?

Surprisingly, in so vast a work as *The Way of the Lord Jesus* is proving to be, in which every question raised is treated in impressive detail, in the two published volumes little attention is given to the question how, even in principle, the data of modern biblical scholarship is to be employed as the *norma normans* of Christian ethics. These volumes do, indeed, contain many citations: the special index to volume one cites most of the biblical books and is over ten pages long, that to volume two, seven pages long. Yet such citation is open to the common criticism that the author is merely "proof-texting," that is, quoting texts that seem verbally to mean what he is saying but which in their proper context have quite a different sense or scope. Moreover, such a procedure, even when the citation is truly probative, does no more than confirm some thesis which the author has developed on the basis of natural reason. It does not root the assertion in the revealed word of God.

There is, however, one chapter in volume one of *The Way of the Lord Jesus*,[7] in which Grisez approaches this question. He writes:

> Along with obvious differences, there are also similarities between the role of the Ten Commandments in the Old Testament and that of the Beatitudes in the New. As God gives the Ten Commandments to Moses, and then the rest of the law is unfolded from them, so Jesus gives the Beatitudes to his followers, and then the rest of the moral implications of the new covenant are unfolded. The Beatitudes provide a properly Christian moral framework. Although their relationship to the rest of the moral content of faith has never been clarified in detail, they have had an important place in moral instruction through Christian history. These are extrinsic, but not insignificant, reasons for taking the Beatitudes as organizing principles in analyzing Christian norms and virtues. . . . Although the New Testament provides no detailed moral code, one can expect to find in Jesus' teaching and example the basic guidance needed for Christian life. . . . St. Matthew's Gospel is in a special way the New Testament book of moral teaching. The Sermon on the Mount is the primary synthesis of such teaching, and the Beatitudes are placed at the start of this synthesis. . . . Hence, it is reasonable to suppose that the Beatitudes express specifically Christian moral principles. . . . It is significant that in his expansion of the ancient creeds, the Credo of the People of God, Paul VI mentions the Beatitudes in his summary of Jesus' teaching. . . . Thus the Pope suggests that the Beatitudes be taken as the model summary of the specifically Christian content of Jesus' moral teaching.[8]

Thus, rightly I think, Grisez relates the moral teaching of the two Testaments by comparing the Ten Commandments to the Sermon on the Mount and then links this to the living catechetical tradition, the *kerygma*, of the magisterium. He is able to quote such noted biblical scholars as John P. Meier, W. D. Davies, and Hans Dieter Betz to back up his claims, along with the moralist Servais Pinckaers, O.P., who has examined the relevant interdisciplinary and historical questions in some depth.[9] Yet Grisez himself goes no further in exploring this topic than to attempt a correlation between the "eight modes of moral responsibility," which are a characteristic feature of his system, and the eight Beatitudes.

My intention, therefore, is first to evaluate this chief effort of Grisez to systematically ground moral theory in the Scriptures, and then to sketch what seems to me a more satisfactory program.

II

In Grisez's moral theory the first moral principle (not norm) is this: "In voluntarily acting for human goods and avoiding what is opposed to them, one ought to choose and otherwise will those and only those possibilities whose willing is compatible with a will toward integral human fulfillment."[10] This fulfillment is possible only by the attainment of certain "basic goods" of two types: (a) "reflexive, existential, or moral goods" in whose definition free choice is included, and these are (1) "self-integration," (2) practical reasonableness and authenticity, (3) justice and friendship, (4) "religion or harmony with God"; or (b) substantive goods in whose definition choice is not included, and these are (5) health, physical integrity and handing on life to new persons, (6) knowledge of various forms of truth and appreciation of various forms of beauty and excellence, and (7) activities of skillful work and play.[11]

Further, Grisez argues that there must be specifications of that first moral principle, which he calls "modes of moral responsibility" each of which excludes "a particular way in which a person can limit himself or herself to a quite partial and inadequate fulfillment."[12] These he formulates as follows:

1. One should not be deterred by felt inertia from acting for intelligible goods.
2. One should not be pressed by enthusiasm or impatience to act individualistically for intelligible goods.
3. One should not choose to satisfy an emotional desire except as part of one's pursuit and/or attainment of an intelligible good other than the satisfaction of the desire itself.
4. One should not choose to act out of an emotional aversion except as part of one's avoidance of some intelligible evil other than the inner tension experienced in enduring that aversion.
5. One should not, in response to different feelings toward different persons, willingly proceed with a preference for anyone unless the preference is required by intelligible goods themselves.
6. One should not choose on the basis of emotions which bear upon empirical aspects of intelligible goods (or bads) in a way which interferes with a more perfect sharing in the good or avoidance of the bad.
7. One should not be moved by hostility to freely accept or choose the destruction, damaging, or impeding of any intelligible human good.

8. One should not be moved by a stronger desire for one instance
   of an intelligible good to act for it by choosing to destroy, damage, or impede some other instance of an intelligible good.[13]

Grisez points out that "much that Scripture and Christian teaching
say about morality is cast in the language of virtues."[14] For him, "distinct
virtues are not separate entities but only aspects of a good person. They,
and their corresponding vices, can therefore be distinguished in various
ways." Thus he argues that it is best to treat the virtues simply as embodi-
ments of the modes of responsibility.[15]

How then are these modes of responsibility specified as Christian?
Grisez's very original proposal is that the eight modes are embodied in
the Eight Beatitudes. Thus the virtues embodying the eight modes of
responsibility specify the first principle of moral theology and are intermediate between it and concrete moral norms, such as the Ten Commandments. In fact, the Beatitudes are even enumerated in the *Gospel According
to St. Matthew* in the same order as Grisez's systematic listing of the modes.

To take only three examples: "Blessed are the poor in spirit" embodies the first mode of responsibility, namely, that one should "accept all
good, including the good fruits of one's own work as God's gift"; "Blessed
are they who mourn" embodies the third mode: "One should not choose
to satisfy an emotional desire except as part of one's pursuit and/or
attainment of an intelligible good other than the satisfaction of the desire
itself"; and "Blessed are the pure of heart" embodies the mode of responsibility that requires that Christians "strive to conform one's whole self to
living faith, and to recognize and purge anything which does not meet
this standard."

Furthermore, Grisez regards the traditional "Seven Gifts of the Holy
Spirit" (Isa 11:1–2) as

> virtues to the extent that they are dispositions to human acts, though of a
> specifically Christian sort, and as gifts insofar as their relationship to faith
> enlivened by charity makes them specifically Christian. Or, perhaps prefera-
> bly, the gifts of the Holy Spirit might be identified with charity considered
> precisely insofar as it is the gift of the Holy Spirit which transforms the
> moral requirements articulated in the modes of responsibility into the char-
> acteristically Christian inclinations (or modes of response) proclaimed
> "blessed" in the Beatitudes.[16]

For the correspondence of each Beatitude to a mode of responsibility
Grisez gives perceptive and plausible arguments, yet one is left with the

feeling that this is an arbitrary and even fanciful accommodation to a system whose origin and justification is not biblical but philosophical. Is it really plausible that Jesus (or Matthew) promulgated the New Law by a series of Beatitudes corresponding to Grisez's modes of responsibility and in just that order? He may reply of course that his accommodation is no more far-fetched than the diverse ways theologians, ever since Augustine, have matched the Aristotelian virtue list to the seven theological and moral virtues, the gifts of the Spirit, the beatitudes, the "spiritual fruits," the Ten Commandments, and the petitions of the Lord's prayer. While some of these enumerations of "sevens" and accommodations to scriptural texts were merely catechetical and mnemonic, it is evident that for St. Thomas Aquinas this matching was a serious theological problem to which he devoted much attention not only in the *Summa* but in many other works.[17]

Nevertheless, it is helpful to compare Grisez's method of accommodation with that of Aquinas. At first sight it appears that Aquinas is a typical medieval who is determined to make everything fit into a neat set of niches. But further study shows he is trying to be true to the deepest principles of his theology conceived as *sacra doctrina,* as a participation in the wisdom of God as God is revealed to us in Scripture and tradition. In that wisdom is revealed all that the Creator intended Adam and Eve and all their descendants to be by nature and by grace, a divine intention finally realized in Jesus and Mary and ultimately in the communion of the saints. In other words, the basis of Aquinas's moral doctrine is a Christian anthropology.

Grisez emphatically concurs with Aquinas in making Jesus the model of Christian life.[18] Too much influenced, however, by the dictum of modern analytical philosophy that the "ought" cannot be derived from the "is," he avoids establishing a Christian anthropology.[19] Hence, he cannot make use, at least in the same systematic way that Aquinas does, of a taxonomy of human powers, habits, virtues, acts, and objects as the basic principle for systematizing biblical doctrine.

But does not Aquinas derive his listing of the virtues from Aristotle rather than from the Bible? I would not deny, of course, that this is the case *in via inventionis.* Divine revelation has to be received into the human intelligence and made intelligible in human experience. Consequently, the word of God in the Bible is expressed in human categories and a variety of literary forms. Theological wisdom has the task of ordering this revealed but humanly formulated data into a scientific order so as to show its unity and increase it intelligibility and credibility. Since theology, while eminently theoretical, is also truly practical, moral theology has the specific task of showing how human persons as free beings can, as it were, complete the work of creation and redemption in themselves and their community by freely chosen acts. Aquinas, therefore, uses Aristotle's psychology to help him read the Bible in a penetrating way but not to impose merely human philosophy upon it.

Does Thomas succeed in doing this as regards the moral data of the Scripture? Not perfectly, of course; medieval psychology and biblical exegesis had serious defects that we today ought to be able to overcome. Aquinas's theological anthropology is first of all based on Genesis 1-2 which teaches that we, like other living things, were created by God from the dust of the earth but also in God's image as stewards of the material creation. Hence we share in the Creator's spirituality and live in spiritual communion with God, not only remotely by nature but intimately by the life of grace. This community in grace has been lost by sin, but is now restored in the God-Man, Jesus Christ. While Aquinas uses the Aristotelian philosophy based on act and potency to formulate this biblical data, the total picture and its certitude transcend human reason.

With this understanding of the unity and complexity of the graced human person comes clarity about those powers which constitute the human species as such. We could not be stewards of God's creation unless we were, like God, intelligent and free, which implies that we have the distinct powers of intellect and will. Yet because we are bodily beings, not pure angelic spirits, our intellectual knowledge requires the sense organs as its instruments, and our will requires bodily affections or passions. These physical, cognitive, and affective powers are instruments for and under the direction of the corresponding spiritual powers: intellect directs the senses; the will directs the passions. Furthermore, the intellect and will are mutually interdependent. The complexity of human nature and its need for a material body subject to chance imply that the human person cannot direct itself toward God or carry out the stewardship committed to it in a consistent and hence successful way without stability of character. This stability, however, is acquired either by discipline or the gifts of God, that is, by virtues acquired or infused. Moreover, success in attaining this goal of life is not an individual accomplishment but happens only through the action of a graced community, a just civil community for temporal life, and a holy church looking toward eternal life.

While this picture of a virtuous Christian character in a just society and a holy Church is nowhere presented by the Scriptures in abstract terms, it is revealed in many concrete ways through images, precepts, exhortations, encomia, and examples. What Aquinas attempted to do, like Augustine and other theologians before him, was to abstract the universal content from the biblical data and express it in appropriate terms taken from Greek philosophy but modified to serve a scientific model. Central to this systematic reformulation of revealed data on the moral life in the New Testament is not a code of conduct like the Ten Commandments, but the *virtues* which form Christian character and community as exemplified in Jesus.

Grisez, while admitting that an ethics which emphasizes individual acts at the expense of a consistent pattern of life is inadequate, argues against the centrality of the virtues so characteristic of St. Thomas's moral theology. He writes:

> Theories which emphasize character and the general trend of one's life nevertheless suffer from a major defect. They fail to realize that character itself—which is one's virtues or vices as a whole—is chiefly (although not solely) the enduring structure of one's choices. . . . Character itself essentially is particular choices, and it manifests itself in further particular acts.[20]

Grisez devotes almost no time to the definition or classification of virtues and tends to reduce them all to modes of Christian response understood as aspects of the single virtue of charity. He is, of course, quite right in saying that character is formed by acts and is expressed in acts. It is entirely Thomistic to insist that virtues are for the sake of acts, not vice versa; and certainly it is entirely Christian to say that "a good tree bears good fruit." Nevertheless, theology as a science is about the universal,[21] and consequently moral theology does not attempt to explain individual prudential acts or to dictate positively, but to develop universal principles and concrete norms to assist prudence in the ultimate judgment of conscience. The importance of the renewed emphasis on virtue theory is that it frees us from the illusion, cultivated by the excessive development of casuistry in the moral manuals, that ethics can replace rather than serve prudence.

Again, for Grisez the Thomistic account of the gifts of the Holy Spirit,[22] and hence of the Beatitudes which are their supreme, paradigmatic acts, is mistaken. It entails

> . . . the notion that human powers are actuated by the gifts of the Holy Spirit in a manner which reason enlightened by faith and human love enlivened by charity cannot account for. Thomas seems to admit an element

of divine activity into the process of human action and to treat it as a principle on the same level with the principles of human action. (If it were not on the same level, it would not be an alternative to the movement of reason.) This appears to be a case of commingling.[23]

By "commingling" Grisez means a kind of monophysitism that confuses the order of grace and nature.[24] A constant theme in Grisez's revision of moral theology is his concern to eliminate what he regards as a certain "other-worldliness" in classical moral theology.

While Grisez's care for balance in this matter is certainly to be commended, it seems to me that his reduction of the gifts and the Beatitudes to mere aspects of faith and charity is subversive of an extensive and deeply rooted tradition in the Church and in magisterial documents that deal with the theology of spirituality. There is not, however, sufficient space to demonstrate that here. What directly concerns my topic is the biblical data regarding the guidance of the Christian by the Holy Spirit.

It is not monophysitic to emphasize that in his human nature Jesus the Christ was not only the divine son, but that he was also anointed and guided by the Holy Spirit, as narrated in the account of his baptism (Mark 1:10 and par.). Aquinas argues that our participation by adoption in the divine sonship is achieved by rebirth through sanctifying grace and the theological and infused moral virtues; yet these virtues, even charity, do not suffice, without the direct guidance of the Holy Spirit, to attain to eternal life in the Trinity.

Hence, in order that the theological virtues should attain God as their object and be exercised in the divine mode appropriate to our life in Christ, we need the gifts of the Spirit to render us flexible to the Holy Spirit's guidance. The effect of this guidance is not spontaneity, as Grisez describes it,[25] but a connaturality with the divine mind and will. No "commingling" of nature and grace is involved, only a transformation by grace in which nature is at once integrally preserved yet elevated. Certainly the theological virtues work such a transformation in the human mind and will or they could not obtain God's self as their proper object. The gifts do not change this object but perfect the mode of union between the power and the object, as analogically an increase in light perfects the union of the eye with color.

Thus I find Grisez's principal attempt to give a biblical foundation to his moral theology by way of the Beatitudes unsatisfactory. What form, then, should this biblical rooting take in a revision of moral theology?

III

My proposal for working out a biblical foundation for a revised moral theology can be reduced to the following points.[26]

1. Such a revision should avoid "proof-texting" and fundamentalism and take into account the solid results of various modern methods of biblical exegesis as explained in the Pontifical Biblical Commission's, "The Interpretation of the Bible in the Church."[27] Of these methods, however, the most directly relevant to the theologian is "canonical criticism," because the guarantee of inspiration and doctrinal inerrancy applies to the canonical text only as it is interpreted in light of the canon as a whole and the tradition of the Church.

2. Consequently, even the finest studies of New Testament ethics—for example the works that Rudolf Schnackenburg[28] and Wolfgang Schragge[29] have produced based on the data supplied by individual biblical authors, or the work that Ceslaus Spicq[30] has done based on biblical themes—do not of themselves constitute a biblically based systematic moral theology.

3. A stance must be taken on the relation of Old Testament ethics to New Testament ethics and this presupposes a position on the canonical unity of the two Testaments, especially as regards their moral teachings. I would opt for the view that Old Testament moral teaching centers in the covenant of the Ten Commandments as "the way of life" chosen against the "way of death" (Deut 30:15). The rest of the Torah, and the narratives and Wisdom literature, render the practical meaning of the Commandments more concrete, while the prophets exhort us to interiorize the law. This interiorization of the law as the law of the Holy Spirit, is the work of Christ, who in the (Matthaean) Sermon of the Mount brings the law to its perfect, universal, and permanent form. Thus the moral law of the Old and New Testaments is one and the same divine law, which includes but transcends the natural law. The ceremonial and judicial elements of this law continue to have instructive but not obligatory force, while the moral elements, in the interpretation given them by Jesus and by apostolic authority in the Church, will remain obligatory until the end of history.

4. Although the law as interpreted by Jesus is permanent and final, not subject to change by any human authority, our understanding of it and its prudential application undergo development in the history of the Church, both positive and negative. At any given time, however, the

understanding and prudential application of the law by the Church's magisterium, even if defective, is obligatory on all members of the Church. Theologians, therefore, although they have a duty to assist in the development of moral doctrine, may not do so by any form of "dissent" that might undermine the authority of the magisterium as the guide of faith and conscience.[31]

5. The New Testament Torah shifts the emphasis from the legal norms of morality, to the formation of the Christian in view of eternal life, and thus to the development of character through the virtues. Central to this virtue theory are the theological virtues of faith, hope, and love (*agape*) which directly unite the Christian to the Trinity. These, however, require support from the infused moral virtues, and are perfected by the gifts of the Holy Spirit through which alone the supreme acts of the Beatitudes become possible and through them connaturality with Christ in the divine sonship.

6. The most difficult problem in systematizing the New Testament data on moral life is the relation of the many virtues named in the texts and illustrated in the lives of Jesus, Mary, and the saints. The four cardinal virtues of prudence, justice, fortitude, and temperance are recognized as such only in a single biblical text, Wisdom 8:7. Yet they are certainly portrayed as principal virtues and characteristic of the Christian in many other places in the New and Old Testament. And they are exemplified in Jesus' own practical wisdom (prudence), his zeal for justice, his patience in martyrdom (fortitude), and his virginity (temperance). They can, in fact, be intimately related to the theological virtues, in that faith is supported in practical matters by prudence, hope by the asceticism of temperance and fortitude, and love by justice. Thus the traditional view that Christian character is formed by the seven virtues of faith, hope, charity, prudence, justice, fortitude, and temperance is a well-grounded systematization of the New Testament picture of the character of Jesus and his saints.

7. Traditional authors differed as to the relation of the seven gifts of the Holy Spirit, the Beatitudes, the fruits of the Spirit, and the Lord's Prayer to the foregoing seven virtues, as Grisez correctly notes.[32] Aquinas himself was not always consistent in statements on this subject, and undoubtedly the fact that the names of virtues are not very stable or easy to translate makes such attributions somewhat arbitrary. Nevertheless, Aquinas sought a sound basis for such attribution in his Christian anthropology in which the human powers involved in fully human, free and morally responsible acts distinguish the virtues through their proper ob-

jects. They can also be systematically related to the basic human needs and to the principal problems that all human beings must meet in attaining integral human fulfillment. Just as the Bible shows us that we cannot be intimately united to God except by faith, hope, and charity and the infused virtues—which enable us to think about what we are to do with a knowledge that is not carnal but spiritual (prudence), to accept the cross (fortitude), to control our fleshly desires in hope of eternal life (temperance), and to love our neighbor as we love ourselves (justice)—so also we need the guidance of the Holy Spirit through the intellectual gifts of wisdom, knowledge, and understanding to enlighten our faith to enter into the mind of Christ. Similarly, we need the gift of counsel to use our prudence spiritually, the gift of fear of the Lord to remain chaste, and the gift of piety to be just to others as our brothers and sisters in Christ.

Only as these gifts free us to follow Jesus in the Holy Spirit is it possible to obtain by fully Christlike acts the blessings promised in the Beatitudes, that is, the poverty of spirit and the mourning for sin that free us to follow Christ in the fear of the Lord, the meekness that accepts the cross, the mercy to the sinful which is true counsel and prudence, the hunger for justice that is true piety, the knowledge that enables us to understand our sinful world and the Creator's original intentions, the purity of heart that enables us to believe truly, and the love of peace that establishes us in the love of God and neighbor.

8. Once the biblical virtues have been given an anthropological and christological foundation, the norms of Christian behavior can be derived from the kind of acts that must be performed and avoided under temptation to conform the Christian to Christ in the community which is the Body of Christ. Among these norms are those of Christian prudence which submit the Christian to the Holy Spirit's guidance in applying these norms to the circumstances of life in a sinful world. The supreme goal of such a life is the contemplation of God in a faith illuminated by the intellectual gifts of the Holy Spirit and conformed to Christ in charity. This life of contemplation is shared by all Christians even in this world, although the vowed life of the practice of the counsels and Beatitudes is (as St. Paul tells us) the most free for its attainment.

9. A moral theology of this type is not only biblically rooted, but also flows from the deepest dogmatic mysteries of the Trinity and Incarnation. It is an ascetic and spiritual theology confirmed by the experience of saints and ordinary Christians. The new *Catechism of the Catholic Church*, developed by a universal consultation of the magisterium, also confirms it.

The moral life of Christians is sustained by the gifts of the Holy Spirit. They are permanent dispositions which make man docile in following the promptings of the Holy Spirit. . . . They belong in their fullness to Christ, the Son of David. They complete and perfect the virtues of those who receive them. They make the faithful docile in readily obeying divine inspirations (nn. 1830–1831).

As for the Beatitudes, which are discussed at some length in the *Catechism* (nn. 1716–1729), it is said: "The Beatitudes teach us the final end to which God calls us: the Kingdom, the vision of God, participation in the divine nature, eternal life, filiation, rest in God" (n. 1726). Thus, the magisterial catechesis of the Church maintains the solid tradition that the Beatitudes are not virtues as such, but the perfect acts of Christian virtue by which the final reward of beatitude is attained. They are the ends, not merely the means, of a fully Christian life. The work of moral theology is to mark out the steps by which that goal can be attained. The collaborative task of revising and renewing moral theology—to which Germain Grisez by his courageous, faithful, and philosophically rigorous work has made so powerful a contribution—will be finally achieved only when we mark out the way of the Lord Jesus in the full light of biblical revelation.

NOTES

1. Vol. 1, *Christian Moral Principles* (Chicago: Franciscan Herald Press) 1983, pp. 13–22. From here on I will refer to this volume as CMP and will use LCL for vol. 2, *Living a Christian Life* (Quincy, IL: Franciscan Herald Press, 1993).
2. CMP, note 20, p. 36–37.
3. CMP, p. 15.
4. *Optatam totius,* n. 16.
5. CMP, p. 606–608, 661–680.
6. *Summa theologiae* I-II. q. 63, a. 4c. Hereafter: S.t.
7. CMP, Chapter 26, "Modes of Christian Response," pp. 627–659.
8. CMP, p. 627–8.
9. CMP. p. 657, notes 1 and 2.
10. CMP, p. 184.
11. CMP, pp. 121–140.
12. CMP, p. 191.
13. CMP, pp. 225–226.
14. CMP, p. 192.
15. CMP, p. 193.
16. CMP, p. 633.

17. For example, in his commentary on the *Sentences*, III, *De virtutibus, De caritate*, and the scripture commentaries.

18. CMP, Chapter 19, "Fulfillment in Jesus and Human Fulfillment."

19. I have already discussed this feature of Grisez's system in "What Is the End of the Human Person: The Vision of God and Integral Human Fulfillment," in *Moral Truth and Moral Tradition: Essays in Honour of Peter Geach and Elizabeth Anscombe*, ed. by Luke Gormally (Dublin and Portland, OR: Four Courts Press, 1994), pp. 68–96.

20. CMP, 193–194.

21. CMP, pp. 31–32. Grisez rejects Aquinas's arguments for theology being an Aristotelian *scientia per causas* which attains certitude and prefers to say that it is a "dialectic . . . in Plato's sense of the word" (CMP p. 7, 27–32). "By this method, one considers truths of faith by comparison (*analogia*) with truths of reason, with one another, and with the ultimate fulfillment to which God calls us in Christ Jesus" (CMP, p. 31). However, in my understanding, although Aristotle's "dialectic" means merely probably knowledge, Plato's "dialectic" attains certitude through at least the formal exemplary cause by an ascent to an innate knowledge of the Ideas. As far as I can see, nothing that Grisez says about theology shows that it is not a *scientia per causes* yielding certitude. Is Grisez, then, by preferring to call theology "dialectical" rejecting an Aristotelian epistemology for a Platonic one?

22. S.t. I-II.q.69.a.1.c.

23. CMP, p. 632–633.

24. CMP, p. 589–590.

25. CMP, p. 634.

26. I first proposed these ideas in "The Scriptural Basis of Moral Theology," *The Thomist*, 1987, also in *Persona et Morale*, Atti del I Congresso Internazionale di Teologia Morale, Rome, 1986, Milano: Edizione Ares, 1987. More recently, they have become the basis of a book, *Living the Truth in Love: A Biblical Introduction to Moral Theology* (Alba House, in press).

27. *Origins*, 23, n. 29 (Jan. 6, 1994): 499–524.

28. *The Moral Teaching of the New Testament*. (New York: Seabury, 1973).

29. *The Ethics of the New Testament*, trans. David E. Green, (Philadelphia: Fortress Press, 1988). See also David Clyde Jones, *Biblical Christian Ethics* (Grand Rapids, MI: Baker Books, 1994).

30. Théologie Morale du Nouveau Testament, 2 vols. (Paris: Lecoffre, 1965); also, *Agape in the New Testament*, 3 vols. (St. Louis: Herder, 1963).

31. I do not deny, of course, the possibility that a Catholic in a rare instance could know with certitude that a particular ordinary teaching of the magisterium is mistaken and may be bound in conscience in his or her personal life to follow the truth, taking responsibility for one's own acts. But even in such rare cases Catholics would not be justified in carrying on a campaign against magisterial teaching, nor in attempting to substitute their authority as theological experts over against the superior doctrinal and pastoral authority of the magisterium. See the Congregation for the Doctrine of the Faith, "Instruction on the Ecclesial Vocation of the Theologian," May 24, 1990, *Origins* 20 (July 5, 1990): 117–26.

32. CMP, pp. 632–633.

Contraception Again—A Conclusion in Search of Convincing Arguments: One Proportionalist's [Mis?]understanding of a Text

EDWARD C. VACEK, S. J.
Paul McKeever Professor of Moral Theology
St. John's University
Jamaica, New York

PREFACE

I accepted the invitation to present this paper because I thought it might be sinful to refuse. The lack of genuine conversation between proportionalists like myself and ethicists in the school of Germain Grisez is unconscionable, and all the more so because most of us are members of the same Church and seek the same truth. Among proportionalists, the overcoming of evil is a priority; and so I had a prima facie obligation to accept.

To his credit, the man we honor, Germain Grisez, asked that some contributors to this symposium be persons who disagree with his thought. That is why I have been invited. And though I can't help but feel like a skunk at a picnic, I would fail in my appointed task if, instead of criticizing Grisez's thought, I gave yet another exposition of proportionalism. I am supposed to stink up matters a bit and then exit quickly. My defense for any offense I might give is that I have been asked to do this to give people something to talk about.

Nevertheless, I am reluctant. Several years ago I wrote an article defending proportionalism and critiquing Grisez's thought. An observation I made there seems especially pertinent: "time and time again intelligent persons read the views of the other side, report them rather accurately, then shake their heads at how someone so smart could be so benighted."[1] That observation is still true, and I fear this paper will further confirm its truth.[2]

When I read the writings of Germain Grisez, I am enormously impressed by his breadth, depth, and erudition. The imaginativeness of his reasoning and the strength of his convictions are remarkable. I especially admire the way he argues so inventively on behalf of the Church's official teachings.[3] Nevertheless, his arguments, far from being compelling, often seem to be counterintuitive.

In my earlier article, I looked *broadly* at Grisez's methodology. I discovered that his methodology and action theory are fundamentally different from my own. In this essay, observing Grisez's counsel that we pay no compliment to a creative author by rehashing old arguments,[4] I concentrate *narrowly* on the thirteen pages (506–19a) of *Living a Christian Life*[5] that deal with contraception as contralife.[6] The topic has the virtue of being focused, while at the same time opening onto major themes in Grisez's thought.[7] The narrow focus seems fair since the topic has long been a concern of Grisez's. The topic itself will illustrate how our two different ethical theories play out when brought to bear on a particular issue.

Grisez begins the section on contraception by saying, "There are two reasons why Catholics should believe that contraception is always wrong" (506a). Those reasons are, first, the Church teaches it and, second, the present pontiff teaches that it is part of divine revelation. In this paper, I do not dispute this teaching. And I will not dispute Grisez's appeals to authority.[8] Rather, I engage Grisez at the level of his supportive arguments (506b).

CONTRALIFE

Grisez does not hide the harsher implications of his thought when, along with our tradition, he holds that contraception is akin to homicide (507a).[9] To demonstrate that contraception, like homicide, is always contralife, Grisez makes four moves. He explains what contraception is not; he defines contraception; he distinguishes contraception from sexual acts; and finally he argues that contraception is contralife. Each step is important to his argument, and each step is questionable.

What Contraception Is Not

Natural law ethics[10] is usually thought to be concerned with what one does, not just with one's intention in doing an action. In my version of natural law, namely, proportionalism,[11] not only one's virtues, relationships, and accomplishments, but also *what* one is doing and how one does it are relevant to moral analysis, though each in quite different ways.[12]

Objective and Subjective Morality

In traditional natural law ethics, the nature of one's act—what one does—featured heavily in what was called "objective morality." Although "subjective morality" was sometimes thought to focus on the ways a person was not fully culpable, it referred more generally to a person's involvement through knowledge and freedom in his or her own acts. This distinction was and is crucial for confessional practice. A related distinction is made today between moral rightness and moral goodness. In brief, rightness has to do with the deed one should do or with the character one should have, while goodness has to do with the uprightness of one's will, which is realized in these deeds and virtues. "Subjective morality," then, refers to the moral goodness or badness of the subject.

Traditional natural law also recognized that we may not actually do what we intend to do. Thus, it was said, we are "formally a liar" if we intend to tell a lie, even if—contrary to our intentions—we speak true words, the "material truth." And we are "formally a truth-teller" if we intend to tell the truth, even if, accidentally, what we say is "materially false." Both aspects were part of morality.

A full analysis of a moral deed, I suggest, reveals at least three "moments": (1) intention, (2) attempting to carry out that intention in an adequate or inadequate way, and (3) actually doing what one intends. The first moment is essential to subjective morality. The second is transitional; it indicates greater subjective involvement, and it is distinguishable from the third because one sometimes makes a decision, but then finds that one "can't go through with it." While the third "moment" depends on contingent factors, it is essential to a complete analysis of the objective morality of a deed. I will argue that Grisez, in his treatment of contraception, emphasizes the first moment, slights the second moment, and makes the third morally irrelevant.

To clarify this difference between how Grisez and I analyze morality, let me introduce one of Grisez's cases: A blind woman intends to commit adultery, but unbeknownst to her she actually has sex with her husband. Is she an adulteress and does she commit adultery? Grisez has written that the blind woman makes herself an adulteress. I think further analysis is necessary. To be sure, since the blind woman intended to commit adultery, she is subjectively guilty. She has set her heart on the path to become an adulteress; she is a would-be adulteress, but prior to the deed, she is not yet an adulteress.[13]

Part of the intellectual intrigue of this case is that she actually does have sex with someone. That is, it is an important addition that she *try* to have sex with someone other than her husband. If intention were sufficient for moral evaluation, then she would be an adulteress even if she never has sex with anyone. Still, more than intention and attempt are necessary for analyzing the objective morality of this and like cases. To really be an adulteress, I think, one has not only to intend, not only to try, but also to commit adultery. In my view, since this woman does not have sex with someone who is not her husband, she cannot properly be said to commit adultery.

Murder is a parallel example in which Grisez and I disagree.[14] I think a man who intends murder is not a murderer unless and until he has killed someone. Intention is not enough. Behavior and accomplishment are also necessary. If we allow intention to suffice, our moral notions are stretched too far. In Grisez's analyses, we have adulteresses who have had sex only with their husbands (or who imaginably might be virgins), murderers who have killed no one, suicides who are alive, liars who tell only the truth, top-flight students who write only failing papers, and good mothers who needlessly kill their children. As we next see, we also have contraceptors who do nothing or who do ineffectual deeds or who even promote fertility.

Contraception Is Not an Issue of Behavior

Grisez locates morality not primarily in behaviors, relationships, adequate attempts, or results but in attitudes and especially in the will. In particular, he locates contraception not in certain techniques, practices or certain effects, but in the *intention* (508a).[15] As evidence for his claim that the particulars of *what* we are doing are morally irrelevant, he offers two observations.

First, he notes that in an effort to prevent births some people employ de facto "useless techniques" (507c). Even if, for example, they take fertility pills or wear amulets, they are, Grisez claims, practicing contraception if they intend thereby to prevent conception. I think this notion is mistaken. Most people, I assume, upon learning that they were using fertility drugs to contracept would shamefacedly acknowledge: "We were not doing *what* we thought we were doing. We were not practicing contraception." Grisez nonetheless holds that in determining whether or not a person is contracepting, "what" they are actually doing is unessential. In other words, "contraception" has no necessary relation to contraceptives or contraceptive practices.

Second, Grisez notes that certain techniques that are chosen by some for the purpose of contraception are chosen by others for quite different purposes. Consider one woman who is not sexually active and another who is. Both take a drug that others use for contraception, but these women take it for its therapeutic effect on some disease they have. Grisez suggests that the first woman could hardly be practicing contraception since she is not even sexually active. Similarly, he argues, the second woman is not practicing contraception because her *intention* in choosing the drug is its therapeutic effect. Therefore it is not contraception, even though it prevents conception. I want here to insist only that certain pills, devices, or patterns of behavior have a contraceptive effect, whether we want them to or not, and that this effect should be part of our moral understanding of contraception. I fear that in discounting our deeds and their effects in favor of intention Grisez here replaces objective morality with subjective morality.

Morality Is Not an Issue of Emotion

Grisez and I have different understandings of the nature of emotions, and accordingly, different evaluations of their role in moral living.[16] He frequently stresses their negative role.[17] In this section on contraception, however, he portrays them as free floating and apart from moral decisions. To wit, he says that, if one woman has a good therapeutic reason to use drugs that aid her health but prevent conception, she can be glad that conception is prevented (508a). Her heart, in other words, can rejoice that she can engage in sex without conception taking place, as long as that is not her intention. He considers a second person who, we may say, chooses to use contraceptive pills to save her life but does so reluctantly (508b) because she really wants a baby.[18] For Grisez, the second woman and not the first is at fault for having a contralife will. The first woman's joy at not having children is outside the moral sphere; the second woman's desire to have children does not mean her will is prolife.

A proportionalist would look differently at these two women: assuming that all other things are equal, the first woman whose heart seems glad that no new life shall be born is less good than the woman whose heart is not glad. For some ethicists, among whom I include myself, emotions ordinarily are highly relevant to moral analysis. Emotions cognitively relate us to value, and so without our emotions we would not be able to be moral. Emotions also frequently reveal the kind of person we are, and this character is often more morally important than the acts that we perform. By contrast, for Grisez, it is our "efficacious volitions, which are morally determinative, rather than feelings" (511c).[19]

Contraception Is Defined through Intention

To those who hold that certain behaviors or devices are contraceptive, Grisez would respond that he is not concerned with how a doctor or even the average person might talk about contraceptives. Rather as a moralist he is concerned with what constitutes the *moral* meaning of contraception. Morality is a matter of the will or of choices, and these are determined by our intentions. He turns to a papal statement to establish this definition:

> In teaching that contraception always is morally excluded, Paul VI defines it in terms of intention: "any action which either before, at the moment of, or after marital intercourse, is specifically intended to impede procreation— whether as an end or as a means" [note omitted]. He could not have accurately defined contraception in any other way, for only certain intentions can render the various things people do ("any action") contraceptive (508a).

Grisez agrees in part and disagrees in part with this statement. Some theologians have held that the pope literally means that "contraception" must be part of *marital* sex; thus, they say, birth control measures in premarital sex are not "contraception" in the proscribed sense and can therefore be recommended. Grisez takes a different approach (509c, 515c). He focuses on how the pope defines (or seems to define[20]) contraception in terms of intention. If one intends to practice contraception, whether as an end or as a means (508a), then morally speaking, one practices contraception. The *intention* to prevent life "renders" *any* device or practice contraceptive.

In defining contraception in terms of intention, Grisez disagrees with the position of those who say that what one does is morally right or wrong "independently of any act of the will" (508c). I find something to agree with and something to disagree with in both positions.

If Grisez is concerned with questions of *subjective morality*, I agree with him that the primary focus should be on the will of the agent. In the sacrament of reconciliation, the penitent should confess the act that she willed to perform, even if that act was not the "pattern of behavior" she actually performed. If she takes a pill to foster her pregnancy but mistakenly takes an abortifacient, she deserves, morally speaking, to be evaluated as one who tried to become a good mother. She should not be forgiven for the abortion because she did not commit the sin of abortion. Her intention is subjectively determinative.

On the other hand, I agree with those who argue that *objective morality* includes the nature of what we are doing "independently of any act of our will." Thus, the woman who unknowingly took an abortifacient should also be told that *what* she actually did was the sort of thing she ought not do. Her good intention does not make this abortive act therapy, nor does it make her a good mother. I disagree, then, with Grisez when he makes intention almost wholly determinative of the moral meaning of contraception. He seems to confuse the centrality of the will in subjective morality with the proper place of intention in objective morality. From my perspective, in this small section of his book, Grisez comes close to practicing a form of constructivism, at least in the moral sphere: acts are whatever we intend them to be.[21]

Where Grisez's critics are wrong is in failing to appreciate how intention properly functions within what I have called objective morality. In fact, I suspect that all of us moral theologians are floundering around on this issue. For example, Grisez's followers disagree on whether the intention involved in capital punishment makes this act a permissible exercise of justice or an immoral form of direct killing. This much should be admitted by all: our intentions often inform or bring coherence to the acts we perform. We do not just do physical behaviors to which we add extrinsic intentions. Rather, our intention often characterizes or coforms the very nature (the object) of our acts. Making love with one's spouse is not "making love" unless there is some sort of loving intention. In brief, intention is often a necessary, but rarely a sufficient, condition for determining *what* we are doing. In my view, Grisez makes intention nearly sufficient when, in his definition of contraception, action serves as a sort of prime matter ("any action," including "useless techniques") which then intentions "render" contraceptive (508a). For him intention can also turn even the nonaction of periodic abstinence into contraception.

Recognizing the role of intention in objective morality should not obscure the idea that using a device or a "pattern of behavior" (507b) is usually also necessary for determining the objective morality of contraception. Some devices and practices really do have a contraceptive effect, and some do not. To be sure, they have these effects only in certain constellations of cause and effect; and they must be used properly. A condom in the closet will prevent neither disease nor birth. But most human actions (and inactions) are not contraceptive, no matter what the intention of the agent; and at least some devices or behaviors are effective contraceptives, no matter what the agent wills.

Let me make my point clearer by contrasting Grisez's approach to contraception with his approach to periodic abstinence. The question commonly raised about natural family planning is how one is "open to procreation" if one engages in sex only during infertile periods. "Openness to procreation," Grisez argues, is not a matter of one's intention. It is not a psychological openness; rather it is a biological "pattern of behavior" (634c–635a). This biological "suitability for procreation" has its own meaning quite apart from anyone's intention (635b). Similarly, he argues that the infertility of certain times in the menstrual cycle "is due to natural conditions" and hence this infertility is outside a couple's intention (511a). I agree with Grisez. I would further argue that these natural facts are part of the objective morality of human sexual practice.

Contraception Is Not a Sexual Act

Grisez holds that using contraception is distinct from a sexual act. If contraception were part of a sexual act, he suggests, then the principle of double effect might be used to justify it (510c). For example, a sexual act that was contraceptive might in unitary fashion bring about both a good effect (e.g., save a life) and a bad effect (e.g., prevent conception), and the latter might be accepted because of the former.

How then does Grisez demonstrate that contraception is not a unitary part of a sexual act? His answer is relatively simple: they are separable. He offers two arguments: first, one can practice contraception (e.g., be sterilized) yet not find a partner for sex; second, when fornicators have contraceptive sex, they make two choices—a choice to have sex and another choice to use contraception (508c). Unfortunately, these arguments may not be conclusive. In the first case, the person who is sterilized presumably intends this sterilized condition to be part of his or her sexual life. Otherwise, the sterilization would be simple self-mutilation. If intentions of themselves can define what one does, then this sterilized condition should be a unitary part of this person's sexual life. If the logic of the second case were applied to sex in marriage, one might have to conclude that such sex is not a marital act, since some people have sex outside of marriage and since other people make two different choices when they choose to be married and when they choose to make love. Thus the arguments need work.

The underlying difficulty, however, is what Grisez means by a sexual act. He defines a sexual act in such a way that contraception could not be a part of it:

> *Sexual act* refers to any act whatsoever—whether thought, word, or deed— in which someone intends, either as an end in itself or as a means to

some other end, to bring about or maintain sexual arousal and/or to cause incomplete or complete sexual satisfaction, whether in himself or herself, in another, or both (633a).

Readers will quickly note two concepts that we have seen before: "any act whatsoever" and "intends." If the distinguishing feature of contraception is the intention to impede procreation, here the distinguishing feature is the intention to foster sexual arousal or satisfaction.

This definition, by the way it insists on intention, understands the meaning of a sexual act very broadly and very narrowly. According to this definition, publishing pornography or washing dishes may be a sexual act. On the other hand, genital intercourse strictly intended by a woman to achieve procreation or to express her love is not a sexual act. I make these observations to point out that some biological and amorous qualities of human sexuality have been slighted.

I propose that sexual acts include far more than arousal or satisfaction. In this expanded understanding, contraceptive measures *might* be included. They might function not just "instrumentally" (509c–510a), but similarly to the way even permanently infertile sexual acts are said to retain their procreative meaning (635ab). Once again, I propose that all of us have yet to figure out how to proceed when we disagree about the object.

Principle of Totality

One point about the object is dear to many proportionalists and deserves to be noted here: much pre-Vatican II moral theology understood the "object" very narrowly. It focused on acts, severed not only from their contexts but especially from their function within the lives and relationships of those who performed them. It tended to overlook the complex ways that human beings, in living a full human life, appropriately perform now one act and now its contrary or even its contradictory. In an aphorism, it tended not to see that wholes (individual persons, life histories, communities) are prior to parts (acts) and that these parts cannot properly be understood without those wholes.

Hence the principle of totality has become a favorite for many proportionalists. It should be admitted, however, that parts and wholes interrelate in various ways. Three examples: If a doctor cuts off my healthy arm, the doctor harms the whole me; and on the whole, I am less able to function as a human being. Second: if a doctor immobilizes my otherwise healthy neck with a cervical collar in order to reduce my debilitating migraines, the doctor helps the whole me. Though a healthy part of me is inhibited, still on the whole I function better with the collar than without it. Third: if a doctor removes my kidney for donation to another person, the doctor somewhat harms me but helps the recipient. This said, allow me to hazard a generalization. Theologians who argue in favor of the official teaching of the Church on contraception tend to argue that it fits the first pattern, while theologians who argue that contraception is sometimes permissible tend to see it in terms of the second or third patterns. The former often argue that sex is different, and so the principle of totality cannot be used.[22] Usually they do not explain why that difference excludes the use of this principle.

How to decide among these competing views? How to decide whether cutting the fallopian tubes is an act that harms a woman, or whether it is an act that, in cases, may contribute to her sexual life, to her whole life, and to the lives of others? I know no convincing arguments. Here we are in the realm of practical wisdom or insight, and on these matters we currently disagree.

Proportionalists tend to consider contraception as part of a person's sexual life and indeed as part of one's whole life. Grisez himself admits that most people think of contraception as an issue of sexual ethics and not, as he wants to portray it in this section, as an issue of life and death (508c). The reason why people consider contraception a sexual issue is, I suggest, because they take a much larger view of the sexual life than Grisez does. They are interested in the whole process. They see both conception and preventing conception as pertaining to their sexual life as it unfolds within and contributes to the flourishing of themselves, their progeny, and others. They ask how contraceptives will fit in and affect a long practice of sexual acts, how fruitful the marriage has already been or will be, and so forth.

The classical axiom is, "Bonum ex integra causa, malum ex quocumque defectu." This axiom is commonly interpreted to mean that if an act lacks goodness in any of its aspects, then it is morally wrong. However helpful that axiom may or may not be for particular acts, it is not so helpful for understanding persons and their lives. All persons have defects, but these defects do not make persons wholly bad. And when acts are understood in terms of the whole life of a person rather than analyzed in isolation, then such acts, if they contain aspects that are only premorally defective, *may* not be evil when they contribute to the lives of one or more persons.

Contralife

We come now to Grisez's central affirmation about the contralife character of contraception. He distinguishes between a technical view and a moral view of contraception. In the former view, "successful contraception does not bear on any human individual's life; it is not as if a possible baby were waiting somewhere to be conceived" (509a). That makes sense to me. But, he says, if we take a moral view, we should focus not on what is done but on the content of our intention.

Grisez makes the claim that contraception necessarily involves *thinking two thoughts*: "a person must think that prospective sexual intercourse might cause a new life to begin, and that this possible effect can be impeded by some other behavior he or she could perform" (508b). The first thought is shared by, let us say, Mr. & Mrs. Contratino, who practice contraception and by Mr. & Mrs. Abstentino who noncontraceptively practice periodic abstinence. Obviously, the second thought could also be shared by both couples, but Grisez says that the Contratinos are different because they turn this thought into a particular choice and a particular intention. That choice is to perform some behavior that can impede the coming to be of new life, and "the relevant immediate intention . . . is that new life not begin" (508b). To the extent that this is so, then, of course, *by definition* contraception is contralife. How does this intention play itself out? According to Grisez:

> Those who choose to contracept often also intend some further good, for example, not to procreate irresponsibly, with bad consequences for already-existing persons. But in choosing contraception as a means to this further good, they necessarily imagine a new person coming to be if he or she is not prevented, they want that imagined person not to be, and they efficaciously will that he or she never be [note omitted]. That will is a contralife will. Therefore, considered as a moral act, each and every contraceptive act necessarily is contralife (509b).

What is perplexing about this description is that Grisez claims to know what contraceptors necessarily have in their minds. They "imagine," they "want," and they "will" quite definite things.

One can imagine any number of interior conversations that would not go as Grisez says they must go. Mrs. Contratino, if sick, might say, "For the sake of my health, I must not get pregnant again, and so I will be sterilized." Contratino might protest that she does not think the thoughts or have the intentions that Grisez says she must have (509c).

She might say, "I really want another baby, but I ought not get pregnant; and so my intention is to become infertile." Grisez, however, rearticulates her statement such that her decision becomes the following: "an efficacious will to prevent the baby it would be best for us not to have" (509c). In other words, what she thinks is her decision to become infertile is really a decision against a particular imagined baby. For Grisez, it is not just that the Contratinos *might* imagine the person they do not want to come into existence; rather they necessarily imagine that person. Grisez seems to picture contraceptors as sadists who dream of the person they are going to make sure will not come into existence. If there are people who so "imagine," "want," and then "will," then these people clearly have a contralife will. I doubt, however, there are many such people.

It is not clear to me how Grisez can read the minds of all who contracept. If he is deducing what they must be imagining, it is not clear to me how he makes his deductions.[23] Even in doing simple mathematics, people do not necessarily follow any one pattern of thought. In ordinary life, all the more, people do not necessarily follow certain patterns of imagination.

Periodic Abstinence

Grisez devotes the longest section of his text on contraception as contralife to showing that the practice of periodic abstinence need not be contraception. Once again, he does not shy from accepting the harsher implications of his own thought. He states upfront that those who choose periodic abstinence *as* a way of avoiding conception *are contraceptors* in the morally relevant sense. Their intention is contraceptive and therefore contralife (510a, 509c).[24] In other words, "sexual abstinence with contraceptive intent" is but another "method of contraception" (511a).[25]

How then does Grisez argue in favor of periodic abstinence? He begins with a reference to tradition. Put simply, nonmarried people have been forbidden to have sexual relations, and the ground for that proscription was that sex would lead to pregnancy. Thus, abstinence was morally required of them *as* a way of preventing pregnancy outside wedlock. The Church also encouraged married people to abstain when they had reason to avoid having a child. Since nobody in the past thought such practices were contraception, Grisez suggests, the practices must not have been contraception (510b).[26] But why? Grisez announces that it "is easy to see why." Unfortunately, it is not so easy for me.

Implausible Choosing

According to Grisez, *both* the contracepting Contratinos and the abstaining Abstentinos might have "a good ulterior end," even ends that morally "should" be pursued. But as we have seen, he claims that the Contratinos also necessarily have the intention "to prevent a baby from coming to be"; and this is wrong (511a). How are the Abstentinos different?

> Their choice is to refrain from intercourse insofar as it might cause a state of affairs which would include not only a baby's coming to be but other things which they think it reasonable, and perhaps obligatory, to avoid. Those who make this choice do not want to cause that state of affairs as a whole; rather than choosing the baby's not coming to be, they only accept it in choosing not to cause the state of affairs which would include it (511b).

In this way of framing the issue, Grisez tries to explain how periodic abstinence need not be a choice against the good of life; otherwise, it too is contralife. The Abstentinos should not think of themselves as "choosing the baby's not coming to be" nor as choosing some larger state of affairs which on the whole includes this lack-of-conception. Rather they choose only that some other undesirable features of this larger state will not occur.

We can imagine that pregnancy presents a severe health hazard to Mrs. Abstentino. Now if she uses periodic abstinence, she should intend to impede only the health hazard. She should also not choose against the larger state of affairs that includes both the pregnancy and the health hazard. Rather, she (reluctantly or even gladly [508a]) only accepts a lack of procreativity. In part-whole analysis, she does not choose in favor of one part (nonconception) or in favor of the whole (in this she is different from a proportionalist), but only against the other part (health hazard). In choosing against this other part, it just so happens that a larger state of affairs including conception will also not occur.[27]

As can be seen, Grisez relies on the ability of the human mind to focus very narrowly on what it is choosing to do and not to do.[28] As I understand Grisez's position, "the baby's not coming to be" will in fact function as the *means* to the nonoccurrence of the health hazard. But it should not be *chosen* as a means. It will function as a means because the "other things which they think it reasonable, and perhaps obligatory, to avoid" would be caused by the conception and would in most cases be subsequent to conception.[29] The Abstentinos may choose to avoid these "other things," and they may recognize that these "other things" will be avoided only if conception is avoided, but the avoidance of conception will be no part of their choice. Rather this avoidance is only accepted as a side-effect. Doubtless, an unsympathetic critic will question how psychologically feasible it is for the Abstentinos (a) to have a good or even obligatory end, (b) to make choices of patterns of behavior that in fact enable them to attain that end, and yet (c) not to see those patterns as means to that good end or, if they do so see them, not to choose them as such. Grisez recognizes that most people will find it hard to see something like childlessness as merely an unwanted side-effect of periodic abstinence.[30] Yet that is the view they must have.

Proportionalist Alternative
Many proportionalists see these mental maneuvers as unnecessary. Contraception is for them a *premoral* evil. Like other nonmoral evils, for example, refusing to plant a beautiful tree or cutting one down, it may in cases be chosen as a means that is part of a complex whole that includes a worthy end. Proportionalists adamantly reject the charge that they affirm using *moral* evil in order to attain that end. Rather, the premoral evil of contraception can be accepted and even chosen as part of a whole that would justify its use. A premoral evil should not be chosen for itself, of course. But it may sometimes be reluctantly chosen if it is a part of a complexus that is required for the attainment of a significant and greater good.

Internal Critique
Rather than pursue this long-standing debate between proportionalists and Grisezian revisionists, I want to look at a difficulty *within* Grisez's approach. I shall rewrite the long quotation given above. I offer two variations:

> [T]heir choice is to 1] *use a contraceptive* {or} 2] *use a pill (diaphragm, condom, etc.)* insofar as *intercourse without this aid* might cause a state of affairs which would include not only a baby's coming to be but other things which they think it reasonable, and perhaps obligatory, to avoid. Those who make this choice do not want to cause that state of affairs as a whole; rather than choosing the baby's not coming to be, they only accept it in choosing not to cause the state of affairs which would include it.

Within Grisez's own framework, variation 1 is incoherent. This is so because a contraceptive is, by definition, anything chosen with the intention of "the baby's not coming to be." So if one uses a contraceptive, whether that involves wearing amulets or using condoms, one cannot coherently make the above statement. But, I submit, variation 2 makes good sense. Or at least as much good sense as periodic abstinence.

Obviously, these different readings are possible only if 1 and 2 are different. In most people's minds, they are not different. They are, however, different in Grisez's system; and therefore in that system, I propose, he should accept the use of condoms and similar devices insofar as they thereby avoid complex states of affairs, at least some parts of which are reasonable or obligatory to prevent.[31]

Importance of Having Certain Thoughts

By now, it should be clear that, in my opinion, basing ethical judgments so heavily on intention is bad business. As we have seen, Grisez acknowledges that persons who practice periodic abstinence may have "contraceptive intentions" (510a). But so might people who play basketball. And he acknowledges that people who use contraceptive pills may not have contraceptive intentions (507c). But so, I argue, might people who use condoms and the like.

Because what is going on in the mind is so important for determining whether one is practicing contraception or legitimately practicing periodic abstinence, it becomes necessary for Grisez to specify exactly what these thoughts must be. If he *defines* contraception or periodic abstinence in terms of having certain thoughts, his task is relatively easy. But then most people using contraceptive devices will likely say that they do not have those thoughts and therefore are not engaging in those practices. If he claims that he is only describing the thoughts that such people must have when they use contraceptives or periodic abstinence, he needs to give a reason for believing that they actually have such thoughts; and the test of his theory is whether in fact they do. Here let me only suggest, without proof, that few people have the thoughts and images Grisez says they have. Indeed, Grisez himself, as we have seen, argues that people can use contraceptive devices or periodic abstinence and not have contraceptive intentions (507c).

Grisez goes two steps further. First, he tells us what is going on in the minds of the Abstentinos when they are engaged in sexual intercourse during the infertile period. Second, he tells us what must occur in the minds of the Contratinos and the Abstentinos when pregnancy unexpectedly occurs.

Thoughts during Infertile Period

When those who use periodic abstinence have normal sexual intercourse at times they have identified as infertile, Grisez says, "their intention in doing so plainly cannot be to impede the beginning of a new life" (511a). Why not? We recall that he has told us that some people "abstain at times when they believe conception is likely and engage in it only when they think conception unlikely," and that if they do so with contraceptive intent, they are in fact practicing contraception (510a). For Grisez, the intention of such people plainly must be to impede the beginning of new life.

I assume Grisez has something else in mind. Presumably he envisions that what the Abstentinos choose when they have sex during an infertile period is simply sexual intercourse all by itself. They do not exercise a choice to *be* infertile at a given time of the monthly cycle; that natural state is not a matter for choice (511a). Still, I am sure that what many people who practice periodic abstinence choose is "sexual intercourse at an infertile time." They make this temporally qualified choice precisely because, for a variety of reasons, they do not want new life to come about. For Grisez, it seems that only those who can keep the infertility of this time out of their intention are morally practicing periodic abstinence.

Thoughts on Becoming Pregnant

Grisez also boldly sets forth what the Abstentinos and the Contratinos will think if there is an unexpected pregnancy. According to Grisez, both couples may legitimately not want to cause a baby, but only the contracepting Contratinos will not want the baby they might cause (512a). Thus, the Contratinos will have to change their minds to accept their baby since otherwise it will remain unwanted. The periodically abstaining, yet nevertheless pregnant Abstentinos, however, will not have to change their minds to accept the baby. According to Grisez, the Abstentinos might be upset at their pregnancy. But this emotional upheaval, Grisez holds, is not morally determinative. Indeed, Grisez imagines the Abstentinos to react in the following way:

> The unexpected pregnancy may even fulfill their emotional desires and volitional wishes for a baby, so that they can truthfully say: "Although we were practicing periodic abstinence because we thought we should not have a baby just now, we are glad we are going to have this baby, for we really wanted it" (511c–512a).

Doubtless people can and do say the very sorts of things indicated by Grisez. My concern is Grisez's apparent blessing of such statements. If— as Grisez imagines—the Abstentinos really *should* not have a baby now, then their rejoicing is problematic, since they are rejoicing in what should not be. If, however, they become glad only after pregnancy, then they may be no different from the Contratinos. They too have changed what they want.

How does this relate to the Contratinos' practice of contraception? Many people who practice contraception are dead-set against abortion. In the Contratinos' minds, one can suppose, thoughts like the following might occur: "We do not want a baby to be conceived. . . . But if a baby is conceived, we will welcome the child." To employ a distinction that Grisez uses—though he denies that contraceptors can use it (512a)—the Contratinos may say that they do not want to cause a baby, but—in case of contraceptive failure—they would quite willingly accept any baby that is conceived. We can see this kind of distinction at work if we consider that almost no one would want to conceive a handicapped child, but many people welcome a handicapped child that they do conceive. The handicapped child does not really begin life unwanted. Similarly, people who practice contraception can accept a child they conceive. Their *conceived* children are not unwanted, and they may not need—any more than those who practice periodic abstinence—to change their minds in order to want their children.

Case of Rape

Grisez concludes the section on the contralife nature of contraception with a brief reflection on the use of "contraceptive measures" in case of rape. His intellectual efforts on the behalf of the raped woman are truly admirable. And his solution is nothing if not ingenious. In this terrible situation, he says, using contraceptive measures is not contraception. Rather, conception should properly be understood as either the continuation or the fullness of sexual union. But since a raped woman is "morally justified in resisting [the violent sexual union's] continuation" (512b), she can also prevent its continuation into conception. Further, she has the moral right to try "to prevent conception insofar as it is the fullness of sexual union" (512b).[32]

I fully agree with Grisez's conclusion; once again, my comments are directed to his arguments. Grisez is aware that some will want to use the same kind of reasoning to argue that, quite apart from rape situations, women are not contracepting when they use various "contraceptive measures" (512c); rather, these women are only cutting short the continuation of the sexual act or they are only preventing its fullness. When that is so, objectors will say, women are not contracepting in the proscribed sense.

Grisez's response is that, if the sexual union is "sought or willingly permitted," then a woman "cannot intend at the same time that it not occur." Grisez is quite right: she cannot. If she seeks sexual union or freely permits it, then it is analytically true that she intends that it occur. Grisez's response, however, misses the point of the objection. The Contratinos might freely intend that their sexual intercourse occur, but they might at the same time or subsequently intend that it not continue into conception or reach its fullness. This is quite possible. To prove his point, Grisez would have to develop a thesis that if one seeks or willingly permits the first step in sexual matters, then one must not stop the process from going all the way. That proof would not be easy.

In summary, let me say that as long as we stay in the realm of intention, I see little reason why those who use contraception, practice periodic abstinence, or protect themselves in rape cannot have the very same intentions. If rape victims can intend to prevent the continuation or completion of the sexual act, so can others. Unless Grisez can figure out a better way of anchoring intention to behavior or technique, his case for the contralife nature of contraceptives appears flawed.

CONTRALIFE IS ALWAYS WRONG

In his first section on contraception, Grisez noted that contraception has been traditionally rejected as contralife. In the second section, which we have treated at length, he argued that it is contralife. Grisez tries in his third section to show that being contralife is always wrong.

The center of my critique thus far has been that Grisez's focus on intention greatly misleads him and opens his arguments to multiple objections. The center of my critique in this section is related: he finds it hard, in moral matters, to distinguish between an idea and a reality. The reason for that difficulty, I suspect, lies in the way he focuses ethics in the act of choice rather than in what is chosen.

Basic Argument

Grisez's argument concerning the immorality of contraceptives consists of only sentences (512c–513a):

> Contraception always involves a choice to impede new human life; life is
> one of the basic human goods [note omitted]; the seventh and eighth modes
> of responsibility exclude choosing to impede any of the basic human goods
> [note omitted]. So, contraception is always wrong.

Establishing the truth of the first clause of the first sentence has been the
burden of the previous section. The meaning of the life prevented by
contraception is the theme of the second clause and the task of this section.

Before taking up that task, let me comment briefly on the third
clause. This clause refers, of course, to two of Grisez's "modes of responsibility."[33] Most proportionalists disagree with the eighth mode, which is
the criterion most relevant here. Proportionalists think that there is a
hierarchy among goods, including basic goods. They think one can rationally compare alternatives that contain various goods. And they think
that at times one can choose to impede, damage, or destroy various goods,
including basic goods, for the sake of other goods. I will not repeat here
what I and others have argued on these points.[34]

Good of Life Prevented

To conclude that contraception is wrong, Grisez tries to show that it
impedes an instance of the basic human good of life:

> basic human goods are morally relevant precisely insofar as they can be
> intelligible ends of acting on which the will bears when one makes choices.
> Considered in this way, *life* refers to the same thing whether one chooses
> to prevent conception or, by abortion, to prevent the birth of a baby already
> conceived (513b).

Grisez says that life in abortion (or homicide [488c]) is the "same thing"
as life in contraception because in each case the life of a particular individual is prevented from going forward. To the contrary, I argue that "life"
is not the same thing in abortion as in contraception. A real hundred
dollar bill is more valuable than a vividly imagined hundred dollar bill.

To show that life in both contraception and abortion is morally the
same thing, Grisez notes that some people decide at one and the same
time to use a contraceptive and, should it fail, to procure an abortion.
This unified intent, he suggests, indicates that a contralife will pervades
both abortion and contraception. Now it is likely that what he says is
true of some people. But other people have a different intent. When the
latter group practice contraception, they have firmly decided that, should

it fail, they will not have an abortion. They so decide because they are not contralife. For them, life is not the same in both choices.

Grisez's approach has a dangerous consequence. If all who practice contraception are as truly contralife as someone who has an abortion, then, should that contraception fail, they could not consistently use "respect for life" to prevent them from getting an abortion. If in using contraceptives they are already contralife or homicidal, then a real abortion would seem to add nothing in this regard.

Earlier in his book, Grisez distinguished between abortion and contraception. The difference between them, he notes, is a difference of existence (504c–05a). But, at this point in his text, Grisez hesitates. He tells us that people prepare for a baby both before and after it is conceived, thereby suggesting that it is the same life in both cases. Grisez draws from these people's activity that "the hoped-for child for whom they prepare is no mere abstraction" (513b). Perhaps. But it is also not real. A hoped-for child may be experienced as something more concrete than what is conveyed by the abstract term "human being." Still, there is a great difference—the difference of reality—between the life of an unconceived, imagined baby and the life of a conceived child.

Morality and Futurables

Grisez claims that human acts generally bear only on the future and therefore only on the possible, not on the actual (513b). In pressing this point—which makes him sound like a consequentialist—he seems to be responding to those who would object that contraception prevents only a possible life and therefore does no real harm. The objection would continue: contraception, therefore, is very different from, say, homicide which kills a real person. Grisez replies that nearly all acts deal only with the possible, and so contraception is not particularly different in this regard: "Homicide only prevents the victim from having a future. So, the homicidal will, like the contraceptive will, is only against life that would be, not against life that is" (512c). In taking this position on the future-bearing of acts, Grisez differs with many proportionalists and many traditional natural law ethicists.

Proportionalism considers inclusively what one is presently doing (traditionally called the *object* of the act), the agent's present character (including the *virtues*), the others who are currently involved, various roles and relationships, the *circumstances* of the act including the *history* that leads up to it, the possible future states (*consequences*) that the person wants to influence, and then, vis-à-vis all that, the role of choice. Likewise traditional natural law theory often focuses on violations of various goods in the *present*. For example, lying is considered a present violation of the nature of speech, quite apart from any future harms that may come from it. For both proportionalists and traditional natural law ethicists, then, if one kills an aging man about to die, the primary moral failing is not that one has taken a few (perhaps miserable) days away from the person's future. The moral failing essentially includes the fact that one has mortally attacked the man's present self. Hence, again, contraception which affects a possible life is very different from abortion or homicide.

Injustice

Grisez raises a different question: is contraception unjust? Justice is not an obvious category for assessing contraception, (unless, e.g., one spouse practices contraception against the will of the other spouse). Grisez thinks otherwise. He makes a two-step argument: if, due to contraceptive failure, a baby is conceived, then (1) that baby would be, at least initially, unwanted; and (2) this is a "position no reasonable person would wish to be in" (514b). The first point is true if, as Grisez claims, contraceptors necessarily imagine the person they don't want (509a). Otherwise it may not be true. The second point is also not so clear, and its import is problematic.

What would a reasonable person wish for? I personally would like to imagine that out of the two to five million children my parents could have conceived on a given day, I was specially chosen and not an accident of nature. But such was not the case. And I would prefer if, upon learning of my conception, my mother did not say something like, "I'm pregnant. I wonder whether *it* will be a boy or a girl." But such probably happened. Being conceived under these conditions does not seem particularly unjust. No one can realistically say that the unique person he or she is was wanted. In that sense, we all were not wanted at the moment of our conception.

Still, one hopes that most of us were not unwanted, and this is Grisez's point. Is it unjust to be unwanted at the moment of conception? Perhaps it is, though it is not clear to me that it is any great injustice. More important, the contracepting Contratinos, as I have argued above, may very well want any baby they accidentally conceive. True, they may not want the upheaval or change that happens when a baby is conceived, but this is quite different from not wanting a baby they do conceive. Their accidentally conceived baby is not unwanted. Thus, it is not clear that "choosing contraception is an injustice" (514b).

Suicide

Perhaps by now it is no shock to read that Grisez analogizes contraception to suicide. He gives three arguments. The first, a variation on the one we have already seen in the analogy to abortion and homicide, is that a contraceptor wills to prevent life and this intention is similar to the will of those who commit suicide (514b). The responses given above about the difference between potential and actual are relevant here.

The second argument is that persons who commit suicide violate "the stewardship which God gives each human person over his or her life. The will to prevent life is likewise irreverent toward God, the Lord of life, with whom couples are called to cooperate in responsibly procreating new persons for the kingdom" (514b). I shall not respond to this argument, not because I do not think it important, but because in writing another essay I have discovered how complicated these issues are.[35] The theological chestnuts buried in this field would populate a forest. Arguments over them would depopulate another forest.

The third argument is closer to the line of thought we have been pursuing in this essay. Grisez writes:

> although a choice to contracept intends to forestall the new person, still it also is a choice to limit the continuity of real human life. For, in preventing the baby whom they project and reject, those who choose to contracept limit their own lives as they tend to become one and to flow beyond themselves. It is as if, by contracepting, they commit a kind of limited suicide; they choose to cut off their life together, as they are about to hand it on, at the precise point at which a new person might emerge (515a).

Against those who have an individualist mind-set, Grisez rightly protests that "this continuity is real and is experienced vividly by a man and a woman who are in love and who joyfully receive the gift of a child as the fruit of their love and its embodiment" (515a).

Having argued something similar elsewhere,[36] I commend Grisez for insisting on the reality of communities like the "one-flesh unity" that is marriage (569–74, 635a). Do I, then, have no points to raise about the way Grisez compares contraception to suicide? I have three. The first concerns the type of realities he speaks of. The second refers to the way he links choices. The third is that the argument expands uncontrollably.

First, I applaud Grisez's efforts to name the reality of the couple as a community and the reality of the continuity of life through the couple. I ask only that he further clarify these ideas. There is in philosophy and theology considerable obscurity about the phenomenological and metaphysical status of "couples" and "life." Until we are clearer about how these realities are the same and how they are different from realities such as individual persons, it is hard to assess Grisez's claim that contraception is akin to suicide.

Second, Grisez moves directly from the "choice to contracept" to the "choice to limit the continuity of real human life" (515a).[37] Grisez can rightly argue that de facto the choice to contracept can limit this continuity. But he wrongly claims that the first choice *is* also a second choice. Similar to what Grisez concedes to those who practice periodic abstinence, one might choose the first and only reluctantly allow the limit. If there is any truth to the oft heard claim that contraceptors are selfish, then it is doubtful that such selfish people would *choose* to commit this sort of suicide.

Third, the argument goes too far. There is a sense in which couples practicing contraception "cut off their life together" and cut off "life's unity as it flows from parents to children" (515a). The problem is how to control this claim. Many couples who have already had children are practicing contraception. Are they too cutting off their lives? Must they go on having children for as long as possible in order not to cut off their lives together? Further, the analogy of suicide would apply not only to persons practicing contraception, but also to couples practicing periodic abstinence, and, in a different way, to single persons, to celibates, indeed, to almost everyone. At some point this becomes nonsensical. Grisez might reply that factually these people are committing this kind of suicide all the time; but unlike contraceptors they are not "choosing" to do so, and that makes all the moral difference. While understandable, this reply does not meet the difficulty. The nonsense is the thought that de facto all people commit something analogous to suicide thousands of times during their lives.

Not a Solution to Other Moral Obligations

Grisez grants that at times it is gravely irresponsible and therefore wrong to risk pregnancy. However, even at such times, he argues that contraception cannot be chosen as the "lesser evil" (515b). He offers three reasons.

Lesser Evil

The first reason is that talk of "lesser evil" belongs to proportionalism, a theory he thinks he has shown to be unworkable (515b). Since over the years I and others have been unsuccessful in persuading Grisez that the method is workable and since his arguments to prove the theory unworkable are unconvincing to proportionalists, this first reason will have to be set aside. That said, let me quickly add that Grisez phrases the problem in an odd way. He claims that it is characteristic of proportionalism to argue that a couple "should choose contraception . . . as the lesser evil" (515b).

There are at least three meanings of the contrast between lesser and greater evil. In the first, some *objective wrongs* are considered to be *less serious* than others. Traditionally Catholic theologians have said that, if for a given person, there would de facto be no acceptable third alternative (classic example: someone in an uncontrollable rage wants either to punch or to kill another, but is not able to peacefully settle differences), then it is permissible to counsel the lesser evil. Properly done, Grisez himself can make such a recommendation of the lesser evil (237–38). Moreover, he lays the basis for it when he distinguishes between grave and light matter [517a–519a]. Indeed, if it were not for his remarks against proportionalism, it would appear that it is this very type of case that Grisez has in mind, since he describes one alternative as "gravely wrong" and the other as a "lesser evil" (515b).

There is a second way of understanding the contrast between grave and lesser evil. It is the contrast between a grave objective wrong and a lesser premoral or nonmoral evil. Surely, no school of philosophy or theology would have trouble with approving the lesser evil in this sort of case.

The third contrast between grave evil and lesser evil is one that divides the schools. Proportionalists hold that various disvalues are "premoral evils." For example, proportionalists would say one can inhibit children from playing (which is a basic good for Grisez, but whose inhibition would likely be a minor and temporary instance of a premoral evil for proportionalists) so that they don't disrupt the congregation's prayer at mass (also a basic good, but whose disruption would likely be a greater premoral evil). Similarly, proportionalists think that the martyr can choose loss of human life over loss of God. For Grisez, these choices are immoral or impossible.[38] The debate over the right way to frame these and numerous other examples seems to have reached an impasse and must here be left unresolved.

Available Alternative

Grisez next argues that contraception should not be used to solve social problems because there is a good alternative, namely, abstinence

(515b). Proportionalists would ordinarily agree that if abstinence is a viable third alternative, then that alternative should be taken. They would readily agree, *as long as* nothing of great significance is lost by abstinence.

It is, however, not easy to prove that nothing great is lost when couples practice abstinence. Sexual intercourse has been a defining activity of marriage, and it is still important for the health of many marriages. Indeed, Grisez claims that it can be obligatory in marriage (634a).[39] Abstinence, then, is a deficit, and for proportionalists this deficit is a reason for considering the use of contraceptives.

Contraceptive Failure

Grisez offers a third argument why those who should not procreate should not use contraceptives: if bearing a child would be "gravely irresponsible, and so gravely wrong," then using contraceptives will also be wrong because contraceptives sometimes fail (515b). In other words, using contraceptives means risking what is irresponsible; therefore, it is irresponsible to use contraceptives. Proportionalists would respond that we constantly risk what would be seriously evil, if it occurred. We do so because we judge that there is a low probability that the evil will occur or that there are serious values that will be lost if we do not entertain the risk. For example, killing people with cars is gravely evil. If there is a viable alternative (Grisez's second reason) to driving and killing, then people ought not drive. But if people kill only rarely, then perhaps they may morally drive, as long as driving itself has its own importance. In brief, Grisez illicitly argues from the gravity of a possible outcome to the gravity of risking that outcome. By contrast, I suggest that if the risk is small in weight or rare in frequency, then the risk, for proportionate reasons, may be run.

Premarital Sex

How does all this cash out? Grisez gives the case of the couple engaged in premarital sex. Like other theologians, Grisez first says that they should not fornicate. But many of these theologians would then say that if the couple is going to have sex, they should at least use contraceptives as lesser evils. Grisez, however, holds that "using contraception aggravates rather than mitigates the sinfulness of fornication, since to the specific malice of fornication it adds a contralife will and the associated injustice to the unwanted child if contraception fails" (515c). That judgment makes good sense in terms of Grisez's system. What he does not tell us, however, is that if they are fornicating and not practicing contraception, they thereby risk a pregnancy and thus they too are adding something "gravely wrong" (515b) to the malice of fornication. In Grisez's system it may be that there is no way of choosing between these two malices, except perhaps by tossing a coin.

Social Consequences

I have just suggested that Grisez takes a one-sided approach in analyzing contraceptive use in premarital sex. In considering the social consequences of using contraceptives, Grisez tells us, the proportionalist's approach is one-sided when it touts the social benefits of practicing contraception: "Like many proportionalist arguments, it ignores the bad effects of the course of action it defends" (515c).

In one limited sense, such a charge should be music to a proportionalist's ears. Proportionalism has too often been identified with consequentialism, and clearly no consequentialist would ignore bad effects.[40] Indeed, looking at those effects is the whole ball of wax for the consequentialist. So perhaps Grisez is finally acknowledging that proportionalism is not consequentialism.

The music is sweet only for an instant, however. Grisez cannot be describing proportionalism, for that method requires consideration of effects. If anything, to most proportionalists, it is, in fact, Grisez's system—in particular the eighth mode of responsibility—that allows one to ignore bad effects. That is, if it is always wrong to impede a basic good no matter what the consequences, then, whenever it is determined that a choice would impede a basic good, there is diminished reason to consider what bad effects might flow from not making that choice.[41] Conversely, when Grisez describes bad effects as merely accepted or "incidentally" occurring, there is a greater danger that these bad effects will be ignored than what occurs through using proportionalist methods.[42]

Finally, Grisez argues that if one honestly considers the social effects of contraception, one will see that it does more of the very harms it is supposed to prevent (516a). To that charge, a proportionalist's response can be brief: if so, then—on proportionalist grounds—people should not practice contraception.[43]

GRAVE MATTER

In his final section, Grisez disagrees with those national episcopal conferences, bishops, and theologians who have suggested that contraception is light matter. He acknowledges that, surprisingly, there is no established theological way for distinguishing a mortal sin from a venial.[44] Grisez admits with Augustine that "even in the light of faith one cannot always easily see why some matters are grave and others light."[45] The best norm seems to be that what the Church has traditionally taught is grave is grave.

With that as background, then it is easy to see why Grisez admits that in evaluating contraception "the gravity of the matter is not obvious" (518c) and why he nevertheless holds that using contraceptives is gravely wrong. The tradition considered contraception akin to homicide. Pius XI did the same (517b).[46] The silence of Paul VI on the issue can be construed as consent to the previous tradition (518ab). Hence, it is serious.

Finally—and as an appropriate pastoral note on which to end—Grisez observes that people may not exercise sufficient reflection or full consent when they use contraceptive devices and so may not be mortally sinning.

CONCLUSION

Supporters of Grisez's thought may judge that this paper is nothing but a series of misunderstandings; and they may conclude that noncommunication would have been the lesser evil. I hope not. Over his long and illustrious career, Germain Grisez has time and time again sought to point out the inadequacies of various philosophical and theological arguments. Few can match the energy he has devoted in pursuit of the truth and in serving the Church. The present essay is intended to pay him the compliment of carrying on that pursuit and that service.

NOTES

1. "Proportionalism: One View of the Debate," *Theological Studies*, 46 (June 1985): 287–314, at 287.

2. Responding to charges from the Grisez school, Richard McCormick repeatedly writes that proportionalists do not hold what they are accused of holding; see "Some Early Reactions to *Veritatis Splendor*," *Theological Studies*, 55 (1994): 488–89, 496ff. Similarly, Grisez has written that proportionalists do not understand his thought; see John Finnis, Joseph M. Boyle, Jr., and Germain Grisez, *Nuclear Deterrence, Morality and Realism* (Oxford: Clarendon, 1987), 201, 271.

3. Grisez is by no means a "conservative." Along with proportionalists, he has been called a revisionist. From his first book to his last, he provides incisive and powerful criticisms of traditional and current teaching.

4. *Abortion: The Myths, the Realities, and the Arguments* (Cleveland: Corpus, 1970), 268.

5. *Way of the Lord Jesus: Living a Christian Life*, vol. 2 (Quincy, IL: Franciscan Press, 1993). Hereafter: *Living a Christian Life*. To help the reader, I will put page numbers in my text. To help even further, I shall roughly divide the page into top, middle, and bottom thirds indicated by the letters a, b, c. Thus 510b refers to the middle of page 510.

6. Because of space limitations, I do not, as I had originally planned, examine Grisez's analysis of contraception as contramarital. I have also resisted the temptation to bolster my own positions by citing from a wide variety of sources. Readers of this long essay will likely be grateful.

7. Grisez, *Contraception and the Natural Law* (Milwaukee: Bruce, 1964), 11.

8. To his great credit, Grisez's thought has in fact often *preceded* developments in papal teaching. See, for example, *Contraception*, 34–35. On the other hand, Grisez himself has various devices by which to distance himself from Church teachings he does not agree with. Consider, for example, *Way of the Lord Jesus: Christian Moral Principles*, vol. 1 (Chicago: Franciscan Herald Press, 1983), 226–28, (hereafter: *Christian Moral Principles*) where he argues that killing in war (commanded by God and done by the people of the Old Testament) and capital punishment (performed by saintly Christians and sanctioned by popes) do not count against his eighth mode of responsibility. In *Living a Christian Life*, 646c, he argues that popes and theologians made a mistake on material cooperation in a serious matter. In *Abortion*, 345, he openly acknowledges how his thinking diverges from the official teaching of the Church.

9. Indeed, some penitentials prescribed more severe penances for contraception than for intentional homicide; cf. John Noonan, Jr., *Contraception: History of Its Treatment by Catholic Theologians and Canonists* (Cambridge: Harvard Univ., 1986), 146–47, 164, 379. Grisez (507a, c) says that the tradition did *not* make the mistake of saying contraception *is* homicide, but then he says that the Catechism of the Council of Trent taught that those who use contraception, like those who procure abortions, "are guilty of a most heinous crime, for this is to be considered an impious conspiracy of homicides." The difference is not made clear.

10. There are many kinds of natural law ethics. I offer one account in "Catholic 'Natural Law' and Reproductive Ethics," *Journal of Medicine and Philosophy*, 17 (1992): 329–46; see also my "Natural Law and the Quest for a New Ethics," *Morality, Religion, and the Filipino: Essays in honor of Vitaliano R. Gorospe, S.J.* (Manila, Philippines: Ateneo de Manila University Press, 1994), 97–111.

11. I disagree with some in the proportionalist school, and some disagree with me. Thus one might fault everything in this essay without thereby refuting all proportionalists.

12. Grisez probably would agree with this complexity. (His frequently used term "proposal," however, distances him from these realities.) My contention is that he does not carry through this complex analysis when he discusses contraception as contralife.

13.   This is not to deny that *what* she did was morally wrong. Sex with her husband was wrong because in the act of sex with her husband she should also have had the intention to have sex with *him*. Her intentions are essential for moral rightness. Because the blind woman did not have this intention, what she engaged in might be called, in Grisezian language, contramarital sex.

14.   Grisez disagrees; see his book written with Joseph Boyle, Jr., *Life and Death With Liberty and Justice* (Notre Dame: Univ. of Notre Dame, 1979), 393: "This definition and moral characterization of killing in the strict sense make no distinction between intent to kill, attempt to kill, and the consummation of the undertaking by successful execution. These distinctions, which are legally significant, are morally irrelevant."

15.   See, however, his early views, *Contraception*, 90–93. In *Abortion*, 327, he notes: " 'Intend' means more than 'foresee,' more even than 'willingly cause.' To intend something is either to aim at it as at one's precise purpose in acting or to embrace it for its positive contribution to the achievement of that purpose."

16.   For an outline of my view, see *Love, Human and Divine: the Heart of Christian Life* (Washington, DC: Georgetown University Press, 1994), Chap. 1.

17.   *Living a Christian Life*, 273–86. He tends to see emotions as subspiritual obstacles to the moral life. His "modes of responsibility" needlessly cast the affective sphere as an obstacle to moral living. See also his work with Russell Shaw, *Beyond the New Morality* (Notre Dame: Univ. of Notre Dame, 1988), 100, 119, 121–30, 179. Nevertheless, in other places, he takes a more neutral and even positive view.

18.   Throughout this essay I will use Grisez's terms "baby" and "child." Other people would write "embryo" or "fetus." I do not intend to enter into any arguments on the topic of abortion, for that would take us too far afield.

19.   For Grisez, character is derivative: it comes from actions and it means simply the "self, regarded as source of further acts," *Christian Moral Principles*, 193; *Life and Death*, 382; *Beyond the New Morality*, 141.

20.   Does the pope so define it? I offer three reservations: First, other translations of this sentence do not or do not so clearly focus on intention. Second, the awkward Latin of the papal statement says that the act itself intends [*actus, qui . . . intendat*], not that the act "is specifically intended" (by the agent). The encyclical's phrasing may not be so strange if the pope is referring to the *finis operis* (that is, the "what") and not, as Grisez thinks, the *finis operantis* (that is, the agent's "intention.") Third, the pope's statement does not have the marks of a definition. It is preceded, first, by a sentence that condemns abortion and then a sentence beginning "Similarly" that condemns sterilization. The sentence that Grisez calls the pope's "definition" also begins with a "Similarly." Since abortion and sterilization would fit within the meaning of the papal sentence, it may be that the pope's statement is meant simply to refer to "anything else" that might be relevant and is not meant to be a definition.

21.   I find ambivalence in Grisez's writings. In *Contraception*, 145–46, 177, Grisez was clearer that "meaning-giving is not an altogether free process . . . [and] concerns the object of the act, not its subjective morality. . . . Moreover, that meaning, which arises from the physical significance of the act, is morally determinative so far as the malice of my will goes." Grisez rejects subjectivism in *Beyond* *the New Theism* (Notre Dame: Univ. of Notre Dame, 1975), 291. On the other hand, see *Beyond the New Morality*, 52, 140–41, at 52: "Thus, we really create situations in a moral sense, because we give the events of our lives and the facts of the world the unique meaning which they have *for us*" (emphasis theirs). And Grisez's claim that goods such as a dollar bill and a copper penny cannot be compared without prior interest on our part or without first choosing to determine ourselves toward some purpose sets up the possibility of an arbitrary voluntarism or a subjectivism; see *Abortion*, 310, 315–16; with Joseph M. Boyle, Jr. and Olaf Tollefsen, *Free Choice: A Self-Referential Argument* (Notre Dame: Univ. of Notre Dame, 1976), 13; *Life and Death*, 349, 362–67. See also my analysis: "Popular Ethical Subjectivism: Four Preludes to Objectivity," *Horizons*, 11 #1 (1984): 42–60.

22.   In *Contraception*, 100–01, 132, Grisez explained that frustration of sexual activity is different from frustration of all other human faculties. The latter should be evaluated in terms of their relationship to human life as a whole, but not the former. For example, if one occasionally overeats or undereats, he says, that is not intrinsically evil. But each and every instance of contraception is wrong. In *Beyond the New Theism*, 292–93, and *Life and Death*, 362–67, and *Beyond the New Morality*, 95, he explains how harming one function must hinder (all?) further expansive living.

23.   For example, Grisez has argued that people who employ useless techniques (507c) as contraceptives are contraceptors. How can these people be said to "efficaciously will" that a person never be? Similarly, since, in the use of contraception, user-failure is often said to result from ambivalence, would Grisez say that such people were not practicing contraception since they seemed not to have the clarity of thought and the effectiveness of will he says are necessary?

24.   By contrast, Ronald Lawler, O.F.M. Cap., Joseph Boyle, Jr. and William E. May, *Catholic Sexual Ethics* (Huntington, IN: Our Sunday Visitor, 1985): 163, write: "In some circumstances, the *intention* not to have a child is appropriate for married couples. But as it is never appropriate or right to do *acts that are direct attacks* on truth or life or other basic human goods, it is never right to attack directly the procreative good" (my emphases).

25.   This position agrees with that of John Paul II. It seems to me, however, that it does not cohere with the "definition" of contraception given by Paul VI. Periodic abstinence, even when chosen as a way to prevent conception, is not an "action which either before, at the moment of, or after marital intercourse . . . ." In fact, I don't think John Paul II and Paul VI are in agreement.

26.   Grisez rightly notes that Paul VI "teaches that contraception and natural family planning are completely different, because only contraception obstructs the natural unfolding of the generative process" (511, note 102). It is not clear, however, whether Grisez himself agrees with this explanation. He has tended to reject arguments based on frustration of the *finis operis*.

27.   I presume that those who practice periodic abstinence would not have to think such thoughts in any very explicit way. See also *Christian Moral Principles*, 892–93.

28.   Grisez often circumscribes the realm of morality quite narrowly. For example, he claims that the physiological conditions of one's own body "are not part of the human act of intercourse, for they are neither included in the couple's

behavior nor subject to their choice" (634c). For most people, this sentence would be nonsense. For Grisez, however, it preserves important moral distinctions.

29. I put it this way to suggest that Grisez's thesis may violate two common versions of the third subprinciple of the principle of double effect. Grisez, however, does not think that this principle is adequate; *Christian Moral Principles*, 307–308; but see "Against Consequentialism," *American Journal of Jurisprudence*, 23 (1978), 54.

30. In *Nuclear Deterrence*, 290–91, Grisez acknowledges: "In ordinary language one hesitates to call something a 'side-effect' if it is foreseen as a certain or natural consequence of the behavior by which one carries out one's choice, even though it is no part of the proposal one adopts. For many, the hesitation becomes positive unwillingness when the foreseen consequence is something of substantial human importance."

31. Even if such devices are not contraceptively contralife, he likely would reject them on other grounds. For example, Grisez argues that those who use condoms to prevent transmission of disease during sexual intercourse may be causing scandal or violating the marital character of their sexual acts; see *Living a Christian Life*, 237–38, 636b, 640c. Here I am trying to critique only his arguments in this section of his book.

32. Earlier, in *Contraception*, 216–17, he gave another imaginative justification: "Self-defense alone must be the object of direct intent. If this is so, the act which prevents conception need not be contraceptive, since it will be the woman's best means of preventing the rapist's abusive violation of her right to choose her own partner in procreation."

33. *Christian Moral Principles*, 216–22. As I understand them, the modes of responsibility generally consist of two parts: first, distorting affections or desires, and, second, proscriptions concerning intelligible goods. Frankly, these modes have always seemed strange to me, in part because the connections between these two parts seem arbitrary.

34. "Proportionalism," 287–314. Unfortunately, as a group proportionalists have not done as much methodological work as Grisez has. He is to be commended for developing his side of the debate. Garth Hallett, S.J., is one of the few who has persistently and at length developed proportionalist thinking. He not only disagrees with Grisez; he also thinks that many who are called proportionalists do inadequate work. See his *Christian Moral Reasoning* (Notre Dame: Univ. of Notre Dame, 1983) and *Greater Good: The Case For Proportionalism* (Washington, DC: Georgetown University, 1995).

35. The essay is entitled "Gifts, God, and Gratitude." See also my "John Paul II and Cooperation with God," *The Annual of the Society of Christian Ethics* (1990), 81–108.

36. Vacek, *Love, Human and Divine*, Chap. 3, 8; "Contemporary Ethics and Scheler's Phenomenology of Community," *Philosophy Today*, 35 (2) (1991): 161–74.

37. It should be admitted that Grisez prefaces his remarks about the continuity of life with the statement that contraception differs from suicide because the former only "prevents a person's coming to be" while the latter means "destroying an actual person" (515a). This distinction, of course, is one that I have been insisting on all along.

38. *Christian Moral Principles*, 588.

39. *Contraception*, 5. Still, he also tries to show that the justified absence of sexual intercourse, though problematic, may not be too serious (640b, 686c–687a).

40. *Nuclear Deterrence*, 201; *Abortion*, 287.

41. *Contraception*, 90, 121; *Abortion*, 327.

42. *Beyond the New Morality*, 144; it should be noted, however, that Grisez does argue (144–45) for a secondary responsibility for these effects, even if, again, he holds that such effects have no real bearing on one's attitudes towards basic goods. See also, *Christian Moral Principles*, 239; *Nuclear Deterrence*, 289–90.

43. Proportionalists surely would agree with Grisez's plea that we "recognize and rectify social injustices" (516b). Proportionalists might also agree that "sound approaches can only mitigate the evils from which humankind suffers" (516c), though some proportionalists would include the use of contraceptives among the sound approaches. These proportionalists, however, would bristle at Grisez's broadside that using contraceptives "facilitates the habitual satisfaction of sexual desire without regard to the reasonableness of doing so, and people with a habit of satisfying desires without regard to reason find it hard to resist even when they recognize special reasons to do so" (516a). Proportionalists would respond that one is speaking of "making love," not simply of satisfying desire; one also is speaking of people who presumably have exercised their conscience, that is, their reason (519a). Hence such actions are not instances of "satisfying desires without regard to reason."

44. See *Christian Moral Principles*, Chap. 16.

45. *Christian Moral Principles*, 396.

46. The quote Grisez gives from Pius XI seems to define contraception not, as Grisez does, in terms of intention but in terms of means; and the reason Pius gives for the immorality of contraception is a reason that Grisez seems to have rejected. See his *Contraception*, 20ff.

Portia's Lament:
Reflections on Practical Reason

RALPH MCINERNY
Michael P. Grace Professor of Medieval Studies
and Professor of Philosophy
University of Notre Dame
South Bend, Indiana

If to do were as easy as to know what were good to do, chapels had been churches, and poor men's cottages princes' palaces.

Merchant of Venice I.2

These words make it clear that if Portia were going to give her kingdom for a horse it would not be the wished for kind that beggars may ride. In her case, of course, it is her hand that is at issue, and her suitor must choose the right casket in order to win it. How would we characterize what is going on in the mind of the young swain come from afar, standing before the three chests, one containing gold, another silver, the third lead? He must choose one of them, in what Nerissa calls a lottery for the lady. Is he engaged in practical reasoning?[1]

I shall take this festive occasion, when we have come together to honor the work and person of Germain Grisez, to reflect on some elementary matters in an area to which he has made significant contributions and stimulated the thoughts of others. My topic is practical reason. What follows is largely a return to the sources, in Aristotle and St. Thomas, in the hope of seeing them afresh. If I am lucky, nothing novel will emerge from this exercise. My ambitions have never gone beyond wanting to be a spear carrier in the grand Thomistic opera—or a mendicant worm munching his way through the Opera Omnia.

When anyone asks what we are doing, our answer might be, at least on a good day, "I'm thinking." Because that is an acceptable answer, we must press on in order to distinguish thought from doing in the way that

Portia does. Her distinction is perhaps better caught by the answer "I'm *just* thinking"—given, let us say, by a two-time loser loitering before the window at Tiffany's. The officer who hurries him on his way and out of temptation does not want him to do what he is thinking of doing.[2] So if thinking is doing, and it is, it is not the kind of doing that is contrasted with thinking.

Is the doing that is distinguished from thinking just choice, an act of the will, something that occurs when thinking has stopped? Or is there another kind of thinking that informs the doing that is contrasted with just thinking?

What exactly is "just thinking"? Let us say that, in an improbable scenario, you come upon me thinking of the rings of Saturn. "Just thinking," I reply to your intrusive question. And what else could I do about the rings of Saturn than think about them? By contrast, the crook looking in Tiffany's window is presumably thinking of something he might do.

So we distinguish thinking about things that do not represent possible projects or doings of ours, on the one hand, from the thinking that does, on the other.[3] The latter is practical thinking, and this is the kind of thinking that is opposed to doing in the lament of Portia. But if there is thinking in the doing as well as in just thinking, what is the relationship between that and practical thinking? Are they two kinds of practical thinking? And how would they differ? Would we appraise them in the same way?

These are my questions. Whether or not I would have raised them independently of reflection on the sources to which I now turn I do not know. That they reflect having been to those sources many times in the past will, I hope, be obvious.

MIND PRACTICAL

The text in Aristotle to which Thomas almost always turns when the question of practical as opposed to theoretical knowledge comes up is the famous passage in III *De Anima 10*.

> Both of these then are capable of originating local movement, thought and appetite: thought, that is, which calculates means to an end, i.e. practical thought (it differs from speculative thought in the character of its end); while appetite is in every form of it relative to an end; for that which is the object of appetite is the stimulant of practical thought; and that which is last in the process of thinking is the beginning of the action (433a13–17.)

A superficial reading of the text would suggest that having an end is what characterizes the practical use of the mind—it calculates means to an end—but of course what the text says is that the practical and speculative uses of our mind differ in the character of their ends. This can surprise us since, after all, it is appetite not cognition that aims at the end or good. One way to handle this difference would be to say that truth can be willed and thus become an end or good, but clearly there is a more fundamental way in which we can say that truth is the good of intellection and not simply something we might choose as a constituent of our integral good. The fulfillment or completion of any process is its end or good; it is in this precise sense that we can speak of truth as the end or good of intellect. Like other changes or movements, thinking is the actuation of a potency. Truth is located in that actuation and is thus the good of the process or movement. This is an extended or analogous sense of "good," and we immediately emphasize that truth is only a partial good of the person, the good of one of his activities, not his good *tout court*. Recalling these matters enables us to see the practical use of intellect as something beyond, something more than, the standard or theoretical use of mind. I take this to be the sense of saying that *intellectus speculativius per extensionem fit practicus*. (*Summa theologiae*, I.79.11, sed contra) We are there referred back to where we began, to *De anima III*.

In the passage quoted, Aristotle has suggested that both appetite and thought can be sources of movement. It seems pretty clear that the speculative intellect does not initiate movement, but how does the practical intellect do so? It is its link with the desirable, the object of appetite, that enables mind practical to move. The desirable, the good, is the principle of practical thinking, and it is the good which gives practical thinking its power to move. Thus the two principles, mind and appetite, are in a sense reduced to one. What moves is the desirable, the object of appetite, and it is what thus addresses appetite that is the starting point of the kind of thinking we call practical.[4]

> It follows that there is a justification for regarding these two as the sources of movement, i.e. appetite and practical thought; for the object of appetite starts a movement and as a result of that thought gives rise to movement, the object of appetite being to it a source of stimulation (III. 10. 433a17–20).

Practical thinking seems to be the servant of desire—if not the slave of passion. Desire of something good stimulates the mind to consider how the desired good can be achieved. As if enjoying our unease, Aristotle adds something even more startling.

> Now thought is always right [*orthos*], but appetite and imagination may be either right or wrong. That is why, though in any case it is the object of appetite that originates movement, this object may be either the real or the apparent good (433a26–29).

Thomas explains this rightness of thought in terms of the grasp of principles and, in the case in point, the grasp of the first principles of practical reasoning. The correctness of reasoning beyond the level of principles derives from the rightness of the first principles; but in this further process of thought, error is possible.

"Next at 'All thought then,' he applies what has been said to a particular accidental factor in movement or action, explaining why we go amiss in our actions. 'All thought,' he says, 'is right,' by which he means that we never err about the first principles of action, about such truths as 'It is wrong to do harm to anyone,' or 'Injustice is never right,' and so on. Those principles correspond to the equally infallible first principles of the speculative reason." [Footnote: *Commentary on De Anima, III, lession 15, n. 826.*]

What moves appetite may be only an apparent good, in which case appetite is not correct, whereas thought, at least on the level of principles, is always correct. It is by taking thought that we will recognize a good as only apparent. Of course, it is not that something just *seems* to attract; the apparent good really engages appetite, but it does so only because it appears to be good. But how can practical intellect, which takes its rise from the good desired, become a critic of its starting point? Before addressing this directly, Aristotle distinguishes senses of the good. "To produce movement the object must be more than this; it must be a good that can be brought into being by action; and only what can be otherwise than as it is can thus be brought into action" (433a29–30; Thomas, n. 827). The good that triggers practical reasoning is in the realm of the contingent, of what can be or not be; whereas the speculative bears on the necessary.[5]

The faculty of thinking and of appetite are parts of the soul, and, as Aristotle notes, there is a need to distinguish quite a number of faculties or powers of the soul. At this juncture, Aristotle needs several senses of appetite, since "appetites can run counter to one another, which happens when a principle of reason and a desire are contrary" (433b5–6). Thomas takes Aristotle to be addressing an objection arising from the fact that the continent man does not follow appetite. The text is reminiscent of the *Protagoras* when it suggests that such a conflict can only occur in beings that have a sense of time and can contrast the present to the future. Desire (*epithumia*) is the desire of the pleasant which is at hand and which presents itself as good when one does not reckon on future consequences of its pursuit. Thomas sketches a little scenario. Someone with fever knows that taking wine will only increase the fever, but desire prompts him to take a glass because it is at hand, and the presently desirable seems simply desirable because one does not think of the future.[6]

But if mind has a role, given the presence of appetite, it begins to emerge that appetite is consequent on mind from the very start. Appetite can only be engaged by a known or imagined good, and this leads Aristotle to speak of appetite as a moved mover.[7] It is the fact that it is only the good as known that moves appetite that provides a basis for the regulative role of reason. The facts that "thought is always right" in its grasp of the starting points of action and that its grasp of the good is what sets appetite in motion, enable Thomas to say that "the desirable is either truly good, when it is grounded in the judgment of right reason, or an apparent good, when it falls away from the judgment of right reason because of desire or imagination."[8]

The moral psychology, as we might call it, in the Anscombian sense, that Thomas finds in Aristotle was not a discovery that had to wait for the time when he wrote his commentary on *De anima*. Scholars are more or less in agreement that the commentary dates from 1268, while Thomas was still teaching in Rome at Santa Sabina, just prior to his return to Paris in 1269. Some eleven other Aristotelian commentaries were to follow over the next four or five years, composed while Thomas was heavily involved in other things, his ordinary magisterial tasks as well as the controversy over Latin Averroism which seems to have been the reason why he was asked to act a second time as *magister regens*.

Tutored by Peter of Ireland in Naples and, after his entry into the Order of Preachers, by Albert the Great, Thomas was immersed in Aristotle from the beginning. In the *Scriptum super libros Sententiarum*, discussing whether or not sacred doctrine is speculative or practical, he is guided by the *Metaphysics* and the *Nicomachean Ethics*, as well as by Scripture and Augustine. In his *expositio* of Boethius's *De trinitate*, also early, Thomas exhibits a sure grasp of the Aristotelian corpus—its editor Bruno Decker lists 140 explicit references to Aristotle. The matters that interest us arise when Boethius, at the outset of chapter two of his *De trinitate*, writes,

"Nam cum tres sint speculativae partes: since then there are three types of the speculative . . ."[9] Speculative as opposed to what? Thomas does not expatiate on this in his *expositio capituli secundi*[10] but takes up the matter immediately in Question Five, article one.[11] Written, if Gils is right, in 1257 or 1258, or perhaps even at the beginning of 1259,[12] it shows the young Thomas already at the height of his powers. This text is not merely the invocation of recognized authorities, drawn from a *florilegium*: the doctrine is argued for in a quite personal way and, indeed, the sequel of this article is the most formal presentation of the distinction of the theoretical sciences to be found anywhere. Notably, the text from *De anima*, with which we began our reflections, though commented on twenty years later, is fully operative in this early text and forms the basis for the discussion.

Also implicit in this text is a point made explicitly elsewhere, namely, that the distinction between speculative and practical "intellects" is a distinction between uses or manifestations of the same faculty, not the assertion that there are two distinct faculties. The basic text is of course *De anima*, III, chapter 11, and the issue continues to be what it is that enables animate things to move themselves. An animal capable of appetite is capable of self-movement, and appetite presupposes at least imagination. Having distinguished two senses of imagination, Aristotle reserves calculative imagination to man, providing a compact statement of the heart of his moral psychology.

> Sensitive imagination (*aisthetike phantasia*), as we have said, is found in all animals, deliberative imagination (*bouleutike*) only in those that are calculative (*logistikois*): for whether this or that shall be enacted [*praksei*] is already a task requiring calculation (*logismou ergon*); and there must be a single standard to measure by, for that is pursued which is greater. It follows that what acts in this way must be able to make a unity out of several images. This is the reason why imagination is held not to involve opinion (*doxav*), in that it does not involve opinion based on inference (*ek syllogismou*), though opinion involves imagination. Hence appetite (*orexis*) contains no deliberative element (*bouleutikon*). Sometimes it overpowers wish, and sets it in movement; at times wish acts thus upon appetite, like a ball, appetite overcoming appetite (*orexis ten orexin*), i.e. in the condition of moral weakness (*akrasia*) though by nature (*physei*) the higher faculty is always more authoritative and gives rise to movement.[13]

What is the "single standard" by which measurement is made in deliberative imagination? "Et in tali consideratione necesse est accipere aliquam unam regulam, vel finem, vel aliquid huiusmodi, ad quod mensuretur quid sit magis agendum."[14] This occasions a summary statement which begins with contrasting "scientific" (*epistemonikon*) reasoning with the sort of reasoning involved in movement. In its speculative or scientific use intellect is not moved but remains at rest. Thomas takes this to be a distinction between two uses of the mind, the speculative and practical, with the first not involved in the pursuit of or flight from anything. He goes on to distinguish a universal and particular form of practical reason, but we must postpone that discussion.

How then to characterize these two uses of the single faculty of intellect? They differ, Thomas suggests, because of something incidental to the object of intellect, a difference insufficient to distinguish separate powers.

> Whether or not it be ordered to some work is incidental to what is grasped by the intellect. But this is how speculative and practical intellect differ, for speculative intellect is that which does not order what it grasps to any work—it is concerned solely with the consideration of truth. Practical intellect, on the other hand, is so called because it orders what is grasped to a work.[15]

This unity of the power of intellect, and the recognition that matters which can and matters which cannot become the start of an activity other than just thinking differ only per accidens, is the basis for seeing a continuity between the principles of the one use of reason and the principles of the other.

THE STAGES OF ACTION

It is clear from such texts that a human action is a complicated process which involves a number of stages as well as an interchange of mind and appetite, of intellect and will. Of course we are reminded of the magnificent analysis of the acts of will constitutive of the complete human action that Thomas sets forth in the *Summa theologiae, qq. 8–17.* Responsible, voluntary action is that over which we have control, and the name for such control is *liberum arbitrium*, which is a capacity involving both will and reason. Thus, properly human actions are those which proceed from deliberate will. But acts which proceed from will so modified—as deliberate—do so under a common formality which is the object of that faculty, namely, the end or good. All human actions are immediately gathered under the common formality of being ordered to the good or end, the object of deliberate will.[16] It is this general truth that must be made ever more specific in the analysis that follows.

The fact that practical reason begins with the end, the good, controls Thomas's analysis of human action. The stress is on the will-acts which make up the complete human act and the structure of the analysis is an end/means one. Thus, Thomas distinguishes will-acts which bear on the end (*voluntas, fruitio, intentio*) from those which bear on the means (*consensus, electio, usus*). The act that bears the same name as its faculty or power is the most basic, the most natural; so it is with *intellectus*, so it is with *voluntas*.[17] Will (or wish, as the translators of Aristotle would have it) is the desire for the known good; it is insofar as something is grasped by the mind as a good, *sub ratione boni*, that it can attract the will. Just as the end is good in a primary sense and the means are good only derivatively, so will bears chiefly on the end and secondarily on the means to it.

Thomas's distinction between the order of intention and the order of execution is, of course, grounded in the end/means analysis of human actions. The end is first in the order of intention and sets off a search for the means of attaining it. The means come first in the order of execution, the actual performance of the deeds that will lead to possession of the desired end.[18] The familiar distinction between the order of specification and the order of exercise enables Thomas to clarify the interaction of mind and appetite.[19]

> If we should consider the movements of the soul's powers from the side of the object specifying the act, the first principle of the motion is from intellect: for it is in this way that a known good moves the will itself. However if we should consider the movement of the powers of the soul from the side of the exercise of the act, then the principle of motion is from will. It is always the case that the power to which the principal end pertains moves into action the power to which pertains what is for the sake of the end.[20]

While this takes care of one puzzle—that mind and will are not mover and moved in the same sense—there is a lingering difficulty. The fundamental argument used to show that our will is free is grounded in the notion that no particular good—that is, no particular kind of good thing—necessitates desire. From the point of view of the exercise of its act, we read, no object moves the will necessarily, whereas from the point of view of the specification of its act, by its object, the will is moved necessarily. The analogy is this: just as the eye naturally sees when color is presented to it, so the will responds to the known good. To continue the analogy, if color is not fully actualized—ill lit, perhaps—the eye does not respond to it. Similarly, should an object be proposed to will that is universally and in every aspect good, the will necessarily tends to it, if it wills anything at all—but it cannot will its opposite.[21] What would such an object be? The ultimate end necessarily moves the will because it is the perfect good. As if to stress its parallel with the famous q. 94, a. 2, Thomas goes on to say that not only the ultimate end, but anything so ordered to it that the end could not be had without it, necessarily moves the will. What might such things be? To be, to live, and the like. Whereas, whatever is such that the end could be had without it, is not necessarily willed. The parallel is with arguments: some conclusions follow necessarily from principles, others are only probable, and only the former command our assent.[22] So what is the lingering puzzle?

It may seem that the issue raised in *De anima* is still with us: what moves us to action? Both mind and will are said to move, the former in the order of specification, the latter in the order of exercise. But will is intellectual appetite; it is the desire of the known good, of an object which specifies it, but what, then, sets the will in motion? Is this an idle question? Thomas both asks and answers it, and his answer is that in the order of exercise the will moves itself. But this turns out on reflection to mean that the will can bring about another movement of itself, will to will that, so to say. Could it mean more? Could it mean that the will, at the outset, sets itself in motion—in the order of exercise? But that seems to make *it* both mover and moved, at once in potency and in act. Thomas poses the problem as one in which someone desiring health moves himself to want a given medicine after deliberating about means to the desired end. In this way, the will is moved and mover in different senses, but then the specter of an infinite regress rears. How does Thomas cut it off? "It is necessary to say," he says, "with respect to the first movement of will, that one who is not always actually willing is moved by an exterior cause, by whose impetus the will begins to will."[23]

It is the very nature of the will to seek the good presented to it by reason. It does this naturally so that the cause of its desire is the cause of its nature. Just as there are certain truths that reason, given its nature, naturally knows, so there are things that will naturally desires—the end or those things without which the end cannot be had. But even here, Thomas qualifies his claim. If there be something that is good from every particular point of view and is grasped as agreeable or suitable (*conveniens*), it will necessarily move the will. Happiness does this, since it is, in Boethius's phrase, a state fulfilled by the coming together of all goods.[24]

To summarize, a human action develops in the following way. Something is grasped by the mind as good and to that extent commends itself to the will. That is, the mind sees it as agreeable (*conveniens*) and the will, attracted, begins to take delight in it.[25] From mere wish (*velle*) it may pass to enjoyment (*frui*) of this mental possession of the good.[26] Intention (*intentio*) is the will's aiming at the agreeable good as an end to be really possessed. It is at this point that the means of achieving the end are sought. Obviously, the will-acts just mentioned follow on corresponding cognitive acts. When Thomas turns to the discussion of means, he first considers choice (*electio*) in q. 13 and then devotes q. 14 to the deliberation (*consilium*) that precedes choice. When deliberation turns up several possible means and will consents to both, it must then choose one. Choice being made of one among the appropriate means, a command (*imperium*, q. 17) is issued and the other powers of the soul as well as the body, its limbs and external instruments, come into play. The command is issued at the hinge of the analysis when, the order of intention being completed, the act is executed.

I apologize for recalling these obvious matters here. Perhaps there are still those who find the discernment of all these elements of the action baroque, an indication of Schoolmen in the grips of intellectual *luxuria*. It was one of the merits of the late Alan Donagan to call attention to the rule that Thomas follows in this analysis.[27] Obviously, Thomas does not mean that each and every human act is an explicit and conscious movement through these moments. It is because an act can be interrupted at any of these points, that we recognize distinct stages. The acts of the virtuous and vicious unfold so smoothly as to seem utterly simple. But every complete human act implicitly or virtually contains these various stages.

DEGREES OF PRACTICAL KNOWLEDGE

What I have been calling the end/means analysis of human action is contrasted with the rule/application analysis. Aristotelian scholars will locate the former in Book Three of the *Nicomachean Ethics*, the latter in Book Seven; and, in the manner of scholars, raise questions about the compatibility of the two: Which came first, and did he embrace the one, then drop it in favor of the other, *et alia hujusmodi*. The same questions could be put to Thomas Aquinas since he follows Aristotle both in seeing the end as the principle of practical thinking and in seeing a kind of discourse in the act, a kind of syllogism, which moves from principles to a conclusion which is their application in this singular action. While there is progress and movement through the stages of the act in the end/means analysis, it does not suggest to us the notion of degrees, whereas talk of principles invites the distinction between more and less common or universal and particular principles, in short, between degrees of proximity to this action here and now. When Thomas does discuss degrees of practical knowledge, he is making more precise the fundamental distinction between the speculative and practical uses of our mind.

When the distinction was made between speculative and practical thinking in the *De anima*, only a single criterion—the end of each—was used. Obviously, if the distinction is to become more nuanced and permit of degrees, there must be a plurality of criteria. Three such criteria are employed by Thomas in a famous passage in which he discusses whether God has speculative or practical knowledge of creatures.

The discussion begins with the remark that, while some instances of knowledge are simply theoretical and others simply practical, there are cases where we say that an instance of knowing is in some respects theoretical and in others practical. There can be such intermediate instances precisely because there is more than one criterion. In the text in question, Thomas proceeds from one end of the spectrum of practical thinking to the other.

The first criterion given here is the *object* of knowledge, the things known. If they are what they are and are not subject to human making or doing, the only cognitive relation we can have to them is theoretical.

The second criterion is the *mode* of knowing. If we take an instance of something that comes within the range of human making or doing, such an object might nonetheless be thought of in a manner indistinguishable from the way in which we think of theoretical objects. Take a house. We might think of and give an account of a house that would be in manner exactly like that we employ when thinking of and accounting for the flowering dogwood. That is, we might define the house, providing its genus—shelter against the elements—and then a difference that would set it off from other things like umbrellas, tents, and geodesic domes. These then are *operabilia*, things we can make, but they are known and defined in the manner appropriate to nonoperable, natural objects. (I say appropriate, because that is the only way we can know the latter objects.) To know operable objects in a manner appropriate to them is to know how they can be brought into being, the steps that must be taken from a mere twinkle in the builder's eye, through many and sweaty stages, until a gazebo appears on the back lawn. Thomas often dubs this the compositive mode, by contrast with the resolutive or analytic mode proper to nonoperable objects.

There is no suggestion here that there is anything wrong with considering operable objects as if they were natural kinds. Indeed, there is reason for saying that this consideration is an inescapable cognitive moment on the way to considering them *modo compositivo*.

The third criterion invoked in this text is the only one invoked in most discussions of the distinction between theoretical and practical knowledge, namely, the *end*. It is because the end of operation defines practical knowing that knowing what is to be done in a way that guides the doing of it is the appropriate way of knowing it. But whether or not the operable object is known in an analytic or a compositive way, we do not have practical knowing in the full sense until that knowledge is actually ordered to operation. The *finis operis* is the *finis operantis* when we have practical knowledge *tout court*.

> Knowledge which is speculative by reason of the thing known is only speculative, whereas that which is speculative in mode or in end is speculative in those respects and practical in another. When it is ordered to the end of operation it is simply practical.[28]

Elsewhere, Thomas suggests a label for knowledge that can be ordered to an *opus* but is not presently so ordered: habitual or virtual practical knowledge. The first designation suggests the kind of knowledge an artisan has but does not use during his lunch hour or in the evening at home. We say he is a builder because he can build a house; he knows how to, thanks to a skill he has acquired but is not at the moment employing. Purely practical knowledge is exemplified by the artisan actually plying his trade, hammering, sawing, raising high the roof tree, and the like.[29] Clearly it is not analytic knowledge of the artifact that the artisan can put into operation.

Having given a twofold way that knowledge can be directed to the end of operation—actually or virtually—Thomas goes on to distinguish two ways in which knowledge is not so orderable, which he calls purely speculative knowledge. When knowledge bears on things that cannot be produced by the one knowing, natural things for us, it is purely speculative. When knowledge bears on things that are operable by the one knowing but aren't being considered as operable, the knowledge is speculative and, the context suggests, purely speculative. If this interpretation is the implication of the text,[30] there is a divergence in usage between the *De veritate* and the *Summa theologiae*. This is clear from the way in which Thomas uses the phrase *speculativa tantum* in the Disputed Question.

There are things which can be separated by intellect although they cannot exist separately. Therefore when an operable thing is considered by intellect, distinguishing things from one another which cannot exist distinctly, this is neither actual nor habitual practical knowledge but is only speculative, as if an artisan were to consider a house by asking after its properties and genus and differences and such like which exist indistinctly in the thing itself. A thing is only considered as operable when it is considered with all the things that must come together in order for it to exist.[31]

The two texts finally embrace the same types of knowledge, but the *Summa theologiae* permits us to call three of them kinds of practical knowledge. If we were to ask ourselves what kind of practical knowledge enters into the practical syllogism, the answer would be easy. Only virtual or habitual practical knowledge can be applied in the actual discourse presumed to be taking place while the artisan is whistling at his work. The virtual or habitual knowledge is actualized in the deed.

Analytic knowledge of something that is operable by the knower— we might call this minimally practical knowledge—is terribly important for architects and engineers, physicians and moralists. Consider how much of the moral part of the *Summa theologiae* is devoted to taxonomic matters—the definitions of virtues and vices and their many subdivisions; with getting clear on the cardinal virtues, to say nothing of saying what precisely the ultimate end is. Such inquiries are the first and necessary stage in practical knowledge.

It is only on the level of virtual or habitual practical knowledge that we have something that might be articulated as a principle or rule that would guide action at however much a remove. "First, kill a chicken," would be threshold advice for someone wishing to make an old-fashioned Sunday dinner on the farm. The addressee is presumed capable of distinguishing birds from beasts and a chicken from a duck. That presumed knowledge might be expressed as "the ones with a coxcomb" or "the ones with two webbed feet." And these descriptions would, of course, be theoretical and remote knowledge of the proposed guest of honor at the dinner table. Doubtless it is because our first knowledge of the things that we can make or do is theoretical that Thomas accepted the claim that *intellectus speculativus extensione fit practicus.* Subsequent more practical thinking moves off from this theoretical moment. Of course, the theoretical knowledge involved is not yet scientific, but it is an instance of knowing what things are that is presupposed by any further scientific development. It would be nonsense to suggest that this priority of the theoretical makes the study of metaphysics a prerequisite to preparing dinner.

PRACTICAL TRUTH

One way of characterizing such minimally practical knowledge would be to say that it will, like the purely theoretical knowledge it mimics, be appraised as true or false. Either one is right about the way to separate the ducks from the chickens, or one isn't. How are the other levels of practical knowledge appraised?

> The truth of practical intellect is something different from that of speculative intellect, as is said in the sixth book of the *Nicomachean Ethics*. For the truth of speculative intellect is based on intellect's conformity with things. Because the intellect cannot be infallibly conformed with contingent things but only with the necessary, there are speculative habits which are virtues with respect to necessary things though not with respect to the contingent. The truth of practical intellect, on the other hand, is based on conformity with right appetite. Such a conformity plays no role in necessary matters which are not brought about by the human will, but only in contingent things which come to be by us, whether these be things done within or things made without. That is why only virtues of practical intellect bear on the contingent, art on makable things, prudence on doable things.[32]

The passage in the *VI Ethics* 2 discusses the origins of human action and singles out thought and desire as what enables us to be responsible for our deeds. Aristotle suggests an analogy between affirmation and denial in thought (*dianoia*) and pursuit and avoidance in desire (*orexis*). Virtue being a habit of choosing and choice being desire's acceptance of what has been deliberated, human action requires agreement between what reason affirms and desire pursues: right action will be the conjunction of right reason and right desire.[33] This gives rise to a virtuous circle. If the truth of practical intellect is determined with reference to right appetite, and the rectitude of appetite results from its conformity with true reason, the explanation seems a clear instance of wheel spinning.

The way out of the difficulty is to note that the end of appetite is fixed by nature; it is the means to the end that reason investigates. Appetite's rectitude with respect to the end is the measure of the truth of practical reason, and it is this practical truth which is the measure of the desire of means.[34] The only way in which a good act can be performed is when the agent is effectively pursuing his true end. Such pursuit involves an act of appetite, not mere knowledge of what the end of appetite is; and this appetitive orientation to the ultimate end guides reason in its pursuit of the appropriate means to the end, that is, of what can be done here and now; and deliberation informs the choice which is embedded in the particular action. Practical truth therefore is the rectitude of the judgment that guides the particular choice. The agent judges as he is inclined to do by his appetitive orientation to the good; that is why the judgment involved is said to be *per modum inclinationis* and not merely *per modum cognitionis*.[35]

Moral science, philosophical or theological, is not true with practical truth, not least because those instructed in moral science can judge the acts of virtue even if they do not themselves possess virtue (moral virtue, that is). Moral science would seem to be located midway between the first principles of the practical order and their particular applications. The moral knowledge most human agents have is uninfluenced by the fifty drachma course of the professional moralist, yet it will exhibit the degrees of moral knowledge we have discovered in Thomas. Everybody has a store of judgments about the things around us, knowing what and how they are, how they are distinguished from one another, that does not qualify as scientific knowledge. Rather, it is from this humble common base—and the nongainsayable principles embedded in it—that the task of devising a science begins. In much the same way, it could be said that moral philosophy and moral theology ape, at a level of abstraction, what goes on informally in all moral agents. It is easy to distinguish the formal thinking from the singular practical judgment in terms of theoretical and practical truth, respectively, but how does this distinction of kinds of truth apply to the informal stages of practical knowledge?

Of course, one might ask what the cash value of such a distinction between formal and informal is. I have come to think that the distinction is far more important than it at first appears. Consider, for example, the discussion of the starting points of practical reasoning under the rubric of "natural law." Thomas gives us two accounts of natural law: first, it is the peculiar human participation in eternal law; second, it is the first self-evident principles of practical reasoning. There was a time when you and I might have heard either of those accounts without understanding what it meant. It could then have been said that we didn't know what natural law is. But if the account of natural law is true, then we could not possibly not know natural law. The knowledge of natural law that is common to all humankind is not knowledge of an account or definition of natural law. The theory articulates what is commonly known.

Just as the starting points of practical reasoning are implicit in everyone's moral reasoning, so less general guidelines that hold only for the most part are presupposed by theory, not conferred by it. The starting points, the first principles, are true with theoretical truth. Less general precepts are true, if they are, with theoretical truth, since they articulate means whereby the end can, if only by and large, be achieved. So long as practical thinking is general, the truth it has will be theoretical. Practical truth applies only to completely practical knowledge, the knowledge embedded in the singular act. Just as practical knowledge as such is an extension of theoretical thinking, so within practical knowledge there is a graded approach to practical thinking *sans phrase* and this alone is the domain of practical truth.

ENVOI

One could go on about this, and doubtless should. My present purpose is a limited one of making clear that it is only practical knowledge in the full sense, completely practical knowledge, that is true with practical truth. The other modes of practical knowledge, if true, will be true with speculative truth—that is, insofar as their judgments are in conformity with the way things are. Thomas's distinction between the judgment of the moral theologian and that of the chaste man on some question of chastity as, respectfully, *per modum cognitionis* and *per modum inclinationis* (*Ia. 1. 8. 3m*) makes that point. Whatever the truth of the moral theologian's judgment, it does not depend on being inclined by virtue to the end. Yet, presumably the judgment Thomas has in mind would be a hypothetical such as, if chastity is to be preserved, then one ought to do such-and-such. That is, it is a judgment about means to the end, but the end is related to it as a *bonum ut verum*, not as a *bonum ut bonum*.

The contrast that Thomas drew between the *iudicium conscientiae* and the *iudicium liberi arbitrii*, the former though not the latter being said to consist *in pura cognitione* (*Q. D. de veritate*, q.17.1.4m), throws light on this matter, though it also raises some interesting questions of its own. Furthermore, the discussions of the virtues associated with prudence, *eubulia, synesis, gnome*, in the commentary on the *Ethics* (VI, 8–9) and in the *Summa theologiae* IaIIae, q. 57, 6, are another rich source of relevant material. It is significant that Thomas distinguishes ethics, economics and politics from the types of prudence relevant to those areas precisely in terms of the fact that these sciences are *in ratione solum* whereas prudence *habet aliquid in appetitu*.[36] The modalities within practical reasoning seem to underscore the truth that we use the same faculty in theoretical and practical matters and that there is more of a continuum than an abrupt break between them.

It should be said that practical intellect has its starting point in a universal consideration and in this respect is one in subject with the speculative, but its consideration terminates in the particular thing to be done, which is why Aristotle says, in *De anima* III, that universal reason does not move apart from particular [reason], so the ratiocinative part of the soul is distinguished from the scientific.[37]

Needless to say, such considerations do not smudge the distinction between speculative and practical knowledge; rather, they clarify it. Completely theoretical knowledge and completely practical knowledge are *toto coelo* different in their ends, in the reason we engage in them. But this distinction does not make the one alien to the other—as if practical reasoning at any level would not be guided by the first principles of reason as such—nor does it preclude that the stages short of complete practical knowledge are governed by theoretical truth. Portia's complaint, after all, has to do, not with the distance between purely theoretical knowledge and practice, but with the fact that practical knowledge, however true, does not always engage the appetite and thus insure that the good known is my good.

NOTES

1. Perhaps the lottery is the best example of the kind of objectless choice prochoice advocates invoke. In any case, buying a lottery ticket, whether with the prospect of millions or a life of bliss with Portia, seems an unhelpful example of practical reasoning.

2. If thinking can be engaged in for its own sake, willing cannot. "Et manifestum est quod omnis appetitus est propter aliquid. Stultum enim est dicere, quod aliquis appetit propter appetere. Nam appetere est quidam motus in aliud tendens. Sed illud cuius est appetitus, scilicet appetibile, est principium intellectus practici. Nam illud quod est primo appetibile, est finis a quo incipit consideratio intellectus practici" (*In III de anima*, lectio 15, n. 821 = Leonine III, ix, 11. 50–57).

3. "Dicit ergo primo quod intellectus qui movet est intellectus qui rationcinatur propter aliquid, non propter ratiocinari tantum; et hic est intellectus practicus, qui differt a speculativo secundum finem. Nam speculativus speculatur veritatem, non propter aliquid aliud, sed propter seipsum tantum; practicus autem speculatur veritatem propter operationem" (*In III de anima*, lectio 15, n. 820 = Leonine III, cap. ix, 11. 43–49). The untroubled use of *speculatur* to signify the activity of practical intellect occurs in the Leonine as well.

4. "Et hoc rationabile est quod haec duo moventia reducuntur in unum, quod est appetibile: quia sit ponebantur haec duo intellectus et appetitus esse

moventia, respectu eiusdem motus, cum unius effectus sit una causa propria, necesse est quod moveant haec duo secundum aliquam communem speciem. Non est autem dicendum quod appetitus moveat sub specie intellectus, sed magis e converso; quia intellectus non invenitur movens sine appetitu; quia voluntas, secundum quam movet intellectus, est quidam appetitus" (*In III de anima*, lectio 15, n. 824 = Leonine III, ix, 11. 78–89).

5. On the necessity of the object of the speculative intellect, see *In Boethii de trinitate*, q.5.a.1c.

6. "Sicut cum febricitanti, ex iudicio intellectus videtur a vino abstinendum esse, ne febris incalescat. Sed concupiscientia incitat ad accipiendum 'propter ipsum iam,' idest propter illud quod in praesenti est: videtur enim quod in praesenti est delectabile, esse simpliciter delectabile et bonum, ex eo quod non consideratur ut futurum" (*loc. cit., n. 829 = Leonine, ll. 161–167*). Sometimes, because of what is foreseen the intellect orders that something desirable not be pursued: "intellectus quandoque ab aliquo concupicibili retrahere iubet propter considerationem futuri (*ll. 159–161*).

7. "The expression 'that which originates movement' is ambiguous: it may mean either something which itself is unmoved or that which at once moves and is moved. Here that which moves without itself being moved is the realizable good, that which at once moves and is moved is the faculty of appetite" (433b14–17). Thomas comments: "Movens autem est duplex: unum quidem immobile, et aliud quod est movens motum. In motu igitur animalis, movens quod non movetur est bonum actuale, quod movet appetitum prout est intellectum vel imaginatum. Sed movens motum, est ipse appetitus, quia omne quod appetit, inquantum appetit movetur, et ipsum appetere est quidam actus vel motus, prout motus est actus perfecti, prout dictum est de operatione sensus et intellectus" (*in. loc.*, n. 831 = Leonine, ll. 190–199).

8. "Hoc autem appetibile, est aut vere bonum, quando persistur in iudicio intellectus recti, aut apparens bonum quando declinat a iudicio intellectus recti, propter appetitum vel phantasiam" (*ibid., n. 827 = Leonine, ll. 120–124*).

9. *Boethius, The Theological Tractates, etc.*, H. F. Stewart, E. K. Rand and S. J. Tester, Cambridge: Harvard University Press, 1978, p. 8, line 5.

10. See Bruno Decker, *Sancti Thomae de Aquino Expositio super librum Boethii De trinitate* (Leiden: Brill, 1958), pp. 158–9. This was the first critical text of the whole of the (incomplete) exposition. Ten years earlier Paul Wyser had published *Thomas von Aquin In librum Boethii De trinitate Quaestiones Quinta et Sexta (Louvain: Nauwelaerts, 1948)*. This edition, which had such an impact on students of Thomas, lacked the *expositio* of Chapter Two of Boethius as well as the first four questions of Thomas's commentary. Both of these editions have been more or less eclipsed by the appearance of Tomus L of the Leonine *Opera Omnia* (Roma: Commissio Leonina, 1992) which contains *Super Boethium De Trinitate* and *Expositio libri Boethii De Ebdomadibus*. The introductions are by Pierre-M. J. Gils

11. "Dicendum quod theoricus sive speculativus intellectus in hoc proprie ab operativo sive practica distinguitur quod speculativus habet pro fine veritatem quam considerat, practicus vero veritatem consideratam ordinat in operationem tamquam in finem. Et ideo dicit Philosophus in III De anima quod differunt ad invicem fine, et in II Metaphysicae dicitur quod 'finis speculativae est veritas,

sed finis operativae scientiae est actio.' Cum ergo oporteat materiam fini esse proportionatum, oportet practicarum scientiarum materiam esse res illas quae a nostro opere fieri possunt, ut sic earum cognito in operationem quasi in finem ordinari possit" (*loc. cit., q.5a.1c*). See also Decker, p. 164, lines 5–14; Wyser, p. 25, lines 26–35; Leonine, p. 137b, lines 93–106.

12. Cf. Leonine edition, p. 9b.

13. *De anima*, III, 11, 434a5–15.

14. Thomas, *in hoc loc.*, lectio 16, n. 841 = Leonine, cap. x, 11. 73–76. The text continues: "Manifestum est enim quod homi 'imitatur' [Thomas's Aristotlelian text *gave imitatur* for *diokei*], idest desiderat, id quod est magis in bonitate, et id quod est melius: melius autem semper diiudicamus aliqua mensura: et ideo oportet accipere aliquam mensuaram in deliberando quid magis sit agendum Et hoc est medium ex quo ratio practica syllogizari quid sit eligendum. Unde manifestum est quod ratio deliberans potest ex pluribus phantasmatibus unum facere, scilicet ex tribus, quorum unum praeeligitur alteri, et tertium quasi mensura, quae praeeligit."

15. "Accidit autem alicui apprehenso per intellectum, quod ordinetur ad opus, vel non ordinetur. Secundum hoc autem differunt intellectus speculativus et practicus. Nam intellectus speculativus est, qui quod apprehendit, non ordinat ad opus, sed ad solam veritatis considerationem: practicus vero intellectus dicitur qui hoc quod apprehendit ordinat ad opus" (*Summa theologiae*, Ia. q.79a.11).

16. "Unde illae solae actiones vocantur prorpie humanae, quarum homo est dominus. Est autem homo dominus suorum actuum per rationem et voluntatem: unde et liberum arbitrium esse dicitur *facultas voluntatis et rationis*. Illae ergo actiones proprie humanae dicuntur, quae ex voluntate deliberata procedunt. . . . Manifestum est autem quod omnes actiones quae procedunt ab aliqua potentia, causantur ab ea secundum rationem sui objecti. Obiectum autem voluntatis est finis et bonum. Unde oportet quod omnes actiones humane propter finem sint" (*IaIIae, q.1a.1c*).

17. "Omnis enim actus denominatus a potentia, nominat simplicem actum illius potentiae: sicut *intelligere* nominat simplicem actum intellectus. Simplex autem actus potentiae est in id quod est secundum se obiectum potentiae. Id autem quod est propter se bonum et volitum est finis. Unde voluntas proprie est ipsius finis" (*IaIIae*, q.8a.2c). This symmetry between mind and will is stressed by Thomas: "*sic enim se habet finis in appetibilibus, sicut se habet principium in intelligibilibus, ut dicitur in VII Ethic*" (*ibid*). There is in Thomas a continuous proportion, expressible in the following way: principles : speculative intellect :: principles : practical intellect :: end : will.

18. In discussing this, Thomas suggests an etymology of 'means' and goes on to link it with the use of 'middle' in the drawing of conclusions. "Ad tertium dicendum quod in executione operis, ea quae sunt ad finem se habent ut media, et finis ut terminus. Unde sicut motus naturalis interdum sistit in medio, et non pertingit ad terminum; ita quandoque operatur aliquid id quod est ad finem, et tamen non consequitur finem. Sed in volendo est e converso: nam voluntas per finem devenit ad volendum ea quae sunt ad finem; sicut et intellectus devenit in conclusiones per principia: quae *media* dicuntur" (*IaIIae*, q.8a.3ad 3m).

19. "Ad tertium dicendum quod voluntas movet intellectum quantum ad exercitium actus: quia et ipsum verum, quod est perfectio intellectus, continetur

sub universali bono ut quoddam bonum particulare. Sed quantum ad determinationem actus, quae est ex parte obiecti, intellectus movet voluntatem: quia et ipsum bonum apprehenditur secundum quamdam specialem rationem comprehensam sub universali ratione veri. Et sic patet quod non est idem movens et motum secundum idem" (*IaIIae*, q.9a.1ad 3m).

20. *Q. D. de malo*, q.6, art, unic. "Si ergo consideremus motum potentiarum animae *ex parte obiecti specificantis* actum, primum principium motionis est ex intellectu: hoc enim modo bonum intellectum movet etiam ipsam voluntatem. Si autem consideremus motum potentiarum animae *ex parte exercitii actus*, sic principium motionis est ex voluntate."

21. Cf. *IaIIae*, q.10, a. 2, c. "Unde si proponatur aliquod objectum voluntati quod sit universaliter bonum et secundum omnem considerationem, ex necessitate voluntas in illud tendet, si aliquid velit: non enim poterit velle oppositum."

22. "Ad tertium dicendum quod finis ultimus ex necessitate movet voluntatem, quia est bonum perfectum. Et similiter illa quae ordinantur ad hunc finem, sine quibus finis haberi non potest, sicut esse et vivere et huiusmodi. Alia vero, sine quibus finis haberi potest, non ex necessitate vult qui vult finem: sicut conclusiones sine quibus principia possunt esse vera, non ex necessitate credit qui credit principia" (*IaIIae*, q.10a.2ad3m).

23. ". . . necesse est ponere, quod quantum ad primum motum voluntatis moveatur voluntas cuiuscumque non semper actu volentis ab aliquod exteriori, cuius instinctu voluntas velle incipiat" (*ibid*). See too *IaIIae*, q.9a.5ad3m: "Deus movet voluntatem hominis, sicut universalis motor, ad universale obiectum voluntatis, quod est bonum. Et sine hac universali motione homo non potest aliquid velle. Sed homo per rationem determinat se ad volendum hoc vel illud, quod est vere bonum vel apparens bonum."

24. "Si ergo apprehendatur aliquid ut bonum conveniens secundum omnia particularia quae considerari possunt, ex necessitate movebit voluntatem; et propter hoc homo ex necessitate appetit *beatitudinem* quae, secundum Boethium est status omnium bonorum congregatione perfectus" (*Q.D. de malo*, q.6, art. un). On Boethius, see *Philosophiae Consolationis, III, prosa* 2, where, speaking of beatitude, he says, "Id autem est bonum quo quis adepto nihil ulterius desiderare queat. Quod quidem est omnium summum bonorum cunctaque intra se bona continens, cui si quid aforet summum esse non posset, quoniam relinqueretur extrinsecus quod posset optari. Liquet igitur esse beatitudinem statum bonorum omnium congregatione perfectum" (*ed. cit.*, p. 232, lines 5–12.)

25. See *IaIIae*, q.11a.1,ad3m.

26. *Ibid.*, a.4c. "Habetur autem finis dupliciter: uno modo perfecte; et alio modo, imperfecte. Perfecte quidem, quando habetur non solum in intentione, sed etiam in re: imperfecte autem, quando habetur in intentione tantum."

27. See *Summa theologiae*, *IaIIae*, *q.17a.3,ad2m*: ". . . ex hoc quod imperium et actus imperatus possunt ab invicem separari, habetur quod sunt multa partibus." The criterion of separability can be applied throughout the series of cognitive and will-acts that make up the complete human action.

28. "Scientia igitur quae est speculativa ratione ipsius rei scitae, est speculativa tantum. Quae vero speculativa est vel secundum modum vel secundum finem, est secundum quid practica. Cum vero ordinatur ad finem operationis, est simpliciter practica" (*Summa theologiae*, Ia.q.14a.16,c).

29. See *Q.D. de veritate*, q.3a.3: "Aliqua ergo cognitio practica dicitur ex ordine ad opus, quod contingit dupliciter: quandoque enim ad opus actu ordinatur, sicut artifex praeconcepta forma proponit illam in materiam inducere, et tunc est actu practica cognito et cognitionis forma; quandoque vero est quidem ordinabilis cognitio ad actum non tamen actu ordinatur, sicut cum artifex excogitat formam artificii et scit modum operandi non tamen operari intendit, et tune est practica habitu vel virtue non actu."

30. "Quando vero nullo modo est ad actum ordinablis cognitio, tunc est pure speculativa, quod etiam dupliciter contingit" (*ibid*). The two ways are those we have given in the text.

31. "Sunt autem quaedam quae possunt separari secundum intellectum quae non sunt seprabilia secundum esse; quando ergo consideratur res per intellectum operabilis distinguendo ab invicem ea quae secundum esse distingui non possunt, non est practica cognito nec actu nec habitu sed speculativa tantum, sicut si artifex consideret dmum investigando passiones eius et genus et differentias et alia huiusmodi quae secundum esse indistincte inveniuntur in re ipsa: sed tunc consideratur res ut est operabilis quando considerantur in ipsa omnia quae ad eius esse requiruntur simul" (*Q. D. de veritate, q.3 a.3, c., lines 109–121 [Leonine]*).

32. "Verum intellectus practici aliter accipitur quam verum intellectus speculativi, ut dicitur in VI Ethic. [1139a26]. Nam verum intellectus speculativi accipitur per conformitatem intellectus ad rem. Et quia intellectus non potest infallibiliter conformari rebus contingentibus, sed solum in necessariis, ideo nullus habitus speculativus contingentium est intellectualis virtus, sed solum in necessariis, ideo nullus habitus speculativus contingentium est intellectualis virtus, sed solum est circa necessaria. Verum autem intellectus practici accipitur per conformitatem ad appetitum rectum. Quae quidem conformitas in necessariis locum non habet, quae voluntate humana non fiunt, sed solum in contingentibus quae possunt a nobis fieri, sive sint agibilia interiora, sive factibilia exteriora. Et ideo circa sola contingentia ponitur virtus intellectus practici: circa factibilia quidem ars, circa agibilia vero prudentia" (*IaIIae*, q.57a.5,ad3m).

33. "What affirmation and negation are in thinking, pursuit and avoidance are in desire; so that since moral excellence is a state concerned with choice, and choice is deliberate desire, therefore both the reasoning must be true and the desire right, if the choice is to be good, and the latter must pursue just what the former asserts. Now this kind of intellect and of truth is practical; of the intellect which is contemplative, not practical nor productive, the good and the bad state are truth and falsity (for this is the function of everything intellectual); while of the part which is practical and intellectual the good state is truth in agreement with right desire" (1139a21–31).

34. "Videtur autem hic esse quoddam dubium. Nam, si veritas intellectus practici determinatur in comparatione ad appetitum rectum, appetitus autem rectitudo determinatur per hoc quod consonat rationi verae, ut prius dictum est, sequetur quaedam circulation in dictis determinationibus. Et ideo dicendum est quod appetitus est finis et eorum quae sunt ad finem; finis autem determinatus est homini a natura, ut supra III (1115b13–19) habitum est, ea autem quae sunt ad finem non sunt nobis determinata a natura, sed per rationem investigantur; sic ergo manifestum est quod rectitudo appetitus per respectum ad finem est mensura veritatis in ratione practica et secundum hoc determinatur veritas rationis practicae secundum concordiam ad appetitum rectum, ipsa autem veritas rationis practicae est regula rectitudinis appetitus circa ea quae sunt ad finem et ideo secundum hoc dicitur appetitus rectus qui persequitur quae vera ration dicit" (*Sententiae sexti libri Ethicorum, 2, lines 109–127*).

    35. *Summa theologiae, Ia.q.1a.6,*ad3: ". . . cum iudicium ad sapientem pertineat, secundum duplicem modum iudicandi, dupliciter sapientia accipitur. Contingit enim aliquem iudicare, uno modo, per modum inclinationis: sicut qui habet habitum virtutis, recte iudicat de his quae sunt secundum virtutem agenda, inquantum ad illa inclinatur: unde in X Ethic. [1176a17] dicitur quod virtuosus est mensura et regula actuum humanorum. Alio modo, per modum cognitionis: sicut aliquid instructus in scientia morali, posset iudicare de actibus virtutis, etiam si virtutem non haberet."

    36. *Sententiae sexti libri Ethicorum, 7, 11. 87–95.* ". . . in quantum enim sunt in sola ratione, dicuntur quaedam scientiae practicae, scilicet, ethica, yeonomica et politica."

    37. "Dicendum est ergo quod intellectus practicus principium quidem habet in universali consideratione et secundum hoc est idem subiecto cum speculativo, sed terminatur eius consideratio in particulari operabili, unde Philosophus dicit in III De anima quod ratio universalis non movet sine particulari, et secundum hoc ratiocinativum ponitur diversa pars animae a scientifico" (*Sent. sexti libri Ethi., 2, ll. 134–141*).

PART TWO

Metaphysics

Practical Reason and Concrete Acts

KEVIN L. FLANNERY, S.J.

Professor of Philosophy
Pontificia Universitas Gregoriana
Rome, Italy

In *Summa theologiae* I-II q.94 a.2, Thomas Aquinas calls the principle that "good is to be done and pursued, and evil is to be avoided" "the first principle in practical reason."[1] The expression 'to be pursued' (*prosequendum*) and its counterpart 'to be avoided' (*vitandum*) can be misleading. In one respect, they can be described as nonethical terms. Thomas takes them directly from Aristotle who often uses them as a pair and who writes, "To perceive . . . is like bare asserting or thinking; but when the object is pleasure or pain, the soul, making a sort of affirmation or negation, pursues or avoids."[2] Thus conceived, there is no more ethical content to the expressions 'to be pursued' and 'to be avoided' than there is when a person sees a plate of *spaghetti alle vongole* as an alluring thing. On the other hand, when 'to be pursued' and 'to be avoided' are applied to good and evil themselves, as they are in *ST* I-II q.94 a.2, they do begin to take on ethical connotations since the good referred to is human good, attacks on which are immoral because they harm human natures.

But even on the more general level, the first principle in practical reason (hereafter FPPR) can be regarded as a straightforward statement about human nature and its general orientation. It says, to use Thomas's own words, that "good is that which all things seek after" (*ST* I-II q.94 a.2). This is just the Aristotelian point writ large. One might not have a particular perception; so with Aristotle we can say that *when* a person perceives a certain object, he perceives it as something to be pursued. But if we are talking about human nature *qua* human nature, this hypothetical aspect must be left out. The point then becomes that persons necessarily *do* seek the good, even if they are often mistaken about what—in general or in particular—the good is.[3] Or, as Socrates puts it in Plato's *Protagoras*, "no one willingly goes after evil or what he regards as evil; nor is it, apparently, in human nature to do so."[4]

Thomas draws a comparison between FPPR and the principle of noncontradiction (hereafter PNC), the difference between the two depending on their diverse objects: being (and not-being) for PNC, good (and not-good) for FPPR—although, as Thomas often asserts, just as every being is good, so every good has being.[5] The intellect itself, Thomas says, is a single "power" which might "accidentally" be directed to one or the other object, being, or good, thus putting into operation either PNC or FPPR.[6]

This close relationship between FPPR and PNC is very important especially for the early sections of the present essay, for what I hope to do is to "prove" FPPR by employing an elenchic demonstration modeled on the elenchic demonstration of PNC in Aristotle's *Metaph.* iv,4.[7] Since Aristotle's demonstration points to some very basic metaphysical notions,[8] applying his method to FPPR should reveal to us some very basic ethical notions—even the foundations of ethics.

There is evidence that Thomas would not resist such an effort to demonstrate FPPR. First, in *Metaph.* iv,4, which Thomas cites in *ST* I-II, q.94 a.2, Aristotle, as part of an argument that even those who deny PNC implicitly hold it, employs as evidence an exercise of practical reason.[9] Second, in the same article, Thomas says that PNC is "founded upon the intelligibility of being and not-being" and that FPPR is "founded upon the intelligibility of good."[10] The remark about PNC is an allusion to the way in which Aristotle in *Metaph.* iv,4 goes below PNC to "significations" that something "is or is not this" (1006a30) in order to prove (elenchically) that PNC is true and necessary. By making a parallel remark about FPPR, identifying its foundation as the intelligibility of good, Thomas appears to be deliberately allowing scope for an elenchic demonstration of FPPR.

I begin by setting out Aristotle's demonstration of PNC in *Metaph.* iv,4, along with my own running commentary. Then I apply the same proof method to FPPR. Next, I discuss some of the implications of the former demonstration for our understanding of practical reason. In particular, I speak of the matter and form of human action—that is, of the necessity of conceiving of human action in terms of concrete acts—and the bearing of the latter conception on the role of options in free choice. Finally, I apply these ideas to Joseph Boyle, Germain Grisez, and Olaf Tollefsen's self-referential argument for the existence of free choice.

ARISTOTLE'S ELENCHIC DEMONSTRATION OF PNC

Preliminaries: Metaph. *iv,3*

Before beginning his elenchic demonstration of PNC, Aristotle says that PNC, "the most certain principle of all," is not an hypothesis.[11] "For a principle which every one must have who knows anything about being, is not an hypothesis; and that which every one must know who knows anything, he must already have when he comes to a special study" (*Metaph.* iv,3,1005b14–17).

This nonhypothetical nature of the demonstration is not always appreciated. R. M. Dancy, for instance, regards Aristotle's approach in *Metaph.* iv,4 as a pragmatic one. "One way of summing up the effect of the argument might be this," writes Dancy, "if you accept a contradiction, you will not be able to give sense to it."[12] But F. Inciarte has shown that this response is a misinterpretation of Aristotle.[13] Aristotle holds not that *if* we are to talk sense, *then* we must assume PNC but that PNC is true and the basis of all communication—therefore, it makes no sense to deny it.

It is not against Aristotle to point out that people (or, at least, philosophers) sometimes do say that PNC does not hold.[14] Aristotle does not deny that—in fact, he assumes it; but he does deny that anyone can actually believe that PNC does not hold. "For it is impossible for anyone to believe [*hupolambanein*] the same thing to be and not to be, as some think Heraclitus says; for what a man says he does not necessarily believe" (*Metaph.* iv,3,1005b23–26). As we shall see more clearly below, Aristotle is employing here a particular sense of 'believe.' To *believe* that PNC is false, one would have to be able to conceive of a world in which the same attribute might "at the same time belong and not belong to the same subject in the same respect" (*Metaph.* iv,3,1005b19–20). But this is impossible; therefore one cannot believe that PNC is not valid.

Aristotle has been criticized for not clearly distinguishing "the ontological formulation" of PNC ("the same attribute cannot at the same time belong and not belong to the same subject in the same respect"— *Metaph.* iv,3,1005ba19–20) and "the psychological formulation" ("it is impossible for anyone to believe the same thing to be and not to be"—*Metaph.* iv,3,1005b23–24).[15] But his insistence that one cannot believe PNC invalid makes it clear that this is no slip. Moreover, as we shall see below, the close relationship between the psychological and the ontological formulation is of key importance to the elenchic demonstration itself. It does not necessarily imply psychologism on Aristotle's part.[16] He does not hold that logical laws are just the laws of human thought, which in other creatures might be quite different; he holds rather that the world (in the sense of "all there is") is not and cannot be illogical—and that our minds *share* in this characteristic.

Metaph. *iv,4*

Aristotle begins the demonstration of PNC proper by identifying his opponents as those who "say" that it is possible that something might be and not be, and who also say that it is possible to "believe" this (*Metaph.* iv,4,1006a1–2). Following Dancy, I shall refer to the holder of this position as "Antiphasis" (from the Greek *antiphasis*, "contradiction").

Antiphasis need only "say something which is significant both for himself and another" and we have him (1006a21). If Antiphasis refuses to signify anything, says Aristotle, he is no better than a plant and we can ignore him (1006a14–15). Although the example that Aristotle uses is an essence—Antiphasis is supposed to select as his signification 'man'—it does not much matter what Antiphasis signifies. Signification, however, as opposed to assertion, must be the basis of the demonstration, otherwise it would beg the question—which is precisely whether a thing must definitely be something to the exclusion of its opposite.[17] Aristotle here moves down a level from asserted propositions to the "significations" upon which they depend. He knows that he cannot ask Antiphasis to admit that the expression, for instance, 'all men are mortal' has a single, definite sense; but Antiphasis, even to say 'all men are mortal' (which he presumably regards as not having a definite sense), must assume that 'man' is doing its proper work as a signifying expression.[18]

What does it mean for a signifying expression to do its proper work? It must mark out a definite thing, but a definite thing that is recognized as such not only by Antiphasis but also by those with whom he speaks. "This is necessary," says Aristotle, "if [Antiphasis] is really to say anything. For if he does not, such a man will not be capable of reasoning, either with himself or with another" (1006a22–24). So, reasoning itself, even reasoning that is done privately, depends on the sort of concepts whose meanings are fixed in conversation with others (1006a21). This is not to say that Antiphasis, having, for instance, identified a previously unknown subatomic particle, might not coin a word for it which he might use in wholly private research; the expression, however, would have to be such that in principle others might be able by means of it to pick out the same thing that Antiphasis picks out.

Aristotle does not believe that a sly Antiphasis might be tempted to signify something that does not have a fixed signification which others might understand. "Not to signify one thing," says Aristotle, "is not to signify at all" (1006b7). Just as no one is told to *follow* FPPR (since one cannot help but follow it), so Antiphasis is not being *instructed* by Aristotle to signify something definite. Rather, we are being told that Antiphasis cannot speak unless he signifies something definite. "The person responsible for the demonstration," says Aristotle, is Antiphasis (1006a25–26). Thus, there is no begging of the question.

Moreover, although Aristotle quite naturally speaks of Antiphasis's saying something to an interlocutor which is significant in a language, the point is not a lingusitic one. "For it is impossible to think of something if we do not think of one thing; but if this *is* possible, one name might be assigned to this one thing."[19] One cannot even reason, says Aristotle, unless the concepts with which one reasons exclude the sense of their opposites—which is to say that one can reason (and also converse), since concepts do exclude their opposites. We see in all this, again and again, the absolute inevitability of the "basis" of PNC—and also the central role of belief in Aristotle's demonstration.

In one section of *Metaph.* iv (1006b11ff), Aristotle also says that, when he speaks of signifying one thing, he does not mean that Antiphasis might simply "signify" predicates that hold of nothing else. Suppose that the expression is 'man.' This expression might be construed as not incompatible with 'not-man' if it were possible to limit its use to "saying things of" (something) and to never bring in that of which it was said (1006b14–15).[20] For predicates can in a sense blend together ('white' and 'musical' and even 'man' might all apply to *a* man, the former three thus "sharing the same space"); but that which constitutes the basis of the reference—let us say, Socrates, that essence—cannot blend with any other reference, if he is to be referred to at all.

Aristotle is in effect admitting here that merely "saying things of" would not constitute the sort of signifying expression he needs for an elenchic demonstration, for no one thing would be signified that need exclude not being that one thing. But this admission is no great sacrifice: "the point in question is not this, whether the same thing can at the same time be and not be a man in name, but whether it can in fact" (1006b20–22). Were Antiphasis only to "say things of" and never "say things of something" (if this can even be imagined), his conversation would never succeed in signifying anything, which is the point from which the elenchic demonstration takes off. Not that Aristotle's demonstration depends on signifying things that actually exist; he means rather that the things to which Antiphasis might refer must at least be capable of existing—as man or Socrates or even sitting-Socrates is capable of existing.

But how, once Antiphasis has signified something in the appropriate way, can PNC be said to be demonstrated? Throughout *Metaph.* iv,4 Aristotle simply assumes that this is obvious; but, as so often in Aristotle, what he proclaims as obvious is far from obvious to us. The key to understanding the force of the argument is the original formulation of the problem. Aristotle's opponents, as we saw, are those who not only say that PNC is not true but who also say that it is possible to believe that it is not true (1006a1–2). His repeated use, especially in the various formulations of PNC, of the expression 'at the same time,'[21] makes it clear that the believing involved is a single act of believing that something is and is not—or could both be and not be—a certain thing. We may indeed be capable of believing, in a way that does not force us to bring our theory to bear upon a particular instance, that PNC is not always valid; but if we try to think of a particular instance in which it does not hold, we shall not succeed. We cannot have before our mind's eye the man Socrates and believe that he is at the same time both standing and not standing (in the same sense of standing). Or to use Aristotle's own example, we cannot have before our mind's eye 'man' and believe that man is both what he is (a two-footed animal) and what he is not (not a two-footed animal) (1006b28–34).

This incapacity is not physical or psychological—although the physical and the psychological are intimately bound up in it. When we try to think of Socrates as both standing and not standing, we realize that the difficulty in doing so has to do in the first place not with Socrates or with posture, nor with an incapacity in us that another person or type of creature might not share. In fact, incapacity is not at issue but an impossibility that is quite general. It is incorrect to speak of Socrates's standing and not standing precisely because it is impossible *logically* for him to be such. Logical positivism bequeathed to the modern world the idea that contradiction is solely a matter of propositions which exclude one another's truth. But Aristotle holds that the impossibility of contradictory propositions being true together is only a manifestation of a deeper and more pervasive "law."[22] According to this law, not only does it make no sense for the propositions 'Socrates is standing' and 'Socrates is not standing' to be true together but neither does it make sense for *Socrates* to be that way (which, of course, is not "a way" at all, for it is utter nonsense).

As elsewhere in Aristotle's philosophy, in this instance too, the general becomes manifest in the particular: PNC is proved in considering the signifying of Socrates. More precisely, the acknowledgment of PNC in a particular instance *is* the acknowledgment of the general principle. Attending to particular significations is the way we get at PNC in order to see it in action. PNC has to do not just with language or even just with thoughts (or beliefs) but with the most general structure of reality: the *rationem entis et non entis*, as Thomas puts it. Or, as I might put it rather germanically, there are logico-psychologico-ontological truths, the most basic of which is PNC.

AN ELENCHIC DEMONSTRATION OF FPPR

The person who denies FPPR—let us call him Antipraxis—denies that the good is to be pursued (in the sense previously identified). There are two ways in which a person might deny this. He might hold that some people (himself, for example) actually choose bad things *qua* being bad things or he might hold that at least some things that a person might choose are morally indifferent, so that it is false to say that everyone seeks good. But if it can be demonstrated that every action is pursued as good, both these positions will have been refuted for together they constitute the contradictory of FPPR. Thus, in what follows, Antipraxis represents the thesis that every action is not pursued as good—that is, he represents the person who asserts the contradictory of FPPR.

As we have seen, practical reason's object—good, instead of mere being—determines its differences from theoretical reason. The elenchic demonstration of FPPR must therefore be different from its counterpart in theoretical reason in any respect that involves good as opposed to being. I shall identify three such respects, making no claims to exhaustiveness.

First, although the denial of FPPR is certainly illogical, it is *practically* illogical. The problem is not in the first place that the denial of FPPR cannot be true (although it cannot be) but that one cannot *do* what it suggests one can do: that is, pursue what one does not consider good. The demonstration of FPPR seeks therefore to show not that the FPPR is true but that, without it, there would be no intelligible human action.[23]

Second, just as we presumed that Antiphasis was willing to enter into rational discourse, so here we presume that Antipraxis is willing to engage in practical reasoning which, by definition, is about things that a person does (or might do) voluntarily—if not necessarily by choice.[24]

Practical reasoning is practical *discourse* in the sense that it leads to things that people do (or might do) and that are (or might be) recognized by others as things that a person does voluntarily. Just as the denier of PNC who refuses to "say something which is significant both for himself and for another" (*Metaph.* iv,4,1006a21) is no better than a plant, so he who refuses even to consider doing anything that might be recognized by others as an intelligible action is beyond refutation but also beyond bothering about. In other words, we presuppose that one cannot consider doing something unless one considers doing *something;* and what might count as doing something is in principle recognizable by others as a definite (intelligible) human action. The definiteness of a "theoretical" signifying consists in the fact that being the opposite of what is signified is excluded by being what is signified. Similarly, in the practical sphere, definiteness consists in the fact that pursuing the opposite of what is signified is excluded by pursuing what is signified. It is because practical significations are this way that they can be part of a shared community of practices and judgments about those practices.

Third, the "signifying" that Antipraxis will be asked to do is not the signifying of a definite thing *as* a being; it is rather the "practical signifying" of a definite thing as a good possibly to be sought.[25] If I signify Socrates, my act is in some sense a signifying of his being. On the other hand, when a person thinks to himself, for instance, 'I will pursue the right theory' (about practical reason), his signifying is not merely a signifying of being but of being-a-good-thing (a thing to be pursued). This means that a practical signifying, instead of being in principle an element of an assertion, is in principle an element of a choice to do something. In theoretical reason, the basic elements are terms ('white' and 'Socrates') which might be brought together into assertions ('Socrates is white'). In practical reason the basic elements are, like terms, delimited ('the right theory' regarded as to be pursued is incompatible with its not being such); but the point is not to combine one element with another in order to assert something but to pursue something as part of a project. For instance, a person might believe that happiness is to be found in having a reputation. Believing that he will gain a reputation if he attains the right theory, he pursues the right theory. The point of associating reputation and the right theory is not to make a claim about the world ("that's the way to gain a reputation") but to get to happiness—or, at least, to apparent happiness.

So then, since we are now dealing with practical (not theoretical) reason, we ask Antipraxis to signify something that might be an object of practical reason: a "*prosequendum.*" This means that he identifies something that makes sense to pursue, although he need not have committed himself to pursuing it.[26] Let us say again that he picks 'the right theory.' We do not want to beg the question by asking him to *decide* to pursue the right theory (which he might argue would be to proclaim that that thing is definitely good, which is precisely what he is contesting).[27] He has, however, agreed to reason practically, so we can ask that he at least signify in a practical way the type of thing that might result in a decision to do that thing. Let us say again that Antipraxis is interested in making a reputation for himself. He considers two ways in which he might do this: by pursuing the right theory about practical reason or by striking his interlocutor. We do not ask him to do one or the other (which would be the practical equivalent of asserting a proposition); the elenchic demonstration of FPPR begins rather from a stage prior to such a choice.

Antipraxis might argue that it is possible to regard pursuing the right theory as being either good *or* bad since it might involve leaving his wife and children destitute or it might mean bringing great happiness to a large number of people. We can point out that he is making the same type of mistake that people often make with respect to Aristotle's elenchic demonstration of PNC. That is, they think that he is concerned in the first instance with what a person might believe in general. But that argument, as we have seen, is concerned in the first instance not with general but with particular beliefs. So also here. We would be foolish to deny that Antipraxis can at 10 a.m. consider the pursuit of the right theory in a positive light and at 3 p.m. as something to be avoided. What is impossible on the present account is that he might (in a practical way) at any *one* time consider having the right theory both to be pursued and not to be pursued. If he is thinking, 'I'll pursue the theory and thereby bring great happiness to others,' he cannot at the same time be thinking, 'I'll not pursue the theory since doing so would hurt the family.'

Antipraxis might reply: "Look, Mr. A, who has no family, can come along and see the right theory as a good; and at the same time Mr. B (who has a family) can come along and see *the same thing* as something bad. Therefore, the act itself is morally indifferent; and it can be so at one particular time." We however have an answer for him: "But you agreed to make a practical signification, didn't you? What Mr. A and Mr. B think about having the right theory does not enter into your signification, which is the basis of the present demonstration. We are saying that *you* cannot both pursue and not pursue the same thing at the same time in the same respect. And that is the basis of our demonstration."[28]

What we are focusing on now is the practical equivalent of trying to see a particular signification under contradictory aspects in the theoretical sphere (Socrates sitting and standing at the same time). What occurs in either practical or theoretical reason is "a kind of flip-flopping of gestalts."[29] Antipraxis might be in doubt at a particular time, but necessarily this involves flipping from one way of seeing the pursuit of the right theory to another way of seeing it. His doubting might consist, for instance, in thinking of the prospect at one moment as a thing to be avoided ("how could I ever support the family?"), at another as a thing to be pursued ("it could make me famous"). But a doubt as such cannot subsist in just *one* of these moments, except insofar as it is conjoined with the other.

Why is this necessarily the case? Why, that is, can pursuing a particular thing not "get into" the same moment as avoiding it? Because practical significations exclude their practical contradictories just as theoretical significations exclude their theoretical contradictories. We tend to think that there is a lack of parallel between practical and theoretical reason in this regard: in theoretical reason, a sort of picture of Socrates standing excludes a similar picture of Socrates not-standing; but the practically contradictory pair 'pursuing the right theory'/'not-pursuing the right theory' seems to be just a matter of different attitudes cast upon the prospect 'pursuing the right theory.' But there is a closer parallel than this unconsidered reaction allows.

Consider again the *prosequendum* 'the right theory.' Its practical contradictory is a wholly different, *positive* prospect. At first it might indeed be specified by no more than the element 'the right theory' plus a negative practical operator—just as a person might learn *just* that Socrates is not standing. But 'not-pursue-(the right theory)' must have a positive aspect, if it is to enter into practical reason at all.[30] That which is pursued must be pursued under the aspect of good. In this sense then it is like 'Socrates not standing.' The negation of 'Socrates is standing' does not represent absolute not-being for it has definite and positive content: Socrates doing *something* (i.e., not standing). Similarly, not pursuing the right theory cannot exist as a pure practical negation: that would be for it to be evil and no one can pursue that. One does-not-pursue the right theory by doing something else—including, perhaps, doing nothing. Even such inactivity can only be considered intelligible to the extent that it is considered under a positive aspect.

How then is Antipraxis refuted? We have asked him to signify something in a practical way—for example, the right theory (as something to be pursued). As with PNC, the claim is that at this point he has refuted himself: the elenchic demonstration is immediate. Just as insisting that

Antiphasis attend not to general beliefs but to significations forces him to concentrate on an indivisible portion of his world and acknowledge in *its* respect that the world cannot be contradictory (since one cannot get an attribute and its contrary into the same "picture"), so also our insistence that Antipraxis attend not to general indecision but rather to practical significations forces him to acknowledge that, if he were to decide to do something, he would have to decide upon it as good and not bad or indifferent. Just as in theoretical signification Antiphasis comes face-to-face with the truth, so in practical signification Antipraxis comes face-to-face with the good (which excludes its contrary). If a practical signification is a possible object of practical reason, it has to be regarded as good. And we know that it *is* a possible object of practical reason since that is a presupposition of the entire enterprise: Antipraxis has agreed to enter into practical discourse.

Someone might object: "But the only reason that Antipraxis is forced to acknowledge definite goods is that you have insisted that he buy into your conception of practical reason, according to which we always choose goods." But we can reply: "We have only insisted that he signify something that might be an intelligible action. It is true that the notion of an intelligible action bears with it the idea that something is pursued (for the action is not yet completed); and this in turn implies that the thing pursued is at least viewed as good (since nothing is sought if it is not considered good). But insisting on this is just to insist that Antipraxis live in the same practical world with us, where we are able to recognize one another's actions as actions that make sense. If he refuses even this, as we admit, we cannot refute him."

So, to conclude this demonstration, apparent *in* practical signification is FPPR: that everyone pursues good things in such a way that pursuing them excludes not pursuing them (i.e., avoiding them). 'The right theory' is a particular good thing, but the impossibility of its including 'not-(the right theory)' is quite general. The fact that we cannot conceive of what it would be like to both pursue and avoid the right theory at the same time in the same respect, shows that the practical world cannot be like that. That is, it shows that "good is to be done and pursued, and evil is to be avoided" or that "good is that which all things seek after."

IMPLICATIONS FOR PRACTICAL REASON

All this has implications for our understanding of practical reasoning. I shall discuss here two such implications, the first having to do with the material and formal aspects of human action, the second with free choice.

Practical Matter, Practical Form

At *Metaph.* iv,4,1006a22, just after saying that for the elenchic demonstration of PNC to get under way Antiphasis must say something significant for himself and for another, Aristotle remarks that "this is necessary, if he really is to say anything." And, as we have seen, at *Metaph.* iv,4,1006b7, Aristotle says, "Not to signify one thing is not to signify at all." Thomas makes a related point with respect to practical reason in his commentary on Aristotle's *De Anima.* He insists that every appetite is for the sake of something: "It is nonsense," he asserts, "to say that someone wants [*appetat*] in order to want [*propter appetere*], since to want is a sort of motion tending toward something."[31] As we shall see more clearly below, Thomas insists that an interior act of the will is always attached to an exterior "something" which it wills. Much of this doctrine derives from Aristotle's *De An.* iii,10.

This idea has important consequences especially for our conception of practical reason. It means that practical reason involves, at every step of the way, what we might call "practical matter," since there cannot be individuation without matter of some type (which is always, of course, tied to the appropriate type of form).[32] This is not to say, however, that the matter in practical reason is physical matter. I am not espousing "physicalism," such as various authors of the Roman Catholic "manualist tradition" are accused of doing. Practical matter is more like logical matter, according to which conception one can say that 'the table is blue' and 'the stove is hot' are of the same form but of different matter.[33] The matter here is neither a blue table nor a hot stove but that which differentiates the one proposition from the other—that is, the fact that one *speaks* about the table's being blue, the other about the stove's being hot, although they are of the same "shape" (or form).

In an article in the *Summa theologiae* devoted to the question whether a human action receives its goodness or badness from its object, the following objection is raised: "the object is compared to the action as its matter. The goodness, however, of a thing is not from its matter but from its form—which is the act. Therefore, the good or bad is not in acts on account of the object." The object spoken of here is not what Thomas calls "the object of the interior act of the will" or *finis;* rather, it is the object of the exterior act.[34] Since the object in this sense is part of the exterior act, there is a temptation to associate it with physical matter. But Thomas, in his reply to the objection, excludes this notion: "the object is not matter *ex qua* but matter *circa quam* and it has thus the intelligibility of form insofar as it provides the species."[35] It is clear here that Thomas is no physicalist. Matter is the individuating principle in Thomas's metaphysics—"that which contracts," allowing one to speak, for instance, not of murder in general but of one particular murder.[36] It is this characteristic that allows this type of matter to have a formal aspect: it *specifies* the act, as the specific form of Socrates specifies him as distinct from man in general.[37]

It also becomes clear, however, in this question of the *Summa* that an action's object is connected with the interior act of the will in such a way that only in *it* (that is, in the interior act) can we speak about an exterior moral act at all: "Now that which is on the part of the will is formal in regard to that which is on the part of the exterior action: because the will uses the limbs to act as instruments; nor have the external actions any measure of morality save insofar as they are voluntary."[38] But these two—the interior and the exterior acts—are not separate *things,* so that an act of adultery, for instance, without an act of the will is still an act of adultery but not a morally relevant one. If the corresponding act of the will is not present, neither is there an exterior act of adultery.[39] The two come into existence together, as matter and form.[40]

This close association, however, between the interior and the exterior act ought not blind us to the fact that the exterior has its own intelligibility and even primacy. Even if it is true that an act of adultery is dependent on an interior act of the will for its very existence, the exterior act of the will is for *something*—that is, for something that might be signified in human moral discourse and as such excludes not being that thing. Writes Thomas:

> We may consider a twofold goodness or malice in the external action: one in respect of due matter and circumstances; the other in respect of the order to the end. And that which is in respect of the order to the end, depends entirely on the will: while that which is in respect of due matter and circumstances, depends on the reason: *and on this goodness depends the goodness of the will, insofar as the will tends towards it.*[41]

Perhaps I can make all this talk of objects, internal acts, and matter more intuitively apparent by employing a rather unconventional image. We might imagine that the practical (as opposed to the theoretical) life is like a penny arcade video game in which a person drives along a simulated road. But instead of the road being preset, it is extemporaneously constructed in front of the driver as he or she considers things to do (*prosequenda*). One can never drive where there is no road, which is to say that practical reasoning is about definite, concrete things (it involves matter); but it is also true that in order to have road to drive on, one need only consider the possibility of taking that road.[42] In practical reason, one cannot fly over a stretch of road, any more than one can in an automobile, since progressing along the road of practical reason just *is* having road on which to drive and so doing. On the other hand, one's practical reasoning is completely free since, given that one can only drive on road, one can take any road one wants. Moreover, even staying by choice on a single road is free since it involves projection of the road and driving down it. Not driving down that road would be another road, a free alternative to driving down the first.

Louis Janssens fails to understand at least a part of this story when, in a recent article, wishing to justify certain types of lying by an appeal to Thomas, he writes: "The end of the person, the protection of the professional secret, is the formal element of the action that [*sic*] justifies what is done, even when, of necessity, telling a *falsiloquium* constitutes the material object of the act."[43] Janssens means that the internal object (or *finis*) determines the goodness of the act regardless of the character of the exterior object. But the two elements cannot be in tension in this way, for the one comes with the other. It is true that the road only comes up if one projects it, but one has to project something and then take that road projected. Practical reason proceeds along *prosequenda*.

This misconception reflects a misinterpretation made earlier in the same article. Janssens writes, "the object is not only the material in which [*sic*] the act consists (*non est materia ex qua*) but the material with which one materially works (*materia circa quam*)."[44] But Thomas does not say in the relevant place that "the object is *not only* the material in which the act consists"; he says precisely what Janssens gives in the Latin: *non est materia ex qua.* The matter of an action is *not* like bricks and stones, matter *from* which we might produce a house. In human action, the material is bound up with the object. It is the thing at which we aim; not that from which we produce what we will.[45]

It is true, of course, that what Janssens calls "the end of the person, the protection of the professional secret," might be the object of that person's intention; but there is no jumping over the stretch of road that leads there—nor does the matter 'protection of the professional secret' (which, of course, must go along with its corresponding form) ever replace the matter 'tell a falsehood.' Both *prosequenda*, each composed of form and matter, are objects of the person's intentions.

Thomas makes this point in a comment on Aristotle's *Metaph.* iii,2,1013a35–b3: "Not only the ultimate thing, for the sake of which the agent acts, is called an end in relation to the things that precede; but also all of the intermediate things, which are between the first agent and the ultimate end, are called end in relation to the things that precede [them]."[46] There is no doubt that in Thomas (and in Aristotle) the "end specifies the act," so that telling a falsehood may indeed be "protecting a professional secret."[47] But it is also telling a falsehood. The form "protecting a professional secret" does not obliterate that. And since telling a falsehood is something that the person protecting the professional secret deliberately *does*, it needs to be assessed on its own merits, since everyone is responsible for what he deliberately does. Accordingly, Thomas, by constant repetition, makes his own the saying of pseudo-Dionysius: "Good comes of a single and perfect cause, evil from many and particular defects."[48] *Any* action in a chain of actions might be deemed wrong.

In a number of places, Thomas seems to speak of the true intention of an act as the ultimate as opposed to the proximate end(s) of an action— as if the individual acts along the way to the goal were the matter, the goal itself the form. Such remarks are easily reconciled, however, with those that speak of the intimate bond between practical form and matter once we take account of the nature of practical matter. Practical matter is practical insofar it is aimed at good; as such, it necessarily contains the ultimate object within itself. Telling a falsehood, as we are considering it here, is not just telling a falsehood (considered in a nonpractical way) but it is telling a falsehood with the aim of protecting a professional secret. Otherwise, it would not be practical matter. Thus, to speak of an action along the way to a goal as matter and the goal as form (to say, e.g., that, if a person robs in order to commit adultery, the matter is robbery, the form adultery),[49] is to exclude neither the idea that the adultery give species (form) *to* the robbery nor the idea that the matter *circa quam* one commits adultery is, at one stage in the process, an act of robbery. We *have* to be able to say the latter (i.e., that sometimes someone committing a robbery *is* committing adultery) if it is to be accurate to say that the form gives species to the act. Of course, since adultery is a movement, the person will not have *committed* adultery until he engages in sexual intercourse with the spouse of another.

Free Choice

Thomas identifies a number of stages that correspond to what we would find an agent doing if we were to stop the process leading up to the action at various points. The stages are *apprehensio, intentio, consilium, iudicium, consensus, electio, imperium, usus* (although in certain instances some stages might not exist independently of others). Various neoscholastic schemes, by adding stages and particularly by putting *iudicium* after *consensus*, attained for the Thomistic theory a certain symmetry between the role of intellect and the role of will: the intellect apprehends, giving rise to simple volition; the intellect settles on the end, the will intends [*intentio*]; the intellect deliberates [*consilium*], the will gives its *consensus;* the intellect makes a judgment about the means [*iudicium*], the will chooses [*electio*]; finally, the intellect issues an *imperium*, the will puts the *imperium* into active use.[50]

Such schemes, however, besides putting intellect and will in separate and sequestered compartments and ignoring what Thomas says about the place of *consensus*,[51] obscure the fact that even after the agent makes a judgment [*iudicium*] about the means he will use, he still has a choice to make. If the process of practical reasoning truly leads to choice [*electio*], at the threshold of choice, there must yet exist options among which the agent chooses.[52] The scholastic ordered pairings *consilium-consensus/ iudicium-electio* suggests that the job of the will is to deliver propulsion (by *consensus* and *electio*) to what is decided only in the intellect (*consilium* and *iudicium*). The genuinely Thomistic order, on the other hand—*consilium, iudicium, consensus, electio*—makes it apparent that the entire moral agent is present right at the very threshold of action. Thus, intellect and will, form and matter are never entirely independent of one another. Or, to employ the above simile, *electio* is a sort of intellectual steering into a particular *prosequendum*. "Choice is either desiderative thought or intellectual desire" (*EN* vi,2,1139b4–5); it involves both intellect and will since steering is choosing a road and there is no choosing that is not the choosing of a road.[53]

One of the advantages of this approach is that it provides an account of choice even when the options are not what we might call "lively options." Essential for any valid system of ethics is the idea that what counts are those things that are "up to us"—the things that we *do* in the sense that we could have done otherwise.[54] By making such things basic, we account for the fact that ethics is necessarily about personal moral character, praise and blame, virtues, and the like. This essential aspect of ethics finds exaggerated expression in ethical theories that place emphasis on the instances in which a person stands at the "moment of decision"— that is, the moment when, for instance, the person hesitates before his options, thinks, then chooses to lie or not, or to become a Mafia hit-man or not, and so on.[55] Certainly such moments of decision are character determining in a strong sense and might even serve as paradigm examples of free choice; but Thomas's scheme, according to which *every* human act remains undecided right up to the last moment, gives a better account of why we praise the person who never lies and would never think of lying and heap the blame on the Mafia hit-man precisely *for* his umpteenth murder, even though it has not been preceded by a moment of decision.

Provided a person is not out of control when he acts (e.g., from drugs or alcohol) and that he is not ignorant of any crucial circumstances of his own action (e.g., that the gun is loaded), then if he commits a blamable deed, he is to be blamed for *that act* since anything one does involves projecting (as a good thing) a stretch of road ahead and taking it. If the person is a habitual killer, for instance, so that he never thinks of *not* taking that road when the possibility presents itself, this does not lessen the blame attached to his latest murder. In fact, his not thinking of alternatives is reason for greater blame. Killing has become quite "natural" for him; it is part of his character. And, as we have seen, character is what ethics is all about.[56]

In short, the moments of decision approach puts undue emphasis on options as an element of free choice. It is true that free choice is and must be among options, but it is not the options *qua* options that makes free choice morally essential. The essential thing is that free choice is an opportunity to go toward or away from the good and thus to become either virtuous or not. One cannot go in the direction of the good if there are no options; but one's character is formed in the doing, not by virtue of having had various options.

One more related point before moving on to the next section. Approaches, such as the neoscholastic approach discussed above, which locate the decisive ethical factor elsewhere than in the actualization of a *prosequendum* composed of practical form and matter, tend to present intention "as if it were a distinct content of consciousness," as John Finnis puts it.[57] They must objectify intention because if the decisive factor does not subsist in the matter of the act itself, other matter must be pressed into service to allow talk about one's "intentions." This approach allows scope for claims along the following lines: "I performed the abortion, that is true; but I regretted performing it. The act itself is horrible, but my intention was right." But the intention with which one does something is not located in the emotions that precede (and in fact follow) an act. One intends in and by means of *significations* that are active, free positings of *prosequenda*. Emotions, on the other hand, are passive things—things we suffer rather than do—and we may well intend something without feeling any emotion at all. But if this is so, we are responsible for what we do, independent of the emotions we have or claim to have.

"FREE CHOICE: A SELF-REFERENTIAL ARGUMENT"

In 1976 Boyle, Grisez, and Tollefsen (hereafter BGT) published a book entitled *Free Choice: A Self-Referential Argument.* In it they present an argument (which I shall call their "main argument") against the person who denies that free will is possible. (They call this person *PNfc*—the Person who holds that No one can make a free choice. *Sfc* stands for the position that Someone can make a free choice; *PSfc*, the person holding the same; and *Nfc*, the position which *PNfc* holds.) The main argument contains a flaw which I should like to discuss now, since it is tied up in an interesting way with the themes that I have discussed here.

The main argument goes something like this:

1. The *PNfc* rationally affirms *Nfc*. (By assumption.)
2. If *Nfc* is rationally affirmed, then the conditions obtain whereby *Sfc* is rationally excluded. (Established independently.)
3. The conditions obtain whereby *Sfc* can be rationally excluded. (From 1 and 2.)
4. If the conditions obtain whereby *Sfc* is rationally excluded, then some rationality norm must be in force. (Established independently.)
5. A rationality norm adequate to warrant an affirmation which excludes *Sfc* is in force. (From 3 and 4.)
6. Any norm by which a *PNfc* can rationally exclude *Sfc* has a normativity which prescribes unconditionally and prescribes one of two open alternatives. (Established independently.)
7. Any norm which prescribes unconditionally and prescribes one of two open alternatives is in force only if the person to whom it is addressed can make a free choice. (Established independently.)
8. Any norm by which the *PNfc* can rationally exclude *Sfc* is in force only if the person to whom it is addressed can make a free choice. (From 6 and 7, plus further clarifications.)
9. Someone can make a free choice. (From 5 and 8.)
10. *Nfc* is inconsistent with 9.
11. *Nfc* is falsified by 9.[58]

The general strategy of this argument is to show that a *PNfc*, in order to assert *Nfc*, must invoke a rationality norm which implies something that is inconsistent with *Nfc*. This "self-referentially falsifies" *Nfc*, which means that the affirmation of *Nfc* has a property that is inconsistent with *Nfc* (p. 133). In other words, the strategy is not to attack *Nfc* directly but to show that it implies a rationality norm that implies free choice (understood in a certain sense), free choice being incompatible with *Nfc*.

An important concept in this argument is rational affirmation (mentioned in 1). BGT acknowledge that the possibility of *PNfc*'s rationally affirming *Nfc* is important to their argument for it constitutes the difference between the main argument and a backup argument they also present.[59] They also assert that among the "necessary conditions for rationally affirming *Nfc*" is the idea that "logical principles are to be adhered to in all one's thinking, even when doing so requires one to give up beliefs based upon experience."[60]

I have no difficulty with the main gist of this argument—although I do take exception to 1 (and to some extent 6). That is, I agree that as part of his argument *PNfc* has to present two lively options to his interlocutor: accept *Nfc* or *Sfc*. And this is to pose a free choice—which is the very thing *PNfc* denies. But it seems to me that what BGT's argument shows is that *Nfc* is an incoherent thesis—in other words, that *PNfc* is "not adhering to logical principles in his thinking." Thus, the main argument never gets off the ground.

Obviously, BGT do not see things this way. They draw, rather, a distinction between rationality norms and "the rules of formal logic":

> [a] The rules of formal logic show how propositions and formally distinct parts of propositions are formally related, while rationality norms indicate only that certain sorts of reasons provide adequate grounds for affirming a conclusion. . . .
> [b] Another consideration further clarifies the distinction between the rules of formal logic and rationality norms, and the bearing on the *act* of affirming. One who violates a law of logic eventually finds himself in formal incoherence; he loses the ability to *mean* anything and *say* anything. One who violates a rationality norm does not thereby become formally incoherent.[61]

The description of formal logic contained in "a" is sound, but it does not distinguish it from rationality norms. Attending to the way that propositions and their parts are formally related is involved in adhering to logical principles. Moreover, if rationality norms indicate that "certain sorts of reasons provide adequate grounds for affirming a conclusion," they also indicate that other reasons are inadequate. Among such inadequate reasons would certainly be those that are logically incoherent. The claim in "b" is certainly false. A person who violates a law of logic can still signify meaningfully and make coherent statements. That is the basis of Aristotle's elenchic demonstration of PNC in *Metaph.* iv,4, and it is certainly reasonable for him to make it such.

But what is the point of this? Why would anyone want to separate being logical from being rational? The point is to ensure that the rationality norms involved in the assertion of *Nfc* leave the relevant question open, so that *PNfc* might offer a real choice to his interlocutor and be thereby caught, hoist with his own petard. According to BGT, if *Nfc* is logically defective, there cannot be such an offer: "There is at least one type of normativity—logical normativity—which prescribes unconditionally and which can actually prescribe even if the person who is directed by it could not make a free choice. A logical norm prescribes the only coherent alternative; thus there are no open alternatives and no need for free choice."[62]

But I see no reason to go along with this conception of free choice. That is, as I have argued, although moments of decision are certainly moments of free choice, free choice extends wider than that. BGT assert: "A choice is free if and only if there is a choice between open alternatives such that there is no factor but the choosing itself which settles which alternative is chosen."[63] But a person faced with a choice between *Nfc* and *Sfc* can freely choose *Sfc* precisely because it is the only logically coherent option—just as a person who knows that *Nfc* is incoherent can freely choose to assert its truth and propagate a supporting theory. Free choice does not require lively options. One simply posits a stretch of road ahead and drives down it.

I am far from thinking that BGT's main argument is an utter failure. With some adjustments, it might be used as a proof that *PNfc* is at least "self-defeating." Such adjustments would perhaps turn the argument into their backup argument.[64] But this is not a topic that I can pursue at the present time.

CONCLUSION

I have argued that Aristotle's method of elenchic demonstration might be used to demonstrate "the first principle in practical reason." Like Aristotle's demonstration of the principle of noncontradiction, the demonstration of its practical equivalent depends on the opponent of the principle's making a signification (his identifying a *prosequendum*).

Identifying *prosequenda* as the foundation of practical reason tells us much about practical reason itself. It tells us, in particular, about the nature of what St. Thomas calls practical matter and practical form; and it tells us much about the nature of free choice.[65]

BIBLIOGRAPHY

PRIMARY

Alexander of Aphrodisias (*in Metaph.*), *In Aristotelis Metaphysica Commentaria*, ed. Michael Hayduck (Berlin: Reimer, 1891) (*Commentaria in Aristotelem Graeca*, v. 1).
Aristotle:
    An. Pr.: *Analytica Priora* (ed. Ross, OCT = Oxford Classical Texts).
    An. Post.: *Analytica Posteriora* (ed. Ross, OCT).
    Cat. = *Categories* (ed. Minio-Paluello, OCT).
    De An.: *De Anima* (ed. Ross, OCT).
    EE: *Eudemian Ethics* (ed. Walzer and Mingay, OCT).
    EN: *Ethica Nicomachea* (ed. Bywater, OCT).
    Metaph.: *Metaphysics* (ed. Jaeger, OCT).
    For translations, see below Barnes (1984).
Thomas:
    De Div. Nom.: *In Librum Beati Dionysii De Divinis Nominibus Expositio*, ed. C. Pera (Turin/Rome: Marietti, 1950).
    De Malo: in *Quaestiones Disputatae*, v.2, ed. P. Bazzi and P. M. Pession (Turin/Rome: Marietti, 1953).
    De Ver. (*De Veritate*): in *Quaestiones Disputatae*, v.1, ed. R. M. Spiazzi (Turin/Rome: Marietti, 1953).
    in An. Post.: *In Libros Posteriorum Analyticorum Expositio*, ed. R. M. Spiazzi (Turin: Marietti, 1955).
    in De An.: *In Aristotelis Librum De Anima Commentarium*, ed. A. M. Pirotta (Turin/Rome: Marietti, 1948).
    in EN: *In Decem Ethicorum Aristotelis ad Nicomachum Expositio*, ed. A. M. Pirotta and M. Gillet (Turin: Marietti, 1934).
    in Int.: *In Libros Peri Hermeneias Expositio*, ed. R. M. Spiazzi (Turin: Marietti, 1955).
    in Metaph.: *In Duodecim Libros Metaphysicorum Aristotelis Expositio*, ed. M.-R. Cathala and R. M. Spiazzi (Rome: Marietti, 1950).
    in Phys.: *In Octos Libros Physicorum Aristotelis Expositio*, ed. P. M. Maggiòlo (Turin/Rome: Marietti, 1965).

in *(I,II,III,IV) Sent.*: *Commentum in Quatuor Libros Sententiarum Magistri Petri Lombardi* 2 vv. (Parma, 1856).

ST: *Summa Theologiae* (ed. P. Caramello) (Turin/Rome: Marietti, 1948). I have used the 1911 Dominican translation of the *Summa Theologiae* (revised in 1920); occasional alterations have not been noted.

SECONDARY

Baker, G. P. and P. M. S. Hacker (1984). *Frege: Logical Excavations* (New York: Oxford University Press/Oxford: Basil Blackwell).

Barnes, Jonathan (1984). *The Complete Works of Aristotle: the Revised Oxford Translation*, 2 vols. (Princeton: Princeton University Press).

Barnes, Jonathan (1990). "Logical form and logical matter," in A. Alberti (ed.) *Logica, mente et persona* (Florence: Leo S. Olschki Editore), pp. 7-119.

Barnes, Jonathan (1994). *Aristotle: Posterior Analytics, translated with a commentary* (Oxford: Clarendon Press).

Boyle, Joseph M. (1984). "The personal responsibility required for mortal sin," in *Moral Truth and Moral Tradition: Essays in Honour of Peter Geach and Elizabeth Anscombe*, ed. L. Gormally (Dublin: Four Courts): 149–162.

Boyle, Joseph M., Germain Grisez, and Olaf Tollefsen (1976). *Free Choice: A Self-Referential Argument* (Notre Dame/London: Notre Dame University Press).

Dancy, R. M. (1975). *Sense and Contradiction: a Study in Aristotle* (Dordrecht: D. Reidel).

Finnis, John (1983). *Fundamentals of Ethics* (Washington: Georgetown University Press).

Finnis, John (1992). "Object and intention in moral judgments according to St. Thomas Aquinas," in *Finalité et intentionnalité: doctrine Thomiste et perspectives modernes*, ed. J. Follon and J. McEvoy (Paris: Librairie Philosophique J. Vrin / Leuven: Éditions Peeters—Éditions de l'Institut Supérieur de Philosophie, Louvain-la-neuve), pp. 127–148. (This is a later and slightly different version of the article bearing the same name which appears in *The Thomist*, 55 [1991]: 1–27.)

Flannery, Kevin (1995a). *Ways into the Logic of Alexander of Aphrodisias* (Leiden/New York/Köln: E. J. Brill).

Flannery, Kevin (1995b). "The Aristotelian First Principle of Practical Reason," *Thomist* 59: 455–478.

Flannery, Kevin (1995c). "Natural law *mens rea* v. the Benthamite tradition," *American Journal of Jurisprudence* 40: 377–400.

Flannery, Kevin (1995d). [Review of] Moral Truth and Moral Tradition: Essays in Honour of Peter Geach and Elizabeth Anscombe, ed. Luke Gormally, *International Philosophical Quarterly* 35, pp. 497–501.

Grisez, Germain (1965). "The First Principle of Practical Reason: A Commentary on the *Summa Theologiae*, 1-2, Question 94, Article 2," *Natural Law Forum* 10: 168–201.

Inciarte, Fernando (1994a). "Aristotle's defense of the principle of non-contradiction," *Archiv für Geschichte der Philosophie* 76: 129–150.

Inciarte, Fernando (1994b). "Die Einheit der Aristotelischen Metaphysik," *Philosophisches Jahrbuch* 101: 1–21.

Janssens, Louis (1994). "Teleology and Proportionality," in Joseph Selling and Jan Jans (ed.) *The Splendor of Accuracy* (Kampen, the Netherlands: Kok Pharos Publishing), pp. 99–113.

Łukasiewicz, Jan (1910). "Über den Satz des Widerspruchs bei Aristotles" in *Bulletin International de l'Académie des Sciences de Cracovie*, Cl. d'histoire et de philosophie, pp. 15–38; translated by V. Wedin as "On the Principle of Contradiction in Aristotle," *Review of Metaphysics* 24 (1970/71): 485–509; retranslated by Jonathan Barnes as "Aristotle on the Law of Contradiction," in J. Barnes, M. Schofield, and R. Sorabji, editors. *Articles on Aristotle, v. 3; Metaphysics* (London: Duckworth, 1975), pp. 50–62.

May, William E. (1984). "Aquinas and Janssens on the Moral Meaning of Human Acts," *Thomist* 48: 566–606.

Penner, Terry (1990). "Plato and Davidson: Parts of the Soul and Weakness of Will," *Canadian Journal of Philosophy*, supp. v.16: 35–74.

Schiaparelli, Annamaria (1994). "Aspetti della critica di Jan Lukasiewicz al principio aristotelico di non contraddizione," *Elenchos* 15: 43–77.

Weisheipl, James A. 1974. *Friar Thomas D'Aquino: His Life, Thought, and Works* (Garden City, New Jersey: Doubleday and Co. [reprinted by Catholic University of America Press, Washington, D.C.]).

Westberg, Daniel (1994). *Right Practical Reason: Aristotle, Action, and Prudence in Aquinas* (Oxford: Clarendon Press).

NOTES

1. The best exegesis of this article of the *Summa theologiae* is Grisez (1965). See especially pp. 187–190, where Grisez explains that FPPR is the principle of all human action—even of morally bad acts. The distinction between practical reason and theoretical reason is traceable to Aristotle's *EN* vi (see especially chapters 1 and 5). In this paper I adopt the common convention of using double inverted commas for quotations and as "scare quotes," single inverted commas in all other places where such marks are called for.

2. *De An.* iii,7,431a8-10. I employ in this paper the *Revised Oxford Translation* [= Barnes (1984)], making however the occasional alteration for the sake of consistency. For Aristotle's use of *diōkein/phugein*, see for instance *De An.* iii,7,431a8-10 & 9,432b28; *EN* ii,3,1104b21-2; *EE* ii,4,1221b33. And see also especially *EN* vi,2,1139a21-22 which is parallel to *De An.* iii,7,431a8-10.

3. See Thomas's *De Malo* q.3 a.12; also q.2 a.6 ad 6; *in IV Sent.* d.16 q.3 a.2 *solutiones* 2 et 3; *in EN* §§507–514 (Thomas's comments on Aristotle's *EN* iii,5,1114a3–31); *in EN* §§807–808 (comments on *EN* iv,5,1126a12–13); *in EN* §1052 (on *EN* v,9,1136a23ff); *ST* I-II q.1 a.6 c; q.8 al c; q.29 a.4 c; q.78 a.1 (especially ad 2).

4. *Protagoras* 358c6–d1.

5. See, for instance, *ST* I q.5 a.1 c: . . . *bonum et ens sunt idem secundum rem, sed differunt secundum rationem tantum. Quod sic patet. Ratio enim boni in hoc consistit, quod aliquid sit appetibile, unde Philosophus, in* I *Ethic., dicit quod bonum est quod omnia appetunt.* See also *ST* I q.17 a.4 ad 2; I-II q.18 a.1 (*sic igitur dicendum est quod omnis actio, inquantum habet aliquid de esse, intantum habet de bonitate*); *De Ver.* q.21 aa.1&2.

6. *ST* I q.79 a.11. In the *sed contra* he says that Aristotle says in *De An.* iii (9,433a1) that *intellectus speculativus per extensionem fit practicus.* Thomas apparently did not read these words when he wrote his commentary on this section of *De An.* (see *in de An.* §§812–815). He repeats or alludes to them, however, in a number of other places: *ST* II-II q.4 a.2 ad 3; *in* III *Sent.* d.23 q.2 a.3 *solutio* 2; *De veritate* q.2 a.8 c; q.14 a.4 c [*unde sola extensio ad opus facit aliquem intellectum esse practicum*]; qu.22 a.10 obj.4. The words apparently go back to the *vetus translatio* of *De Anima:* see the Leonine Commission edition of *De Veritate* (= *Quaestiones Disputatae de Veritate, tomus* 22, v.1), *apparatus criticus* for p.69 (q.2 a.8), line 55.

7. The expression 'elenchic demonstration' refers to *Metaph.* iv,4,1006a55ff, where Aristotle acknowledges that, since PNC is a first principle (*archē*), it cannot be demonstrated. It can however, he says, be "demonstrated by elenchus" (*esti d' apodeixai elegktikōs*—1006a11–12). For the sake of brevity, in what follows I shall sometimes drop the qualifier 'elenchic.' Aristotle actually proposes in *Metaph.* iv,4 a series of arguments for PNC; I shall be concerned, however, almost solely with the first in this series (i.e., 1005b35–1007b18). Accordingly, I shall speak in the singular of Aristotle's "elenchic demonstration."

8. Inciarte argues very convincingly that the kernel of Aristotle's *Metaphysics* (or, at least, of books iv, vii–ix and xii) is to be found in the elenchic demonstration of PNC (Inciarte [1994b]).

9. *Metaph.* iv,4,1008b14ff; see also Thomas in *Metaph.* §658. Can we be sure that Thomas was immediately aware of *Metaph.* iv,4,1008b14ff when he wrote *ST* I–II q.94 a.2? The various books of *in Metaph.* are difficult to date, but Weisheipl claims that the one on *Metaph.* iv was probably written at roughly the same time as *ST* I-II (Weisheipl [1974], pp. 361, 379]. Indeed, Thomas's *in Metaph.* §595 (on *Metaph.* iv,3,1005b5-8, i.e., Aristotle's remarks immediately prior to his elenchic demonstration of PNC) is so close to what is said in *ST* I-II q.94 a.2 about the things which are *per se nota* that it is difficult to believe that he did not have the demonstration in mind as he was writing *ST* I-II q.94 a.2.

10. *Et ideo primum principium indemonstrabile est quod non est simul affirmare et negare, quod fundatur supra rationem entis et non entis, et super hoc principio omnia alia fundantur, ut dicitur in iv metaphys. . . . Et ideo primum principium in ratione practica est quod fundatur supra rationem boni, quae est, bonum est quod omnia appetunt.*

11. *Metaph.* iv,3,1005b14. At *Metaph.* iv,4,1006a3 Aristotle says that he has previously "assumed" [*eilēphamen*] that the same thing cannot be and not be. But this must be interpreted (as both Alexander of Aphrodisias [*in Metaph.* 272.6] and Thomas [*in Metaph.* §606] do) in terms of the previous passage which denies that PNC is an hypothesis.

12. Dancy (1975), p. 34.

13. See especially Inciarte (1994a), p. 135, n.11.

14. Dancy (1975), pp. 35–36; Łukasiewicz (1910), p. 21.

15. These phrases, "the ontological formulation" and "the psychological formulation" come from Łukasiewicz (1910), p.16. Łukasiewicz also speaks of the "logical formulation" ("the most indisputable of all beliefs is that contradictory statements are not at the same time true" [*Metaph.* iv,6,1011b13–14]).

16. For a good exposition of the history of psychologism and (especially Fregean) antipsychologism, see Baker and Hacker (1984), pp. 33–62.

17. "I don't think it matters a *lot* what he says. . . . All that matters is that he utter a word, and one which signifies something, to himself and to others; and his uttering of any such word is also not a matter of saying that anything is so, or that it is not so" (Dancy [1975], p. 31, omitting references and footnotes). The range of possible significations must be very wide in order for Aristotle to be demonstrating PNC—whose application, of course, is as wide as being itself.

18. Aristotle makes a similar move to a lower level in several places in the *Prior Analytics* (*An. Pr.*), particularly when he employs the proof method known as *ekthesis*. For instance, when early in *An. Pr.* he proves that universal negative propositions convert (i.e., that, if A holds of no B, then B holds of no A), because he cannot rely on the logical apparatus that he is yet to construct, which itself depends on the conversion of universal negatives, he argues in this fashion: "Now if A holds of no B, B will not belong to any A; for if it does belong to some (say to C), it will not be true that A belongs to no B—for C is one of the Bs" (*An. Pr.* i,2,25a15–17). "C" belongs not to the syllogistic (i.e., to the theory set out in *An. Pr.*); it constitutes rather Aristotle's recourse to something more basic than the syllogistic in order to avoid begging the question. This is Alexander of Aphrodisias's interpretation and I believe it is the correct one. See Flannery (1995a), pp. 16–19, 38–45.

19. 1006b10–11; emphasis in *Revised Oxford Translation* (= Barnes [1984]).

20. See *Cat.* v.2a14–17.

21. The Greek word is *hama;* it appears at *Metaph.* iv,3,1005b19,27,29,30; *Metaph.* iv,4,1006b21,33, 1007a18, 1007b13,18,19. On this point, see Schiaparelli (1994), p. 51.

22. I put the word 'law' in scare quotes because (at least in a certain sense) PNC is not a rule that a person might choose to violate. For the sense I have in mind, see Wittgenstein's *Tractatus Logico-Philosophicus* 5.4731.

23. Practical contradiction does, however, involve real logical contradiction: see Flannery (1995b) *passim.*

24. See *EN,* iii,1–2.

25. For the sake of simplicity and where I can do so without causing confusion, in what follows I will sometimes drop from 'practical signification' (and similar phrases) the qualifier 'practical.'

26. In order to signify practically, Antipraxis must consider the thing signified as a thing possibly to be pursued (as a *prosequendum*), just as, in order to signify theoretically, Antiphasis must consider something as if it were one existent thing. If Antipraxis somehow manages to limit himself to act descriptions (the practical equivalent of only "saying things of"), he would not succeed in signifying practically. Also, even a *prosequendum* which involves a not-doing-something (i.e., an avoiding of it) is a positive *prosequendum* (i.e., *something* one might do) since its avoidance would involve a definite course of action. Similarly, according to

Thomas, negation is always "reducible to the genus of affirmation" (*in Int.* §61; see also §§10,108). Pure not-doing cannot be the object of practical reason any more than pure not-being can be the object of theoretical reason (see above note 10). Thus, a *prosequendum* which is a something-not-to-be-done is a practical signifying.

27. Cp. *Metaph.* iv,4,1006a1821.

28. This argument is related to Thomas's position that an act might be morally indifferent *secundum speciem* but not in *individuo consideratus* is discussed in *ST* I-II q.18 a.9 (see also q.18 a.8).

29. These very apt words come from Penner (1990), p. 69. Penner is speaking, however, solely of practical reason.

30. I understand 'not-pursue-(the right theory)' not as the *mere* not pursuing of the right theory—a person who has never thought of pursuing any theories is not pursuing a particular right theory when, for instance, he is playing golf—but as a positive prospect having to do with the possible pursuing of the right theory.

31. *In De An.* §821; comment on Aristotle's *De An.* iii,10,433a15–17: "Every desire is for the sake of something (*heneka tou*), for that for which there is a desire, this is the beginning of practical intelligence. For the ultimate thing <desire> is the beginning of action."

32. For matter as the principle of individuation in Thomas, see for instance *ST* I q.3 a.3 c; q.39 a.1 ad 3; q.39 a.2 c; I-II q.63 a.1 c.

33. On logical matter, see Barnes (1990) and also Flannery (1995a), chapter 3. Aristotle (and also Alexander of Aphrodisias) were well aware that logical matter could not be something in the world, otherwise it would never be possible to utter a false statement: see Flannery (1995a), pp. 95–96, 111–114. At *in An. Post.* §2, Thomas says that the *materia circa quam* of logic is the act of reason.

34. *ST* I-II q.18 a.6: *In actu autem voluntario invenitur duplex actus, scilicet actus interior voluntatis, et actus exterior, et uterque horum actuum habet suum obiectum. Finis autem proprie est obiectum interioris actus voluntarii, id autem circa quod est actio exterior, est obiectum eius. Sicut igitur actus exterior accipit speciem ab obiecto circa quod est; ita actus interior voluntatis accipit speciem a fine, sicut a proprio obiecto. Ita autem quod est ex parte voluntatis, se habet ut formale ad id quod est ex parte exterioris actus, quia voluntas utitur membris ad agendum, sicut instrumentis; neque actus exteriores habent rationem moralitatis, nisi inquantum sunt voluntarii.*

35. *ST* I-II q.18 a.2 ad 2: *Dicendum quod obiectum non est materia ex qua, sed materia circa quam, et habet quodammodo rationem formae, inquantum dat speciem.* See also ad 3. For more on the notion of *materia circa quam*, see *ST* I-II q.55 a.4 c; q.60 a.2 c; q.65 a.2 c; q.72 a.3 ad 2; q.73 a.3 ad 1; q.75 a.4 ad 1; also *in I Sent.* d.48 q.1 a.2 c; *in II Sent.* d.36 q.1 a.5 ad 4. The expression *materia circa quam* comes originally from Aristotle's *peri ti* at *EN* iii,1,1111a4: see *in EN* §415 and *ST* I-II q.7 a.3 c.

36. See *ST* I-II q.18 a.7 ad 3. See also *ST* I-II q.75 a.4 obj.1 and ad 1.

37. See *De Malo* q.2 a.5; also q.9 a.2 ad 10.

38. *ST* I-II q.18 a.6 c.

39. I discuss this issue in Flannery (1995c).

40. In fact, at *ST* I-II q.20 a.3 c, Thomas says that *actus interior voluntatis et actus exterior, prout considerantur in genere moris, sunt unus actus* (see also ad 3; see also q.17 a.4 c).

41. *ST* I-II q.20 a.2 c (my emphasis). I am much indebted in this section to William May's excellent article on this topic. See, especially, May (1984), pp. 580–85.

42. In accordance with the above elenchic demonstration, perhaps we would have to say also that as the driver posits one possible turning, any other possible turning that he may be considering necessarily disappears from vision. But we should not, I think, make this analogy do more work than it is capable of.

43. Janssens (1994), p. 111. The word *falsiloquium* is normally translated falsehood.

44. Janssens (1994), p. 105. He cites *ST* I-II q.18 a.2 ad 2 (see above, note 35).

45. Janssens also writes: "it appears that the end toward which the subject strives in each case is not merely an element of the object of the action but the formal element that is so important that it determines whether the material element is *materia debito modo disposita*" (p. 111). The phrase *materia debito modo disposita* is a reference to Thomas's remark at *ST* I-II q.4 a.4: "just as matter cannot receive a form, unless it be duly disposed thereto [*debito modo disposita ad ipsam*], so nothing gains an end, except it be duly ordained thereto." Thomas's point is that in the practical sphere, just as for example a saw cannot be made of wax, so a good act cannot be a good act unless the material of which it is "composed" is also good. But the "formal element" cannot "determine" anything about the "material element," in the way that Janssens suggests. Travelling along the strange road of practical reason where options suddenly appear as we deliberate, we might choose not to turn onto a particular stretch of road that we regard as immoral; but certainly our choosing it cannot make it moral.

46. *In Metaph.* §771. See also *in Phys.* §181; also Finnis (1992), pp. 134–137.

47. See for instance *in De An.* §§305–308 (ad *De An.* ii,4,415a17–22); also Finnis (1983), pp. 20–21, 25 and Finnis (1992), p. 138, n.33.

48. *Bonum [procedit] ex una et perfecta causa, malum autem [procedit] ex multis [et?] particularibus defectibus* (*De Div. Nom.* §572). As I said, Thomas quotes or cites this remark often: *ST* I-II: q.18 a.11 obj.3; q.19 a.6 ad 1; q.19 a.7 ad 3; q.71 a.5 ad 1; q.72 a.9 obj.1; in *De Malo:* q.2 a.4 ad 2; q.2 a.7 obj.3; q.2 a.9 ad 12; q.4 a.1 ad 13; q.8 a.1 obj.12 et c; q.10 a.1 c; q.16 a.6 ad 11; *in EN* §320 (ad *EN* ii,6,1106b29–30).

49. See the end of *ST* I–II q.18 a.6 c (the first portion of which is given in note 34 above): *Et ideo actus humani species formaliter consideratur secundum finem, materialiter autem secundum obiectum exterioris actus. Unde Philosophus dicit, in V Ethic., quod ille qui furatur ut committat adulterium, est, per se loquendo, magis adulter quam fur.*

50. See Finnis (1992), pp. 129ff; also Westberg (1994), pp. 119–135, 168.

51. See *ST* I-II q.15 a.3 c; q.74 a.7 ad 1.

52. *In II Sent.* d.24 q.1 a.2 c; *ST* I-II q.13 a.4 ad 3; q.15 a.3 ad 3; *De Ver.* q.22 a.15 c.

53. At *ST* I-II q.15 a.3 ad 3, Thomas writes as follows: "Choice [*electio*] includes something that consent [*consensus*] has not, namely, a certain relation to something to which something else is preferred: and therefore after consent there still remains a choice. For it may happen that by aid of counsel [*consilium*] several means have been found conducive to the end, and through each of these meeting with approval, consent has been given to each: but after approving of many, we have given our preference to one by choosing it. But if only one meets with approval, then consent and choice do not differ in reality, but only in our way of looking at them; so that we call it consent, according as we approve of doing that thing; but choice according as we prefer it to those that do not meet with our approval." Even if *consensus* does not present multiple options of the sort that belong to its domain, there is still a choice to be made, since the person can always choose not to effect the one option. To do or not to do the one thing are not the sort of options that *consensus* is concerned with, since it considers alternative means to an end.

54. See *EN* iii,5,1113b6; also iii,1,1110a15–18, iii,5,1113b21–1114a7,1114a21–31.

55. See Boyle (1994) and also Flannery (1995d), pp. 498–500.

56. See Thomas's *De Malo* q.3 a.13 ad 5, where he discusses the bearing of passion on culpability. He says that if the impulse to sin comes from without, it decreases culpability; if, however, it comes from within—that is, from the will—it increases culpability and, the more vehement the will, the greater the sin. Then Thomas says that habit makes the will to sin more vehement; thus, he who sins from habit, sins more gravely—and more vehemently! The murderer need not furrow his brow or slap his thigh with a determined exclamation, "I'll do it." Although such behavior might be good indication of a committed will, better indication (as the *De Malo* passage would suggest) is the fact that the murderer *does not* give external expression to his consent but simply goes ahead and kills.

57. Finnis (1992), p. 127; see also pp. 146–148.

58. Boyle, Grisez and Tollefsen (1976), p. 163. I have left out some remarks that BGT make within this argument.

59. They argue that (1) if *Nfc* can be rationally affirmed, it is self-referentially falsified; (2) If *Nfc* cannot be rationally affirmed, then any attempt to do so will be self-defeating (Boyle, Grisez, and Tollefsen [1976], pp. 137, 153). The protasis of "2" (the backup argument) is granted "for the sake of argument" (p. 154). Two is also discussed at pp. 166–168. On p. 167, they say that "if *Nfc* cannot be rationally affirmed, then [the main argument] is inadequate, since that argument proceeds on the assumption that the *PNfc* can rationally affirm *Nfc*."

60. Boyle, Grisez, and Tollefsen (1976), p. 144.

61. Boyle, Grisez, and Tollefsen (1976), p. 145. I have inserted the markers "a" and "b."

62. Boyle, Grisez, and Tollefsen (1976), p. 166. "There are cases in which deliberation becomes clarification; one's established priorities determine which of the available alternatives one accepts. Choices of there sort are not free . . ." (p. 78; see also pp. 74–77). Certainly among one's "priorities" might be logical consistency.

63. Boyle, Grisez, and Tollefsen (1976), p. 164.

64. See note 59.

65. For comments on earlier drafts of this essay, I especially thank Stephen Brock, Patrick Lee, William May, John Finnis, Lawrence Dewan, O. P., and other participants at the Princeton conference on the thought of Germain Grisez; also Hugh MacKenzie who provided some helpful criticisms; and "the White Russians" who discussed a shorter version of the paper at a meeting in Rome in March 1995.

Human Beings Are Animals

PATRICK LEE
Professor of Philosophy
University of Steubenville
Steubenville, Ohio

That bodily life is an essential component in the make-up of a human person is a central thesis in several works of Germain Grisez. Its denial, though often only implicit, has led to false ethical conclusions on contraception, abortion, euthanasia, sex ethics in general, and the roles of men and women in marriage.[1]

It seems to me, however, that the argument for biological life as an essential part of the human being that is found in the Grisez-Boyle-Finnis corpus needs improvement or reworking. In this article I propose an improvement and an explanation of how this theoretical proposition is linked to ethical positions.

The argument in the books on euthanasia and nuclear deterrence appeals to our direct experience of composite actions, such as writing a sentence on a piece of paper, since the unity of such actions involves both the body and the mind in a single action.[2] From there, Grisez, Boyle, and Finnis argue that the subject of this action, which involves both conscious and bodily actuations, is experienced as a unified whole.[3]

If successful, however, this argument only refutes a body-soul substance dualism. It does not directly address a position such as that suggested by David Hume or Derek Parfit, namely, the position that the person is not a substance at all but a set of experiences united by memory and other psychological connections (hereafter, the "no-subject view"). Further, the appeal to introspective experience, combined with the brevity of the argument, almost inevitably make it appear question-begging to readers influenced by the analytic tradition. An argument is needed that not only defends the thesis that a human person is a substance, but also, at least initially, approaches the issue from a third-person perspective.

The main argument I propose is very similar to the one in Grisez-Boyle. Although it begins from a third-person perspective, it centers on the human agent's unity of action, and it is, like the Grisez-Boyle argument, a development of Aquinas's argument against Plato's position on the relation of the soul to the body.[4] The main argument is as follows:

1. Sensing is a bodily act, that is, an act performed by a bodily entity making use of a bodily organ.
2. It is the same thing which senses and which understands.
3. Therefore, that which understands is a bodily entity, not a spiritual substance making use of the body.[5]

I will explain each of these steps in the argument more fully. Providing support for the first premise, is, however, of most importance, since substance dualists and proponents of the no-subject view typically deny that premise.

MAIN CHALLENGES TO ESTABLISHING THE FIRST PREMISE

To establish the first premise of this argument, I shall begin by considering sensation in *nonhuman* animals. My argument is this: first, sensation in nonhuman animals is an organic, bodily act. It is an act performed by a bodily organism, an act intrinsically ordered to the survival or fulfillment of a bodily organism. Second, sensation in human beings is the same kind of act as the act of sensation in nonhuman animals. It follows that sensation in human beings is an organic, bodily act.

I believe that four theories can, in various ways, block our acceptance of the proposition that sensation in nonhuman animals is an organic act. Two theories of material entities go against this proposition: mechanism and eventism (or process philosophy, the position that the ultimate entities are events rather than substances). And two theories of mind go against it: the no-subject view and substance dualism (that is, the identification of mind with an independent spiritual substance).

When we see a dog chase a rabbit or sniff out the place of a hidden bone, and observe that dogs have bodily structures similar to our eyes, ears, and noses, we understand that dogs see, hear, and smell. But there are various ways of denying this position. First, someone might say that sensation is not a unitary action at all, but an aggregate of electrical and chemical reactions: a mechanist would take this sort of position. Second, someone might say that sensation is really a mental episode associated with the body: a proponent of the no-subject view might take this position. Third, someone might say that nonhuman animals have no sensation: it only appears that they do, but they are, in fact, automata, as Descartes held. Fourth, someone might say that nonhuman animals have sensation but these animals are—like Plato's humans—beings who have substantially distinct minds. To defend the first premise in the main argument, we must defend the position that animals are enduring entities (against mechanism, eventism and the no-subject view); the position that they really do sense (against the idea that they are automata); and the position that in them sensation is an organic act (against substance dualism).

Animals Are Enduring Agents

A mechanist holds that the dog is an aggregate of smaller entities, perhaps molecules, and perhaps these molecules are aggregates of atoms, and so on. On this view, dogs and cats are only aggregates of smaller entities, and their actions are determined not by any intrinsic unitary direction but merely by the interaction of the smaller units. A proponent of this view might add that it is *convenient* to think of objects as unitary substances, but this convenience hardly translates into a true description of the world. This mechanistic view may then be harmonized with either a functionalist view of the human mind or the identification of the human self with a distinct substance as Platonists or Cartesians hold.

It is more than convenience, however, that moves us to see dogs and cats as real substantial units rather than as mere aggregates, *entia per accidens*.[6] Our viewing the dog as a unit is similar, as Aristotle pointed out, to our viewing a house or other composite artificial objects as units. Why do we think of the boards and bricks of a house as one? Because we grasp a unity, a functional unity, in those materials. We understand that the materials of the house are all organized for the purpose of providing shelter and warmth. In this case the unity is extrinsic, or imposed from outside by human agency.[7]

Analogously, when we see a dog chase a rabbit or come up to us drooping his head and wagging his tail, we apprehend a unity in the materials that go into the make-up of the dog. In the dog's chase of the rabbit we understand the canine feet and back and head as organized and directed to a single end, the catching of the rabbit. Even while the dog is sleeping, we understand the various parts of the dog—the cells, the tissues, the organs—as functional parts of a whole. In this case however, the dog, unlike the house, has its unity from within.

The things around us, most obviously, the living things and animals, are really various types of agents. And agents endure. An agent is a source of regular actions and reactions. As we observe recurrent and predictable actions, we identify the source or center of such actions as a thing or agent. It is not reasonable to think of reality simply as events or as particles in random motion, because the existence of agents or natures is required to explain the recurrence of definite actions and reactions. We must think and act in relation to dogs as units, for example, because only in that way can we understand and predict the actions of the materials that together we refer to as a dog. The materials that form a dog are in some ways similar to a multiplicity of chalk marks on a blackboard: why those bits of chalk dust are there can be explained mechanically, by reference to the properties of the chalk dust and the wood and other chemicals in the blackboard. But beyond that, is an intelligibility in the chalk marks that can be understood only by grasping their unity, which allows them to express a meaning. Similarly, we cannot fully explain why the dog zigged and zagged exactly as he did without seeing the dog as a unitary agent, as an animal in pursuit of prey. True, the motions of parts of the dog can be explained on lower levels, that is, by reference to the smaller particles in the make-up of the dog. We can explain the dog's turning to the left by reference to muscle contractions, and these contractions can be explained as electricochemical reactions. But the unity in its zigging and zagging can be understood only by seeing the materials in the dog as parts of a single agent. But again, the dog, unlike the house or chalk dust, has its unity from within. It is the same with trees, and other composite substances.

Thus, the unity of the materials consists in their intrinsic organization. Dogs, cats, trees, and, on the lower level, molecules and even atoms, are composite units understood as one in that they are distinct types of agents.

The position that animals and other entities are things or substances that persist through time is not an a priori necessary truth. It is not inconceivable that we could have a world with entities that do not persist at all, or for a very short time.[8] The evidence that there are persisting substances, and that animals are persisting substances consists in the phenomena that show beyond reasonable doubt that animals and other entities are *agents,* and that they remain the same sort of agents, and numerically the same agents, throughout stretches of time. The actions initiated and sustained by animals—such actions as chasing prey, eating meals, mating—are actions that take time. To suppose that there are only events or experiences strung together in various ways is to lose sight of the fact that in countless cases an action and its structure is explained by the kind of agent that produced and sustained it. A dog will chase a rabbit, whereas a horse will not. This is partly because a dog is a carnivore while a horse is a herbivore. But this is more reasonably interpreted as meaning that a dog is a certain type of agent, that is, a persistent source of predictable actions and reactions—given certain circumstances this type of agent will act or react in certain ways.[9]

This account of dogs and other animals is also challenged by process philosophy, more specifically, eventism. Whitehead recognized that both difference and continuity must be included in our account of the realities we experience.[10] But rather than locating the continuity in a persisting substrate, such as a substantial agent, he located it in the commonality of universal features. For example, an animal is not a persisting substance, but a society of events, and the continuity is the commonality of features shared by the series of events (which Whitehead calls "actual occasions").[11]

But the continuity that he recognized is serial and still calls for explanation. If the commonality is not intrinsically determined, then the regularity with which such continuous sequences occurs remains unexplained. If the *explanandum* remains the same throughout some stretch of time, then the *explanans*, to provide explanation, must also persist through time. That is, if what requires explanation is the order in a sequence of events spread throughout time, then the *explanans* must persist throughout that sequence. But the order of sequence of events is precisely what requires explanation, especially on the level of living things.

So it is reasonable to hold that the dog is a persisting organism. The dog chases the rabbit on Monday because the dog is a carnivore. The dog chases the rabbit on Tuesday because he is still a carnivore, and he remembers where and how he chased it on Monday. (This memory is shown by the fact that as the dog approaches the tree where he first saw the rabbit on Monday he begins to salivate and turn his head quickly in various directions.)

Animals Do Sense

Descartes denied that nonhuman animals sense. He held that animals are automata, that is, like machines, mere aggregates.[12] However, this position is untenable. Their movements are clearly specified by information obtained through sensation. They turn their heads to obtain sensations; they cry out with pain when struck, and groan or cry when suffering constant pain. Much of their behavior can, also, be explained only by admitting that they remember and have images. Dogs that seem to be sleeping cry out or moan, clearly reacting to what they are dreaming. There is, then, sensation in nonhuman animals, or, at the very least, sensation is associated with animals (perhaps it occurs in minds associated with them).

Sensation in Nonhuman Animals Is an Organic Act

Both Descartes and St. Augustine held that sensation in human beings is not, strictly speaking, a bodily act at all, but an act performed by the soul on the occasion of the change produced in the body by stimuli acting on it.[13] According to this view, having a sensation is in my consciousness and in my soul, even though it informs me of how things are modifying my body. Descartes did not believe that animals have minds, so he concluded that they do not sense. I argued against that in the last section. However, one could hold that nonhuman animals have sensation but that it occurs in souls or minds associated with their bodies. In this section I rule out that position.

The functional unity in the material body of the dog is intelligible only if it includes sensation. The dog zigs and zags meaningful, which is why we rightly understand the dog as a unit. But its act is unintelligible unless the dog can sense. That is, the various bodily parts of the dog are reasonably understood as unified precisely as instruments or organs for acts of sensation. The dog's parts are unified only as participating in the act of sensing an external object and reacting to it—only in this way is the scene of the dog chasing a rabbit coherent. And these unified actions are intelligible only as acts of sensation intrinsically ordered to the survival or perfection of the organism. Sensing is an action done by the organism, one in which, for example, the eyes and ears of the dog participate as intrinsic instruments or organs.

We can see this point another way. Suppose sensation were *not* an organic act, an act intrinsically ordered to the survival and perfecting of the animal organism, but was, as Cartesians hold with respect to human sensation, an act performed by an immaterial substance associated with the dog's body. What would follow from that? If that were the case, then the bodily parts of what we call a "dog" would lack all intrinsic unity. One would have to analyze quite differently the scene that we now interpret as an action performed by the composite unit called "dog." Its *movement* as well as its *sensation* would have to be viewed as performed by the dog-mind as a distinct agent. The dog's body would be an extrinsic instrument, somewhat as chalk is an extrinsic instrument for writing on a blackboard. But would the dog's body be one? What intrinsic unity would the body parts have? The answer, I think, is that it would not be intrinsically one at all. It would be like the chalk dust, which is really an aggregate rather than an intrinsic unity. But that brings us back to the excessive pluralism rejected earlier.

Again, if sensation in nonhuman animals were *not* an organic action then it would be, the way Descartes claimed sensation is in humans, an act performed by the animal's mind, on the occasion of a change produced in the animal's body. The nonhuman animal's body would be an extrinsic instrument for the spiritual act of sensation. Now, this notion is initially plausible as an account of sensation in human beings, because persons have a rich mental life. One can abstract from various aspects of human living and think of sensation in human beings as serving only their mental life. But, this view is quite implausible when presented as an account of sensations in nonhuman animals. If it were true, the animal's mental life would be the end or goal and its body an extrinsic instrument serving the animal-mind. The animal-mind would have a life of its own, to which its body was extrinsic. But all the evidence about nonhuman animals refutes this possibility. Nonhuman animal sensations are subordinated to the survival and flourishing of the bodily organism rather than vice versa. Their mental life has no contemplative aspect but is regularly oriented toward obtaining food or mates or prey.

If we observe the body of any animal, we see various cells organized into tissues and the tissues organized into organs, and the organs into systems. These are reasonably viewed as parts of the organism insofar as each performs a function that supports the way of life of the organism as a whole. But consider the life of wild animals, such as lions or hyenas. Their lives center on hunting, and hunting cannot be done without sensation and perception. If we subtract from the lion his sensory functions, there simply is no lion at all. These functions are so inextricably bound up with the lion's life that the rest of the systems—the digestive, the circulatory, and so on—are unintelligible without them. The bodily structures regularly exercised in sensation are clearly functionally parts of the lion as a whole. We conclude that in nonhuman animals sensation is an organic act.

Sensation in Human Beings Is the Same Kind of Act as Sensation in Nonhuman Animals

Only when considering sensation in human beings is anyone tempted to say that it is a purely spiritual act occasioned by changes in the body. And the reason is that sensation in human beings is often subordinated to speculative understanding, that is, to understanding pursued for its own sake. For this reason, I began with sensation in nonhuman animals.

Once one grants that sensation occurs in nonhuman animals, it becomes clear that sensation in human beings is the same sort of act. We have the same type of bodily structures functioning as sense organs, the same type of nerve cells and organization in the brain relevant to sensory impulses, and we perform the same types of actions. Thus we are led to say that the behavior of nonhuman animals and human beings is specified by sensory information in basically the same manner. Human beings do not usually chase rabbits, but they do sometimes chase dogs. It would be very odd if the zigging and zagging of the dog chasing a rabbit was an entirely different act than that of the boy chasing the dog chasing the rabbit. Clearly, the chasing of a dog by a human is the same sort of act as the dog's chasing of a rabbit. Hence the argument that proves that the dog's sensation or perception is bodily applies equally to the sensation or perception of human beings.

THAT WHICH SENSES IS THE SAME THING AS THAT WHICH UNDERSTANDS

We turn now to the second premise in the main argument: that which senses is the same thing as that which understands. Evidence for this proposition can be found by analyzing singular judgments. When one affirms, for example, that *This is a tree,* it is by understanding, or an intellectual act, that one apprehends what is meant by "tree" and apprehends objects as unitary, living things. Viewing such an affirmation or judgment as having a subject-predicate structure, we can say that the predicate of the judgment is grasped by one's understanding. The subject of the judgment, however, what one refers to by the word "this" is apprehended by sensation or perception. What one means by "this" is precisely that which is perceptually present to one. But, clearly, it must be the same thing that apprehends the predicate and the subject of a unitary judgment. So it is the same thing, the same agent, that understands and senses or perceives.

From these two points, the conclusion follows that *the thing* that understands—what everyone refers to as "I"—is an animal.

In sum:

1. Sensation in nonhuman animals is an organic act.
2. Sensation in humans is the same sort of act as sensation in nonhuman animals.

3. Therefore, sensation in humans is an organic act.
4. If sensation is an organic act, then what does the sensing is a bodily, organic being.
5. What senses is a bodily, organic being. (from 3 and 4)
6. The thing that senses is identical with the thing that understands.
7. The word "I" refers to the thing that understands.
8. Therefore, the word "I" refers to a bodily, organic being. (from 6 and 7)

Since organisms that sense are classified as animals, it follows that human beings are animals.

ANOTHER ARGUMENT TO SHOW THAT SENSATION IN HUMAN BEINGS IS A BODILY ACT

Another argument can be presented for the first premise of the main argument, namely, that sensation in human beings is a bodily act (see premise 3 on the longer form of the main argument). This argument moves from the object of the act to the nature of the act. What is sensed is never a quality or quantity per se, but always a quality as it appears from this or that direction. For example, I do not simply see red or blue but a surface from this or that angle, that is, from the perspective of my eyes. I visualize a house, for example, necessarily from this or that perspective. Perspective is different from position. I can understand position mathematically, through coordinates, but perspective is something I can grasp only by experiencing it. I may know something about a perspective without actually seeing from it, but it is significant that I can do so only by imagining what it would look like to someone seeing it from that individual place.

So, what is seen—and the same is true analogously with the other senses—is internally characterized by spatial location. It is not just that what is known is a spatial location. Rather, what is known is the physical effect that the object has on the physical subject. That is, the very act of knowing seems to be characterized by spatial location. The facts about perspective are best explained by supposing that what we sense is neither a quality itself, nor something purely subjective, but something relative, namely, the thing in its physical action on us. Thus, the subject that has the sensation is a bodily thing. What senses is not a mind associated with a body, but an animal. The rest of the argument continues as before.

THE LINK BETWEEN HUMAN INTELLIGENCE
AND THE BODY

Some philosophers view understanding and willing as so independent of sensation and the body that the soul, the principle of understanding and willing, must be conceived as complete in itself, without any intrinsic orientation to matter or the body. I believe it can be shown, however, that human intelligence has an intrinsic need and functional orientation to the body. Showing this dependence will answer an objection against the position that human beings are animals (namely, that this position leads to materialism, or that it ignores the transcendence of the intellect and will). It will also provide an additional argument for the position that human beings are animals; for if the most spiritual of human actions require distinct bodily acts to attain their goals, then the principle of these acts must be understood as incomplete—as being by nature a part.

The basic argument is from Aquinas. The human soul is by nature a partial, incomplete nature. Again, what a thing is is revealed in its actions. But the distinctive actions of the human soul, such as understanding, have an intrinsic need for bodily actions. So the principle of understanding (and willing) is by nature a part, or incomplete.

Some philosophers argue that the act of understanding, unlike sensation, is an act performed without a bodily organ. To establish whether they are right (as I think they are) would require another article.[14] However, if human understanding is a purely spiritual act, an act performed without a bodily organ,[15] nevertheless, it is naturally tied to sensation. It may not be contradictory to think that the act of understanding could occur in some instance without sense presentations, say, after death. However, we cannot conceive what such understanding would be like. What we directly understand is always an intelligible content or pattern in a sense presentation. What we understand is not just occasioned by sense presentations, but is specified by them. Proof of this idea is the fact that some sense presentations are appropriate for understanding a point while others are completely unhelpful. That is, the sense presentation is not merely an occasion for one's act of understanding, which might then be informed by something else. Rather, we intellectually grasp the point, when we do so directly—*in* the presentation of sense.[16] After direct understandings, we can move on to understand by relation and analogy objects for which we do not have sense presentations. Also, while directly understanding an external, physical object, we are concomitantly (or reflexively) aware of our act of understanding. However, knowledge of our mental acts cannot be primary, but only concomitant to the primary and direct knowledge of material things. Our acts of understanding are always into sense presentations, or concomitant to, or by comparison or contrast with, what we first understand in sense presentations.

Thus our intellect is by its nature oriented to sense presentations. The human intellect is not designed to turn away from matter to obtain its information elsewhere, as the Platonists and Cartesians hold. Rather, there is intelligibility *in* the material world; and it is that intelligibility which is proportionate to our human minds. Our minds are not designed to turn away from or bypass the material world. As the human intellect cannot naturally perform its function without the aid of the body, so it manifests its incompleteness. The principle of human understanding is an incomplete nature.

Further, the human act of understanding is incomplete in that it is abstract. By understanding, one directly grasps only a feature held in common by many things, abstracted from other features with which it is one in reality. For example, one directly understands such features as *animal, human,* or *triangular,* whereas to know concrete animals, human beings, and triangular things, one must exercise one's perception or imagination, as well as one's intellect. One must grasp those features as concretized in things; but to do that requires bodily perceptions, not just intellectual acts. All the human intellect by itself can grasp is an intelligible aspect of some thing. But to understand an abstract intelligible aspect of a thing just by itself is not to understand the thing in the manner in which it exists. To understand a thing in the manner in which it exists is to understand an intelligible aspect precisely as an aspect of a thing. But this involves a reference back to sense experience. For it is by sense experience that we are initially aware of the whole of which the intelligible aspect is understood. This reference occurs, of course, in all intellectual acts of judgment.

Not that every judgment is singular or its evidence narrowly perceptual. There are universal judgments and necessary ones for which the evidence is not just a perceptual link. Still, the abstract intelligible aspect must be conceived as joined to a thing or things, and the notion of a thing is dependent on our initial perceptual experience. Even when we refer to, and infer truths about, immaterial things, we do so by analogy with material things, and we conceive of them in the manner that is really only fitting to material things. (Thus, as Aquinas points out, our understanding and language about God are in certain respects unsuited to his nonmaterial nature; the abstractive mode of our understanding fits material things, which exist as composites, not God who is not a composite.[17])

So, even though the act of understanding is done without a bodily organ, the human soul cannot complete its act—in the sense that it cannot succeed in understanding a thing in the manner in which it exists—by itself alone. This point is an important one, because one cannot hold that the soul and the body constitute a single substance and, at the same time, that the soul is complete in its nature.[18] Although the soul can survive without the body (since it is possible for it to perform some type of act without the body), it is intrisically oriented to the body because its operations cannot attain their end without the aid of the body.

ON PRIVILEGED ACCESS

An argument that moves many people to a dualist view is from the privileged access or privacy of our mental acts. How can sensory acts be bodily events when bodily events are open to public inspection, at least in principle, whereas my sensory acts are observable only by me? Other people can perhaps in some way observe me having a sensation but they cannot have my sensation. The essential argument is this: That to which one has privileged access is not identical with that to which there is public access; we have privileged access to our sensations as well as our thoughts and desires while there is public access to bodily acts; therefore sensations are not bodily, organic acts.[19]

The difficulty is in the first premise. It is often the case that the same thing can be known in various ways. If *A* is known in one way and *B* is known in another, this does not mean that *A* is really distinct from *B*.

Descartes made the same mistake in his argument to identify the self with the mind, where he said that the fact that I can doubt the existence of the body but not the existence of the mind shows that the mind and the body are different things.[20] But as Peter Geach points out, using a slightly different counterexample: a boy may doubt the existence of the postman while being certain of the existence of his father even though the two are identical.[21] The moral is that the same reality may be apprehended in various ways; the diversity of apprehensions in no way proves the diversity of what is apprehended. One may apprehend a sensation from the standpoint of the one who is having the sensation, and one may apprehend the sensation from the standpoint of an external observer. The apprehensions differ, but only one thing is apprehended.

IMPLICATIONS FOR ETHICAL THEORY—
THE BODILY PERSON AND INTRINSIC VALUE

I have suggested that significant ethical implications follow from the conclusion that biological life is an essential, intrinsic aspect of the human person. How it is so presents a puzzle. Biological facts by themselves do not imply ethical conclusions, for the conclusion cannot contain more than its premises.[22] That is, the naturalistic fallacy is indeed a fallacy. What, then, is the relationship between this factual conclusion and ethical positions?

When one chooses an action one chooses it for a reason, that is, for the sake of some good one thinks this action will help realize. That good may itself be a way of realizing some further good, and that good a means to another, and so on. But the chain of goods cannot be infinite. There must, then, be ultimate reasons for one's choices, some goods that one recognizes as needing no further support, that are not mere means to some further good.

What is the character of these ultimate reasons, these ultimate goods? Such ultimate reasons must be reasons for oneself. That is, there must be in an object that which makes it suitable to oneself, or to the kind of agent one is. Conversely, there must be in oneself a natural interest or tendency toward that sort of object.

Of course, we have acquired tendencies as well as natural ones. Natural tendencies are those we have simply in virtue of the kind of thing we are. Acquired tendencies, on the other hand—for example, a taste for caviar, or for betting on races—can only be obtained by actions through which we experience the objects of such tendencies. But all such actions exercise preexisting tendencies. Thus, acquired tendencies are determinations of natural tendencies. It remains that something can be an ultimate reason for acting only if one has a natural interest in the sort of object it is.

But that to which an agent has a natural interest or tendency must be the actualization or fulfillment of its natural potentialities.[23] This is an essential proposition: If A naturally tends toward X, then X must be the actualization of the type of thing A is. X must be a something, a positive activity. If Y is the ceasing to be of A, for example, one would not think of it as the object of its tendency; rather, one would say that A is just short-lived, that it tends toward whatever it regularly attained prior to its ceasing to be. And X must be the actualization of a potentiality in A;

the only actions to which *A* can naturally tend are those of which *A* is capable.

The self in whose fulfillment one is naturally interested, however, is not an isolated individual. One has various unions with other people and is interested in the fulfillment not only of oneself but also of all those with whom one is in communion: family, co-citizens, neighbors— all persons ultimately. The fulfillment of other people naturally interests one; it is an improvement of one's condition since one is not an isolated individual but has various unities with other people. The ultimate reasons for choosing something consist in expectations that this object can really fulfill oneself or others with whom one is in communion. In other words, every intrinsic good (ultimate reason for choosing) is an essential perfection of the self (or other selves).

Thus, every ultimate reason for acting, every basic good, is an intrinsic aspect of a human person. We have not, however, shown the converse, namely, that every intrinsic aspect of a human person is a basic good. Indeed, the converse is not true. There can be an entity composed of *A* and *B* where *A* is wholly instrumental, or merely instrumental, to *B*, or the whole *A-B*. For example, the heart is wholly instrumental to the animal. That is, bodily parts of a bodily entity can be instrumental to the bodily entity. However, could one say that the whole body of an animal is wholly instrumental to something else in or of the animal? If one could say that the whole body was instrumental to the mind, say, then it would have to be a dispensable part of the whole. Perhaps one could view it like the placenta a baby grows, or baby teeth, which serve a temporary function. But then, although one could still view the body as part of the whole human being, one would be forced to deny that the human being is an animal. One would be forced to view the human being as essentially a mind, even though its having a body would somehow be a dispensable but in some ways valuable part of it.

However, what we have shown already is that a human being is an animal, not a mind-cum-bodily-parts. The human agent which performs the various actions a human being performs is a living bodily, sensing being, that is, an animal.

What I am arguing is in some ways so obvious that it is difficult to state. The perfection of *S* cannot consist in its ceasing to be *S*. If human persons are essentially animals, then their perfection cannot consist in their ceasing to be animals, for that would be their destruction.[24] Moreover, if S is essentially an animal then the condition which is S's perfection must include S's being an animal. The perfection of an animal must include the well-being of its body; otherwise, the body is an appendage and what exists is not an animal. There can, of course, be internal ordering among the bodily parts of an animal, but to make the body as a whole merely an instrument in relation to another activity or to other activities, is implicitly to deny that the entity is essentially an animal. In general, then, one can say that any theory that implies that the body will not be a participant in the complete fulfillment of the human person implies a dualistic view of the human person and is therefore mistaken.

Suppose, then, someone holds that pleasant experience is the only intrinsic good. He or she holds that biological life is not itself a good but only a means for realizing pleasant experiences. This person is viewing pleasant experience as the only thing which in itself improves one's condition. He identifies his condition as of the sort that can be improved only by an experience. Therefore he is viewing his condition as consisting only in consciousness. The same point applies to any view of what the intrinsic good is or intrinsic goods are. If the complete intrinsic good is identified with intellectual contemplation, then the human person is implicitly viewed as a nonmaterial entity. The perfection of the human person, the good viewed intrinsically (as opposed to merely instrumentally) must include, although not be limited to, bodily perfection.

One might object that this argument presupposes a teleological view of human action. But suppose one holds that human action is not always for the sake of one's fulfillment. Suppose one holds a deontological ethical theory, that in acting morally one acts, not for the sake of fulfillment, but to do one's duty, or to respond adequately to values, or from some other motive?

In this case one who does not include bodily fulfillment in what is intrinsically good need not suppose dualism, even implicitly. However, as a matter of psychology, whenever one chooses, one does so to improve one's condition. One cannot choose otherwise, for the objects one deliberates about and chooses must be objects one *can* choose, and one can choose only that which has a natural appeal. Deontological theories cannot actually prescribe choices of objects unrelated (as such) to our fulfillment; therefore, they are *in effect* identifying the only intrinsic human good with moral goodness. Thus, although such theories need not presuppose dualism, their effect is dualist.

NOTES

1.   See, for example, the works of Grisez and, in some cases, Grisez and Boyle, on contraception, abortion, and euthanasia. See also Grisez's "Dualism and the New Morality," *Atti Del Congresso Internazionale (Roma-Napoli - 17/24 Aprile 1974) Tomasso d'Aquino nel suo Settimo Centennario,* vol. 5; *L'Agire Morale* (Napoli: Edizioni Domenicane Italiane, 1977), 323–33.

2.   See Germain Grisez and Joseph Boyle, *Life and Death with Liberty and Justice,* (New York: University of Notre Dame Press, 1979), 378; John Finnis, Germain Grisez and Joseph Boyle, *Nuclear Deterrence, Morality and Realism* (New York: Oxford University Press, 1987), 308.

3.   Ibid.

4.   See St. Thomas, *Summa theologiae,* I.q.76.a.1.

5.   Ibid.

6.   On the distinction between a composite substance and a mere aggregate, see Richard Connell, *Substance and Modern Science* (Houston, Texas: Center for Thomistic Studies, 1988), 3–39.

7.   Aristotle, *Parts of Animals,* I, 1 639b15-640a10; *Metaphysics,* Bk. VII, Chap. 17.

8.   This is not to say that a world without substances is logically possible, but a world with substances whose duration was so short it was not detectable is possible.

9.   Cf. Benedict Ashley, O. P., *Theologies of the Body: Humanist and Christian* (Braintree, Mass.: Pope John Center, 1985), 253–296; R. Harré and E. H. Madden, *Causal Powers: A Theory of Natural Necessity* (Totowa, New Jersey: Rowman and Littlefield, 1975), 44–118; Ivor Leclerc, "The Problem of the Physical Existent," *International Philosophical Quarterly* 9 (1969): 40–62; Ivor Leclerq, *The Philosophy of Nature* (Washington, D.C.: Catholic University of America Press, 1986), 107–189.

10.   A. N. Whitehead, *Process and Reality* (New York: Macmillan, 1929), 34–35; 59–66; 240–248.

11.   Ibid.

12.   Rene Descartes, *Discourse on Method,* 5; *Replies to Objections,* 4, 1.

13.   Rene Descartes, *Meditations on First Philosophy,* Meditation II; St. Augustine, *De Quantitate Animae* XXIII, 41; XXV, 48. Cf. Vernon Bourke, *Augustine's Quest for Wisdom* (Milwaukee: Bruce, 1945), 111–112.

14.   Cf. Peter Geach, "What Do We Think With," in *God and the Soul* (New York: Schocken, 1969), 3–41; James Ross, "Immaterial Aspects of Thought," *Journal of Philosophy,* 1992: 136–150; Mortimer Adler, *Intellect: Mind Over Matter* (New York: Macmillan, 1990), 41–54. In each case, the argument is that understanding has a characteristic which is incompatible with being an act performed with a bodily organ. Geach argues that the basic act of understanding is atemporal (understanding is not a process extended in time). Adler defends the position that understanding has a universal as its direct object. And Ross argues that understanding can discern functions indiscernible to any material system (roughly, those that are extensionally equivalent and yet intentionally distinct).

15.   It is important to see that, if human understanding is a purely spiritual act, it should still not be thought of as an act "performed by the soul." Rather,

the human being performs the acts of understanding, as it is the human being who performs acts of sensing or walking. The difference is only that sensing and walking are done with bodily organs and understanding is not. See especially Peter Geach's careful way of phrasing the question, in "What Do We Think With."

16. Cf. Bernard Lonergan, *Insight*, 3rd ed. (New York: Philosophical Library, 1970), 3–19.

17. St. Thomas, *Summa theologiae*, I.q.13.aa.1 and 2.

18. To his credit, Descartes wanted to hold that the body and the soul together make up one substance. However, he also held, and emphasized, a position incompatible with that, namely, that the soul is complete in its nature. For discussion and texts: Daisie Radner, "Descartes' Notion of the Unity of Mind and Body," *Journal of the History of Philosophy* 9 (1971): 159–170; Paul Hoffman, "The Unity of Descartes' Man," *Philosophical Review* 95 (1986): 339–392.

19. Cf. Richard Swinburne, *The Evolution of the Soul* (Oxford: Oxford University Press, 1986), 45–61; Jerome Shaffer, *Philosophy of Mind* (Englewood Cliffs, N.J.: Prentice-Hall, 1968), 39–60.

20. Rene Descartes, *Meditations on First Philosophy*, Meditation II.

21. Peter Geach, *God and the Soul*.

22. Cf. Alfonzo Gomez-Lobo, "Natural Law and Naturalism," *Proceedings of the American Catholic Philosophical Association*, 59 (1985): 232–249.

23. This point is true of any agent, whether voluntary or not. For example, a plant grows, takes in nourishment and repairs damages to its structure. We say, then, that it is a unitary, living substance. To say so is to understand the various parts of the plant as organized toward an end, as an enduring source of regular activities. Of course, many things also happen to the plant coming from outside. The wind blows the plant, a rabbit brushes against it breaking off one of its leaves. To understand a plant at all one must distinguish those activities (and reactivities) that come from within the plant from those that do not. The activities to which it internally tends must be viewed as actualizations of its potentialities. For that is what it means to say that the plant is the source of its regular activities and reactivities.

24. This realization, by the way, is the reasoning behind Thomas Aquinas's remark that a person is not saved unless his body is saved, even if his soul has been saved, for, "*Anima mea non est ego.*" ("My soul is not I.") Thomas Aquinas, *Commentary on St. Paul's First Letter to the Corinthians*, chap. 15, lect. 2, on verse 19, #924.

PART THREE

Politics

No Intentional Killing Whatsoever: The Case of Capital Punishment

GERARD V. BRADLEY

Professor of Law
University of Notre Dame
Notre Dame, Indiana

Ask a Catholic neoconservative or the editors of *Commonweal* what the last "social encyclical" was. They will answer that it was *Centisimus Annus*. They will tell you that there Pope John Paul II settled the central question of "Catholic social teaching," the question of basic institutional form in political economy. "Democratic capitalism has prevailed!" If you inquire further, they will tell you that *Veritatis splendor* (VS) was about morals, especially about academic moral theology. Neither it nor *Evangelium vitae* (EV) was a "social encyclical." EV was, to be sure, about "life" issues, but it addressed culture not political economy. They will add, finally, that EV articulated a nice ideal for the conformity of civil law to moral truth, but an ideal that is unsuited to our secular, pluralistic society.

Even if we stipulate that "Catholic social teaching" is about what public authority—the state—may do and must not do, this common account is grossly misleading. For it presupposes precisely the divisibility of morality into "public" and "private" realms that VS and EV deny. The common view just sketched misses, if it does not implicitly deny, the heart of Catholic social teaching, namely, this arresting assertion by Pope John Paul II in VS:

> *When it is a matter of the moral norms prohibiting intrinsic evil, there are no privileges or exceptions for anyone.* It makes no difference whether one is the master of the world or the "poorest of the poor" on the face of the earth. Before the demands of morality we are all absolutely equal.[1]

The universal applicability of exceptionless norms establishes the moral equality of all persons. By declaring the basic human goods (the backbone of exceptionless norms) absolutely immune from direct attack, Catholic social teaching insures that no one may rightly be made the instrument of the purposes of another—not of the Cabinet, the "community," or the "great man".

Twenty-five years ago[2] Germain Grisez argued from pretty much that foundation against capital punishment. The tradition within which he worked, Grisez conceded, held that "the lives of those who attack the common good"—in unjust warfare and by committing capital crimes—"are not always considered inviolate" (p. 65). Grisez argued nevertheless that "human life can never rightly be directly attacked" (p. 66), a norm I express in this paper as, "No intentional killing whatsoever." Grisez built his position partly on the Second Vatican Council's clarification of the "common good" of political society as limited, even instrumental: the sum total of social conditions which are required to *allow persons to perfect themselves.*[3] "If no human society," Grisez wrote in 1970, "is complete, if civil society is merely one form of community with limited concerns, then it is by no means clear that men associated in states may rightly kill wrongdoers to protect the common good if such killing would be morally forbidden by individuals" (p. 69).

Grisez recognized that legitimate defense required effective separation of dangerous malefactors from the community, "often" achieved by ostracism or banishment or by imprisonment (p. 67). The important thing for Grisez is that the morality of capital punishment was a matter of specifying the exceptionless norm against all intentional killing and that specification leaves open the possibility—neither investigated nor denied in 1970 by Grisez—that, occasionally, capital punishment might be the necessary vehicle of effective separation.[4]

I aim to show in this paper that the Church's teaching on capital punishment, as found in EV[5] and the *Catechism,*[6] is best understood as essentially Grisez's view of 1970. The texts are, admittedly, too obscure to permit a compelling argument for my claim. I shall argue, though, that the texts make considerably more sense on the assumption that the death penalty is permissible *only* where it is consistent with a norm against all intentional killing whatsoever, than on any other assumption.

The Church teaches that capital punishment may be approved where necessary to the "defense of society." In EV the Pope says that in developed societies such cases are "rare, if not practically nonexistent." I shall argue that this statement rules out the common justification for capital punishment, which might be described as "defense of society," as a deterrent to future, would-be offenders. "Necessary" to the defense of society means *just* this malefactor's continuing threat to others. Thus, EV and the Catechism seem to assimilate capital punishment to ordinary self-defense, a matter of causing death while intending strictly just to halt aggression.

Does the Church mean to deny the possibility defended by John Finnis and rejected by Grisez, that capital punishment may be specified morally by the intention to restore the order of justice disturbed by the criminal's bad act? The teachings do not explicitly say. I develop an argument in the later sections that even recognizing that possibility, retributive executions are, at least in developed societies, contrary to Church teaching.

I

"The source of all other rights" is "the right to life" (EV 72). This right is the obverse of the commandment "You shall not kill" which, the Pope teaches in *EV*, "is at the basis of all life together in society" (EV 53).

What acts does the commandment exclude? It must not exclude all acts that foreseeably create risks to the lives of others. Otherwise, we could not drive our cars or build bridges. Does it exclude all acts that intend death as either an end or a means? The tradition, at least as far back as Aquinas, held that it did so for "private" persons, though they may defend themselves with deadly force where necessary. But the tradition held that intentional killing may be licit in three situations: justified armed rebellion, just war, capital punishment. All are acts of "public authority," even if only by analogy in the case of rebellion (where "private" persons act directly for the common good against its enemies, who may claim to exercise legitimate public authority). The upright use of force in justified rebellion, however, depends on a combination of the other two cases: legitimate "private" defense, and killing in defense of the common good. The former I do not question; the latter two cases, I aim to show, are assimilable to the former.

Now consider the case of just warfare. Grisez has argued cogently that warfare does not require combatants to violate the stricture against intentional killing.[7] How could that be? Consider a limited case, U.S. Marine Corps operations on Iwo Jima. The Marines knew that the Japanese army had evacuated all civilians and that the defenders would never surrender. A Marine would, as a practical matter, have to direct lethal force against enemy forces until they were all dead. Is *this* not intentional killing?

Members of the Third, Fourth, and Fifth Marine Divisions on Iwo Jima may well have intended to kill Japanese soldiers. All certainly behaved much of the time in a way indistinguishable from the behavior of intentional killers. But they need not have. Marines need only have intended to render harmless enemy soldiers, killing them in the process. Sound fantastic? On Iwo Jima, some Japanese must have fallen mortally wounded. While no Marine, practically, was obliged to attend to their medical needs (given the continuing battle, and the medical needs of fallen Marines), none would have been morally justified in shooting the helplessly wounded enemy. And many Marines, I am sure, had an opportunity to finish Japanese off and did not precisely for moral reasons. What could those reasons be, if not (at least in an intuitive sense) that to kill helpless soldiers was akin to murder.

Maybe we can imagine the massive bloodshed on Iwo Jima as (strictly) the foreseen effects of actions intended to disable aggressors. But how can capital punishment—an act that necessarily includes death— be similarly imagined? The executioner is supposed to finish off the helpless prisoner! Is this not a clear case of intentional killing, albeit justified? The Church does not teach that it is never permissible to execute a convicted criminal. How, then, could its teaching on the death penalty, whatever it is, be governed by a norm against intentional killing?

One means of reconciliation might be to say that the criminal forfeits his right to life by his bad actions, that he descends to the moral status of a beast. I doubt whether anyone ever considered this assertion an argument, as opposed to a loose way of stating a conclusion in favor of capital punishment. However, this possibility of reconciliation is now foreclosed by Church teaching: *"Not even a murderer loses his personal dignity,* and God himself pledges to guarantee this" (EV 96, emphasis in the original).

Another possibility of reconciliation has been to hold that the state shares a divine prerogative to take the lives of those who attack the common good by committing capital crimes. If so, one might say that capital punishment involves no intentional killing—that the executioner's intention is simply to carry out God's judgment. But to hold this view, one would have to hold that God might intend to kill (as perhaps in the case of Abraham and Isaac,[8] and elsewhere in the Old Testament and that public authority is delegated divine authority (on one common interpretation of Romans 13:1).[9]

The Pope in VS denies both these propositions. He says that God "preferred the correction rather than the death of the sinner" (EV 9). Whatever might have been the case in the Old Testament, with Jesus and the New Covenant it is clearly revealed that God never intends anyone's death. "Life is always a good" (EV 30), and the Pope means to judge "public authority" *by* its adherence to the commandment not to kill. We are invited to test anyone's claim to be doing God's will by this prescription. Once we figure out what acts the Commandment excludes, we will know whatever there is of importance to know about God's delegation of authority.

But the Pope says in *EV* that God is the "absolute Lord of the life of man" (53); no one may "arbitrarily choose to live or die"; the absolute master of "such decisions is the Creator" (58). Does this not mean that capital punishment, which is surely sometimes permissible, *must* somehow share in this prerogative? The Pope's attestations to God's mastery over life evidences, not delegated divine authority to kill, but God's will that no human person whomsoever shall have a homicidal will. If so, it rather seems that where capital punishment is permitted, it involves (somehow) no intention to kill.

The norm articulated in *EV* usually includes the term "innocent": "the direct and voluntary killing of an innocent human being is always gravely immoral" (57); "No one . . . can claim for himself the right to directly destroy an innocent human being" (53); the absolute inviolability of "innocent human life" (57). If capital punishment is, even in rare cases, morally permissible, is it not clear that intentional killing, albeit of noninnocent persons, is sanctioned? But if so, *someone* has to have a homicidal will (even if we disagree about who that someone is).[10] Condemnation to death by competent public authority might, in this construal of EV, justify the executioner's act, but it does not change the nature of it: justified *intentional* killing.

Given the deliberateness and apparent intentional structure of the act of building a scaffold, parading the condemned to it, and (as the judicial sentence commonly put it) "hanged by the neck until dead," how *could* capital punishment be a case of *un*intentional killing? It is not "unintentional," as in "accidental" or "surprising." Death is expected as a matter of cause and effect in the natural order. But it does not follow that, for moral analysis, death is intended, even if the behavior that causes death is a necessary part of the performance. It might be an act of legitimate defense. It might be an act intended to restore justice. Capital punishment might be a case of *non*intentional killing.

II

Do EV and the Catechism indicate that the general norm about killing *is* that no one may intentionally kill? There is considerable textual warrant (the use of "innocent") for supposing not. But the language varies, and the meaning of individual statements of the norm (whatever exactly it is) is unclear. The Pope in EV defines euthanasia ("in the strict sense"), for instance, as an action or omission which of itself and by intention causes death" (64). Euthanasia violates God's law, he continues, because it is the "deliberate and morally unacceptable killing of a human person." "Deliberate" probably denotes "freely chosen." If so, euthanasia is the freely chosen, morally unacceptable killing of a human person insofar as it intends death, by whatever means. "Innocent," so often used in statements of the norm, is nowhere used regarding euthanasia. Abortion is, the Pope declares, "the deliberate killing of an innocent human being" (EV 62). Innocent means here, though, that the unborn are in no sense "aggressors," so that lethal force may be used against them (EV 58).

The commandment is most often stated simply as "You shall not kill." The Holy Father frames his key discussion in EV of a "fuller and deeper understanding of what God's commandment prohibits and proscribes" [55] by reference to §§2263–2269 of the Catechism. The title of the section comprising the later paragraphs in the Catechism is "intentional homicide." The commandment forbids *direct and intentional killing*" as gravely sinful (§2268, emphasis in original). Intending death by *any* physical means (i.e., by any causal nexus in the natural order) is always wrong.

The textual signals in EV and the Catechism are mixed enough, it seems to me, to turn to specifications of the general norm for evidence of what that norm actually is. I submit that the surest route to the intended meaning of the norm against killing goes through capital punishment. If the teaching on capital punishment is consistent with and seems consciously designed to specify a norm compactly stated as, "No intentional killing whatsoever," then we have good reason to believe that it is the general norm, and consequently that capital punishment is never permitted where it would be an intentional killing.

III

The Pope introduces his discussion of capital punishment in EV by conceding that ordinary persons may, in some circumstances, use deadly force. This concession is the question of "legitimate defense," which the text (and, more, the footnote in EV to the Catechism) makes clear is a concession to the morally licit use of lethal force, *not* to intentional killing. The Pope's citation includes St. Thomas's statement that an "act of self-defense can have a double effect: the preservation of one's own life; and the killing of the aggressor. ... The one is intended, the other is not." The portion of the Catechism to which the Pope refers continues:

Someone who defends his life is not guilty of murder even if he is forced to deal his aggressor a lethal blow. If a man in self-defense uses more than necessary violence, it will be unlawful: whereas if he repels force with moderation, his defense will be lawful. . . . Nor is it necessary for salvation that a man omit the act of moderate self-defense to avoid killing the other man, since one is bound to take more care of one's own life than of another's.

EV cites this passage for the textual proposition that "the fatal outcome is attributable to the aggressor whose action brought it about," even if the aggressor is morally irresponsible due to lack of the use of reason (EV 55).

Both *EV* and the *Catechism* treat private defense of "persons" and of the family as belonging to the same moral species as defense of "societies" and "state" (see EV 55; Catechism §2263). Public authority's use of force, in other words, seems to be assimilated to the one set of actions which would disable aggressors without intending to kill. In any case, public authority is the referent of the Pope's statement in EV 56: "This is the context in which to place the problem of the death penalty":[11] "[r]endering the aggressor unable to inflict harm."

Precisely on the question of when capital punishment is permitted, the Pope says: (1) only "in cases of absolute necessity: in other words, when it would not be possible otherwise to *defend society*"; and (2) "If bloodless means are sufficient to *defend human lives against an aggressor and to protect public order and the safety of persons*, public authority must limit itself to such means . . ." (EV 56, my emphasis).

The second of these propositions reiterates §2267 of the Catechism, save that, in the English translations with which I have been working, "must" appears in EV 56 where "should" appears in the Catechism.[12]

IV

The Pope's intended meaning may still be obscure. Both 1 and 2 are at least equivocal, as is one prominent commentator's expression of what the Pope has in mind: "The continued existence of the malefactor himself" must present a threat for death to be imposed.[13] The apparent ambiguity was not relieved by Cardinal Ratzinger's commentary on EV. He said at its publication that it contained "a development of doctrine" on capital punishment, and that the *Catechism* would have to be revised to reflect the new teaching. This comment is unlikely to have been a reference to the Pope's specification of the Catechism's "in cases of extreme gravity" (to "absolute necessity"; such cases "are very rare, if not practically nonexistent"). While that is a development or extension of previous papal statements, it is not a doctrinal teaching at all.

Richard John Neuhaus sought a clarification of the Cardinal's comments, and received what *National Review* published as a "reassuring word." The excerpt below is, according to Neuhaus, an accurate quotation of the Cardinal's entire remarks on the subject:

> Clearly, the Holy Father has not altered the doctrinal principles which pertain to this issue [the death penalty] as they are presented in the Catechism, but has simply deepened the application of such principles in the context of present-day historical circumstances. Thus, where other means for the self-defense of society are possible and adequate, the death penalty may be permitted to disappear. Such a development, occurring within society and leading to the forgoing of this type of punishment is something good and ought to be hoped for.[14]

The editors concluded, happily, that there is no question of recalling the Catechism. "The Cardinal meant only that the official Latin text, which is being prepared after the publication of the vernacular versions, will refer to what *Evangelium Vitae* says about capital punishment. So Catholics relying on the Church's official teaching as expressed in the Catechism may in good faith disagree over whether, in today's circumstances, the self-defense of society requires the death penalty."[15]

What *National Review* (NR) has in mind—and supposes Cardinal Ratzinger had in mind—is the standard conservative argument for the death penalty, the argument from "deterrence." Will executing this prisoner deter other, unknown, would-be criminals from their bad acts by threatening them with the same fate—death? NR is saying that faithful Catholics must limit their support of the death penalty to where it deters criminals and thus "protects" society. But whether capital punishment deters is a factual question which governs applications of the principle. On that question, faithful Catholics can and do disagree. Hence (and I suppose this is why the editors are happy), the Pope says nothing that challenges what many conservatives presently hold.

NR's interpretation is against the weight of the textual evidence in EV and the Catechism. The latter point squarely to the continuing threat of *this* malefactor, and *not* to the future threat(s) of unknown would-be criminals. Besides the texts already mentioned, consider §27 of *EV*: "There is evidence of *growing public opposition to the death penalty,* even when such a penalty is seen as a kind of 'legitimate defense' on the part of society.

Modern society in fact has the means of effectively suppressing crime by rendering criminals harmless without definitively denying them the chance to reform" (emphasis in original). "Legitimate defense" of society, the whole context makes clear, refers to neutralizing those already apprehended, and excludes the notion of killing harmless prisoners as an example to the population at large. The Pope's settled conviction is that "today," because of "improvements in the organization of the penal system," cases in which death is needed "are very rare, if not practically nonexistent" (56). If the Pope had in mind the conservative interpretation (the deterrence theory), he could not say this at all, much less say it without adverting to the legitimate diversity of views on the subject. That is, *whether* capital punishment "deters" in modern society *is* debatable. The Pope does not seem to think the question to which the answer is "rare" is one permitting much disagreement. The Pope must not be talking about deterrence when he uses the phrase "protect society." This does not imply that the Pope means to settle a question of application of norms to contingent circumstances. Rather, I am using the Pope's application to get at the principle he has in mind.

To effectively deter future criminals, some substantial number of executions is necessary. Otherwise, those who are supposed to be deterred will rightly conclude they have a greater chance of being hit by lightning than of being the "very rare" fellow electrocuted in prison. It would seem that only if the Pope has in mind *this* malefactor's continued dangerousness could he plausibly conclude that the death penalty is "very rare[ly]" necessary.

On the conservative interpretation, finally, capital punishment would certainly be intentional killing, at least a case of doing evil that good may come of it. For the choice could not be other than to kill this person, unlike the possibility, (to be explored) of restoring the order of justice here and now, *by* and *in* this very act.[16] Thus, the evidence adduced here to support the proposition that the teaching is "No intentional killing whatsoever" is evidence against the conservative interpretation.

V

Does the Pope mean to say that in developed societies there will (should?) be a *few* executions ("very rare") or that *as* a practical matter, there will be none? What *would* warrant the conclusion that execution of this prisoner is "necessary" to protect society against his or her further aggression? The Pope does not say. What can we say? It is always possible that a prisoner will escape custody and do harm, or in anger kill someone inside the prison. Complete isolation is impossible. Even prisoners in solitary confinement need to be fed and bathed. They are entitled to basic medical care, if not to limited social interaction with other prisoners and, possibly, with family. The prisoner may ask for a priest, minister, or other pastor. Since this point is obvious, it must not be sufficient, in the Pope's mind, to justify an execution. Otherwise, executions would be common, not "rare."

A more serious possibility is to treat a certain history of criminal acts as sufficient proof that an individual will advance his interests violently, in derogation of others' rights, whenever the opportunity to do so without incurring unpleasant consequences presents itself. I do not doubt there are many such persons. Nor do I doubt that this type of judgment is within human competence. It is precisely the kind of judgment that sends persistent offenders to prison for life. While that is not the same as being executed (though it entails dying in prison), life imprisonment should be imposed only on the basis of a judgment that is morally certain. This class of persons is also very large. That is obvious enough. The Pope must not have this group in mind either. Otherwise, capital punishment would be common.

The problem is that as a practical matter, no legal system of which I am aware authorizes a sentence which corresponds precisely to the apparent requirements for capital punishment to be licitly imposed. Our society comes closest in civil commitment procedures. Individuals who suffer from mental disorders sufficient to make them, in a standard statement of the legal norm, "dangerous to others" may be restrained against their wills, even where they have committed no crime. But there is no authority whatsoever to put any such person to death. (Of course, in no case would this be "punishment.") No doubt the restraints and drugs necessary to render the most troubled of these individual safe for interpersonal dealings are quite severe. May they be imposed on mentally healthy but deeply antisocial persons?

If the moral requirements for capital punishment were transposed into criminal law, the requisite sentence would seem to be a conditional, long-term imprisonment: jail time terminable by execution if, but only if, one proves later to be unmanageably dangerous. There is no such possible sentence in America. "Conviction" technically occurs in our justice system after a jury verdict, when the court pronounces a sentence of imprisonment or a sentence of death. There is no possibility down the line of converting the former into the latter—and for good reason: the decision to "convert" a term of years into a death sentence is no minor, administrative matter. Further misconduct—say, the murder of another inmate—gives rise to the possibility of more severe penalties (including, in our law, death), but they may be imposed only after the entire criminal process again runs its course. Thus, our system effectively bifurcates the possibility held out by the Pope into successive, separate criminal prosecutions, in which the already sentenced prisoner is tried (while in custody) for additional crimes. Are capital crimes, therefore, specified to include, say, murder by life-termers, consistent with the teaching of EV? Capital prosecutions would then be pretty "rare," though *not* "nonexistent." My reservation about this possibility is that it crudely translates the moral framework proposed by the Pope, and does so in a society (ours) which seems inclined to punish with death all heinous crimes, entirely apart from questions of continued dangerousness. The prudent course might well be to support abolition of capital punishment by constitutional amendment.

VI

Might one abide the norm against intentional killing *and* punish with death, apart from questions of *this* malefactor's continuing dangerousness to prison guards, medics? Does the Pope reject the possibility defended by Finnis and rejected by Grisez that capital punishment might be an act which intends retribution, and not, strictly, death? The Pope does not explicitly say. But the Pope in EV self-consciously considers just how— on what basis—capital punishment *could be* a case of nonintentional killing. While he affirms that retribution is the aim of punishment (EV 56), the *only* case of nonintentional killing in capital punishment that he seems to think legitimate is the case of *this* malefactor's continuing dangerousness. Capital punishment would likely be imposed as retribution on a whole class of offenders, specified by their complicity in a category of offenses. But the Pope calls for the practical extinction of the death penalty, suggesting that retributive imposition of death is excluded.

I concede however that the textual evidence does not permit much more that speculation on the status of Church teaching on this point. I shall try to piece together a freestanding argument that is consistent with EV which grants the possibility defended by Finnis. That is, let us suppose that one responsible for capital punishment *can* intend only retribution (and I shall sketch how that might be). The death penalty is, in my view, still justifiable in developed societies only where necessary to neutralize this dangerous convict.

What is the aim of punishment? Finnis provides an account at once sound and faithful to the tradition (and I presume the Pope has something very much like it in mind):

> The defining and essential (though not necessarily the exclusive) point of punishment is to restore an order of fairness which was disrupted by the criminal's criminal act. That order was a fairly (it is supposed) distributed set of advantages and disadvantages, the system of benefits and burdens of life in human community. The disruption consisted in a choice to take the advantage of following one's own preferences rather than restraining oneself to remain within that fair order (or, where the crime is one of negligence, an unwillingness to make the effort required to remain with the legally or morally required pattern of actions and restraints). Since freedom to follow one's preferences is in itself an important human good, the criminal's act of self-preference was itself the gaining of an advantage over those who restrain themselves to remain within that legally and/or morally required pattern. So the essential point of punishment is to restore the disrupted order of fairness by depriving the criminal of his ill-gotten advantage. And since that advantage consisted at least primarily in (wrongful) freedom of choice and action, the appropriate means of restoring the order of fairness is by depriving the criminal of his freedom of choice and action.[17]

To better appreciate the aim or point of punishment, one should hold in the mind's eye a diachronic view of a society's interaction, a broad pattern of restraint, action, and opportunity established by custom, morality, and law. As Finnis suggests, public authority administers punishment so that, over a period of time, it is the case that no one is made a "sucker" by choosing to remain within the law's path for pursuing one's projects in cooperation with others.

The essential (but not exclusive) moral wrong in criminal behavior is the selfish (i.e., unfair) grab of more freedom than is one's due, more than others enjoy by virtue of their continuing to abide by the law. Besides whatever substantive harm criminals do, Grisez recently wrote, they "freely prefer their own interests . . . and in doing so they seize more than their fair share of liberty to do as one pleases." In suffering punishment, which as such need be only the unwelcome deprivation of the liberty to do as one pleases, criminals "lose their advantage over law-abiding citizens."[18]

This understanding of the aim of punishment allows us to see that while death would be a punishment (i.e., a most unwelcome deprivation) no crime *implies* punishment by death. The implication would be true if *lex talionis* were a sound guide to administering the criminal law. But it is not, and it is surely not our guide. We do not sodomize rapists or mutilate those convicted of assault. One who faints behind the wheel of a car, and careens into and kills some children standing on the street corner, has committed no crime at all. Yet one who fires a gun at—but misses—the same kids goes to jail for attempted murder, even if the children were never aware of the attack. Attempted murder is, to be sure, punished more severely than pickpocketing or shoplifting. So there is some relationship between (we might say) the substantive harm caused by a crime and its appropriate punishment. But that relationship actually results from the greater self-preference exhibited by the criminal: one who is so opposed or indifferent to others' rights and interests as to deliberately (or recklessly) kill them, has acted that much more unfairly.

It might be that the death sentence is fair retribution, apart from *lex talionis*, for massive self-assertion at the extraordinary expense of others. Then it would seem that punishing such offenders at all would entail capital punishment. But the conclusion follows only if death is the only fair punishment, *and* if fairness is the only criterion relevant to punishment.

The latter proposition is false. Fairness is not the only criterion. Fairness is one very important element of the common good. But the more inclusive common good, not fairness, is the principle of legitimate public authority, including its exercise in administering punishments. Finnis says that "if it is unfair to law abiding citizens not to punish criminals, it is more unfair to them to punish criminals when it is clear that the punishment will lead to more crime, more unfairness by criminals and more danger and disadvantage to law-abiding citizens." Cases of immunity from prosecution—for diplomats, legislators during session, sitting presidents—are justified by reference to the common good, even if otherwise letting such persons "get away with it" is unfair. Short of such wholesale exceptions from criminal liability, a variety of evidentiary privileges (priest-penitent, doctor-patient, husband-wife) and limitations on police investigation (no torture, no illegal search and seizure) make it practically difficult to prosecute certain types of offenses. I am not sure if prosecuting to the detriment of values protected by these crosscutting norms is "unfair." It seems more appropriate to say that, while it would be fair to prosecute, the common good is better served if we do not.

The important point that emerges from the few preceding paragraphs is that punishment is not logically tied to *any* particular *form* or *kind* of unwelcome imposition. How malefactors should be punished— both as to kinds of deprivations imposed on them and as to the extent of the imposition of any one kind—is entirely a matter of specification, save that the scale of punishments should exhibit a rough coherence: larceny should be punished less severely than robbery (which is forcible larceny), and robbery less severely than murder. Thus, we simply cannot say, as a matter of any kind of rational necessity or entailment, that death (or *any* particular punishment) is the *only* fair one, unless all the other available punishments are inadequate.

VII

"The problem" of capital punishment, the Pope says in EV, "must be viewed in the context of a system of penal justice ever more in line with human dignity and thus, in the end, with God's plan for man and society" [56]. The Pope does not say that premodern societies violated man's dignity or acted contrary to God's plan to the extent that capital punishment was not, in those days, "very rare." The opportunity we now have to punish adequately without taking life did not then exist. In less developed societies, execution might have been the only means of effective defense. It might also have been—and here is the possibility of nonintentional killing in capital punishment as retribution—that death was the existential *condition* for imposing a deprivation (of opportunities, freedom) which was the *only* adequate punishment available. If so, public authority might well have been morally obliged to punish by death (if the alternatives available were, say, uncertain detention in the sheriff's barn or payment of a fine). One could then impose death without choosing it, choosing instead to restore the order of justice by the deprivation effected in and by the execution. One's choice would be just that deprivation which death makes possible, and which the restoration of justice demands.

But capital punishment, in any place or time, kills (and thus creates great possibility for scandal), and eliminates any chance for the malefactor's reform. It seems to me, then, that the burden of proof should be placed on one who claims that alternative available punishments are all *in*adequate to show that *in*adequacy. That might well have been the case before prisons. But where secure prisons are available, I think that *in*adequacy cannot be shown.

Someone might object: legislators should be morally free to choose from among the available adequate punishments, including death. But, they may not choose, strictly, death. And where one selects electrocution from among available adequate punishments (say, life imprisonment, exile, and death), then one has chosen death. One has integrated one's will around killing, in the morally decisive sense of "choice."

Can we say that death—the suppression of life—is precisely the imposition needed to restore the order of justice, *and* that we do not choose death but simply choose to punish?

I think this case cannot arise once the point of punishment is properly identified. There are different *forms* of punishment—torture, fines, imprisonment, death—which are more or less repugnant and more or less unwelcome. But they are all forms *of punishment*, and as various forms of unwelcome impositions they are commensurable. However crudely done, public authority can and does compare and rank them as greater or lesser impositions upon the criminal's autonomy, and freedom to do as he or she pleases. Thus, death (the suppression of life), as such—and *not* the existential condition (and in that sense transparent) for a massive imposition—cannot be deemed the uniquely suited punishment for any crime.

The posited case either misapprehends the nature of punishment or is a different way of claiming that death is the only adequate punishment available.

VIII

One sense of the indeterminacy of punishment—its precise form and measure are to be settled not by logic but by choice—is the premise of my argument against the possibility of retributive capital punishment in developed societies. But is the concept of punishment expansive enough (in a different sense) to allow for any cases of licit capital punishment in developed societies as acts of "self-defense"? More exactly, in what sense can executing a prisoner not because he committed a certain type of crime but because he is chronically dangerous, be an act of *punishment* at all?

I have already *practically* responded to this challenge. Mature legal systems do not impose "punishment" for "chronic dangerousness" as such. Crimes are constituted by discrete acts, not dispositions or habits, even if punishment is something greater for habitual offenders. Persons in or out of prison who threaten others may well be dealt fatal blows (without intending to kill them). But they are not "punished," capitally or otherwise. Thus I conclude that faithful application of the Church's teaching to our society leads to abolition of the death penalty. My conclusion here is consistent with Church teaching, which says not that anyone *should be* executed, but that "very few" may.

The deeper question. Whether calculations of prison terms may take account of concerns—deterrence, defense against this dangerous character, rehabilitation—which are foreign to the retributive point of punishment. Are these *non*retributive (social hygiene, moralistic) considerations, which would not suffice by themselves to "punish" anyone for a day, properly the basis for years of additional imprisonment for a convicted robber or kidnapper?

CONCLUSION

Developing societies which suffer from shortages of various basic goods—education, health care, food—have to make choices about which needs to address first from the available common stock. Among those needs is the need for resources sufficient to position the criminal justice system so that it has adequate punishments available, short of execution. But even if the right to life *is* the source of all other rights, so long as a decision to leave prisons unconstructed is not intended as a means to kill (say, where those in power foresee that some disfavored racial or ethnic minority will disproportionately suffer capital punishment), it is a choice consistent with the Church's teaching. But in developed societies, and anywhere a prison system exists, abolition of the death penalty seems to be the practical way of observing the norm, "No intentional killing whatsoever."

NOTES

1. See also EV 57: "Before the moral norm which prohibits the direct taking of the life of an innocent human being there are no privileges or exceptions. . . ."

2. G. Grisez, "Toward A Consistent Natural-Law Ethic of Killing," 15 *Am. J. Jurisprudence* 64 (1970).

3. *See Gaudium et Spes* 26.

4. In Volume II of *The Way of the Lord Jesus: Living a Christian Life* (1983), Grisez says that the "defensive function" can be served in ways other than executing criminals, notably by having a secure prison system (p. 892).

5. The relevant part of EV is as follows: As time passed, the Church's tradition has always consistently taught the absolute and unchanging value of the commandment 'You shall not kill' . . .

> 55 This should not cause surprise: to kill a human being, in whom the image of God is present, is a particularly serious sin. *Only God is the master of life!* Yet from the beginning, faced with the many and often tragic cases which occur in the life of individuals and society, Christian

reflection has sought a fuller and deeper understanding of what God's commandment prohibits and prescribes. [43] There are in fact situations in which values proposed by God's Law seem to involve a genuine paradox. This happens for example in the case of *legitimate defence*, in which the right to protect one's own life and the duty not to harm someone else's life are difficult to reconcile in practice. Certainly, the intrinsic value of life and the duty to love oneself no less than others are the basis of *a true right to self-defence*. The demanding commandment of love of neighbour, set forth in the Old Testament and confirmed by Jesus, itself presupposes love of oneself as the basis of comparison: "You shall love your neighbour *as yourself*" (Mark 12:31). Consequently, no one can renounce the right to self-defence out of lack of love for life or for self. This can only be done in virtue of a heroic love which deepens and transfigures the love of self into a radical self-offering, according to the spirit of the Gospel Beatitudes (cf. Matt 5:38–40). The sublime example of this self-offering is the Lord Jesus himself. Moreover, "legitimate defence can be not only a right but a grave duty for someone responsible for another's life, the common good of the family or of the State". [44] Unfortunately it happens that the need to render the aggressor incapable of causing harm sometimes involves taking his life. In this case, the fatal outcome is attributable to the aggressor whose action brought it about, even though he may not be morally responsible because of a lack of the use of reason. [45]

56 This is the context in which to place the problem of the *death penalty*. On this matter there is a growing tendency, in the Church and in civil society, to demand that it be applied in a very limited way or even that it be abolished completely. The problem must be viewed in the context of a system of penal justice ever more in line with human dignity and thus, in the end, with God's plan for man and society. The primary purpose of the punishment which society inflicts is "to redress the disorder caused by the offence". [46] Public authority must redress the violation of personal and social rights by imposing on the offender an adequate punishment for the crime, as a condition for the offender to regain the exercise of his or her freedom. In this way authority also fulfills the purpose of defending public order and ensuring people's safety, while at the same time offering the offender an incentive and help to change his or her behaviour and be rehabilitated. [47]

It is clear that, for these purposes to be achieved, *the nature and extent of the punishment* must be carefully evaluated and decided upon, and ought not go to the extreme of executing the offender except in cases of absolute necessity: in other words, when it would not be possible otherwise to defend society. Today however, as a result of steady improvements in the organization of the penal system, such cases are very rare, if not practically nonexistent.

In any event, the principle set forth in the *Catechism of the Catholic Church* remains valid: "If bloodless means are sufficient to defend human lives against an aggressor and to protect public order and the safety of persons, public authority must limit itself to such means, because they better correspond to the concrete conditions of the common good and are more in conformity to the dignity of the human person" [48].

6. The following are the relevant sections of the Catechism:

2263 The legitimate defense of persons and societies is not an exception to the prohibition against the murder of the innocent that constitutes intentional killing. "The act of self-defense can have a double effect: the preservation of one's own life; and the killing of the aggressor . . . The one is intended, the other is not."

2264 Love toward oneself remains a fundamental principle of morality. Therefore it is legitimate to insist on respect for one's own right to life. Someone who defends his life is not guilty of murder even if he is forced to deal his aggressor a lethal blow:

If a man in self-defense uses more than necessary violence, it will be unlawful: whereas if he repels force with moderation, his defense will be lawful. . . . Nor is it necessary for salvation that a man omit the act of moderate self-defense to avoid killing the other man, since one is bound to take more care of one's own life than of another's.

2265 Legitimate defense can be not only a right but a grave duty for someone responsible for another's life, the common good of the family or of the state.

2266 Preserving the common good of society requires rendering the aggressor unable to inflict harm. For this reason the traditional teaching of the Church has acknowledged as well-founded the right and duty of legitimate public authority to punish malefactors by means of penalties commensurate with the gravity of the crime, not excluding, in cases of extreme gravity, the death penalty. For analogous reasons those holding authority have the right to repel by armed force aggressors against the community in their charge.

The primary effect of *punishment* is to redress the disorder caused by the offense. When his punishment is voluntarily accepted by the offender, it takes on the value of expiation. Moreover, punishment has the effect of preserving public order and the safety of persons. Finally punishment has a medicinal value; as far as possible it should contribute to the correction of the offender.

2267 If bloodless means are sufficient to defend human lives against an aggressor and to protect public order and the safety of persons, public authority should limit itself to such means, because they better correspond to the concrete conditions of the common good and are more in conformity to the dignity of the human person.

Intentional homicide

2268 The fifth commandment forbids *direct and intentional killing* as gravely sinful. The murderer and those who cooperate voluntarily in murder commit a sin that cries out to heaven for vengeance.

Infanticide, fratricide, parricide, and the murder of a spouse are especially grave crimes by reason of the natural bonds which they break. Concern for eugenics or public health cannot justify any murder, even if commanded by public authority.

2269 The fifth commandment forbids doing anything with the intention of *indirectly* bringing about a person's death. The moral law prohibits exposing someone to mortal danger without grave reason, as well as refusing assistance to a person in danger.

The acceptance by human society of murderous famines, without efforts to remedy them, is a scandalous injustice and a grave offense if, without proportionate reasons, he has acted in a way that brings about someone's death, even without the intention to do so.

7. See II *Way* at 904–6.

8. But see P. Lee, "Permanence of the Ten Commandments: St. Thomas and His Modern Commentators," 42 *Theological Studies* (1981): 422.

9. But see II *Way*, at 851.

10. It might be that the hangman's act is specified by obedience to a valid order of some higher, competent public authority (e.g., a death warrant signed by the governor). I use "executioner" to identify whoever it is (governor, juror, judge, legislator) that, on the supposition that capital punishment is an intentional killing, actually intends the prisoner's death.

11. The Latin "Hoc in rerum prospectu de poena capitali oritur quaestio" seems clearer, as "In this context arises the . . ."

12. The French version of the Catechism might best be translated (with my emphasis) as "*will* limit itself to such means": "l'autorité s'en tiendra a ces moyens." The Catechism, in still another indication that capital punishment and participation in just war are specifications of the one norm, goes on to say that "for analogous reason" public authority has the right to repel by "armed force" aggressors against the community.

13. J. Haas, *Crisis*, July/August 1995: 23.

14. *National Review*, July 10, 1995, p. 14.

15. Id.

16. See Part VI.

17. J. Finnis, *Fundamentals of Ethics*, 128 (1983).

18. II *Way* at 891.

Public Good: The Specifically Political Common Good in Aquinas

JOHN FINNIS
Professor of Law and Legal Philosophy
Oxford University, England
Robert and Frances Biolchini Professor of Law
University of Notre Dame, Indiana

As Grisez has recently argued, in his philosophical theology of politics:

> Even though a political society cannot flourish without virtuous citizens, it plainly cannot be government's proper end directly to promote virtue in general, since not all justice and neighborliness are included in political society's common good. Moreover, both the limits of political society's common good and its instrumentality in relation to the good of citizens as individuals and as members of nonpolitical communities set analogous limits on the extent to which government can rightly concern itself with other aspects of morality, especially insofar as they concern the interior acts and affections of hearts rather than the outward behavior which directly affects other people.

In a footnote to this text, following a reference to Aquinas's *Summa Theologiae* (II–II. q.104 a.5) and *De Regno* (15), Grisez adds, however, that both Aristotle and Thomas

> . . . hold that the general promotion of virtue and suppression of vice should be the main component of the common good of political society; in this, they overlook limits on the competence of the state which have been clarified by recent Church teaching regarding the instrumental character of political society's common good, the principle of subsidiarity . . . and religious liberty.[1]

But Aquinas, as I will argue, not only gives substantial support to the positions asserted in Grisez's text, but rejects the position attributed in the text's footnote to Aristotle's *Ethics* (10.9. 1179a–1180b28) and Aquinas's own *De Regno* (15 or 2.4).[2]

I

Grisez's powerful treatment of patriotism, politics, and citizenship distinguishes *nation* from *state* or political society/community, state from *government* (the political community's apparatus for making and implementing decisions),[3] and government from *regime* (the particular set of people holding governmental office).[4] Aquinas, though aware of these distinctions, is not generally concerned to differentiate between nation and state, or between the state's structure of governing offices and the particular rulers or regime of office-holders.[5] Still, Grisez's terminology corresponds with Aquinas's in its central usage: *civitas* and synonymously *communitas politica*[6] or *communitas civilis*,[7] in Aquinas, can usually be translated by "a state," "states," or "the state," though never in Maritain's sense ("the State" as government, organs of government, or subject of public law), but as signifying the whole large society which is organized politically by the sorts of institutions, arrangements, and practices commonly and reasonably called "government" and "law."[8]

Aquinas's treatise on law (S.T. I–II, qq.90–108) is the context for his most important treatment of political matters. It is shaped by a methodological decision and a theoretical thesis. The thesis is that law exists, focally or centrally, only in complete communities, *perfectae communitates*. The methodological decision is to set aside all questions about which sorts of multifamily community are "complete," and to consider a type, usually named *civitas*, whose completeness is simply posited.

The decision has important consequences. Aquinas is well aware that in his own world, though there are some city-*states* (civitates), there are also many cities which do not pretend to be complete communities but exist (perhaps established rather like castles to adorn a kingdom) as parts of a realm;[9] and *civitates*, kingdoms, and realms may be politically organized in sets,[10] perhaps as "provinces" (of which he often speaks) or empires (about which he discretely remains almost wholly silent). He is well aware of the idea, and the reality, of peoples (gentes; populi) and nations (nationes)[11] and regions (regiones). His methodological decision allows him to abstract from all this.[12] It also allows him to abstract from a number of deep and puzzling questions: how—and indeed by what right—any particular *civitas* comes into being (and passes away); how far the *civitas* should coincide with unities of origin or culture; and whether and what intermediate constitutional forms there are, such as federations or international organizations. Liberated from such questions, Aquinas will consider the *civitas* rather as if it were, and were to be, the only political community in the world and its people the only people.[13] All issues of *extension*—of origins, membership, and boundaries, or amalgamations and dissolutions—are thereby set aside.[14] The issues will all be, so to speak, intensional: the proper functions and modes and limits of government, authorititative direction, and obligatory compliance in a community whose "completeness" is presupposed.

Can a state's common good, being the good of a complete community, be anything less than the complete good, the fulfillment—*beatitudo imperfecta* if not *perfecta*[15]—of its citizens? That is the question with which this essay is concerned; it will be answered with a distinction: yes, and no. At the outset, however, it is sufficient to note that the question seems equivalent to another: What type of direction can properly be given by governments and law? The questions seem to be equivalent, in Aquinas, because he has stipulated that a state is a complete community,[16] and has given *complete community* a purely formal description:[17] a community so organized that its government and law give *all* the direction that properly can be given by human government and coercive *law* to promote and protect the common good, that is, the good of the community and thus[18] of all its members and other proper elements.

II

It is easy to read Aquinas as holding that the state's common good is the fulfillment (and thus the complete virtue) of each of its citizens, and that government and law should therefore promote that fulfillment. Of course, Aquinas teaches the unwisdom of legislating against every act of vice,[19] and the need to proceed gradually in inculcating virtue by law,[20] not attempting the impossible.[21] But it is easy to read him as holding that such legislation, though unwise, is not *ultra vires*—does not reach beyond the state's common good or the purpose, functions, and jurisdiction of state government and law.

This reading could begin with Aristotle's critique of the Sophists' social-contract or mutual-insurance theory of the state. The law "should be such as will make the citizens good and just,"[22] since "a *polis* is a community (partnership, *communicatio, koinonia*) of (clans and) neighborhoods in living well, with the object of a complete and self-sufficient (*autarkous*) life . . . , it must therefore be for the sake of truly good (*kalôn*) actions, not of merely living together."[23] Surely, one may ask, Aquinas didn't dissent from Aristotle here? Doesn't the *Summa Theologiae* reaffirm Aristotle's teaching that our need for state law is primarily to ensure the effective promotion of *virtue*, by way of laws enforced with penal sanctions, where parental capacity runs out?[24] For surely parents rightly try to educate their children into complete, all-round virtue and fulfillment? Doubtless, parents will exceed their authority if they try to reinforce their education with coercive measures of the kind the state can use.[25] But in all other respects, surely state law holds the same place in the state as parental precepts hold in the family,[26] precisely because it has the same purpose and jurisdiction of promoting fulfillment and therefore inculcating virtue, without restrictions of *goal*?

Plausible as it is, as a first reading of many passages, this interpretation of Aquinas must be rejected. No passage requires to be read in this way, and it is inconsistent with a number of clear passages in mature texts.

Clearest, perhaps, are the passages in which Aquinas argues that "the purpose (finis) of human law and the purpose of divine law are different."[27]

> For *human law's purpose is the temporal tranquility of the state* (temporalis tranquillitas civitatis), a purpose which the law attains by coercively *prohibiting external acts* (cohibendo exteriores actus) to the extent that those are evils *which can disturb the state's peaceful condition*) (quantum ad illa mala quae possunt perturbare pacificum statum civitatis).[28]

In other words, divine and civil government, in Aquinas's view, differ in method—the latter's prohibitions, unlike the former's, being restricted to external acts—because they differ in purpose. This double difference is insisted upon repeatedly:

> The form of community (modus communitatis) to which human law is directed (ordinatur) is different from the form of community to which divine law is directed. For human law is directed to *civil community*, which is a matter of people *relating to one another* (quae est hominum ad invicem).[29] But people are related to one another (ordinantur ad invicem) by the *external* acts in which people communicate and deal (communicant) with each other. But this sort of communicating/dealing (communicatio) is a matter of *justice* (pertinet ad rationem iustitiae), which is properly directive in and of human community (directiva communitatis humanae). *So human law does not put forward precepts about anything other than acts of justice* [and injustice] (non proponit praecepta nisi de actibus iustitiae);[30] if it prescribes acts of other virtues, this is only because and insofar as they take on the character of justice (assumunt rationem iustitiae).[31]

Aquinas's point in the last sentence is: derelictions of duty by soldiers, police, and emergency service personnel can readily be caused by want of courage; the injustices of adultery, child abuse, or other sexual assaults typically arise from lack of sexual self-control; and so forth; so the law can rightly require choices characteristic of other virtues besides justice. But the law of the state cannot rightly regulate the full range of choices required by practical reasonableness.[32]

> Types of virtue are distinguished by their objects, and each virtue's object can be related either to someone's private good or to the common good of the group. Take courage, for example: one can act out of courage either to save the state or to preserve the rights (ius) of one's friend. But law is for the common good. So, although there is no [type of] virtue the acts of which cannot be prescribed by law, *human law does not make prescriptions about all the acts of all the virtues, but only about those acts which are relatable (ordinabiles) to the common good*, whether *immediately* (as when things are done directly for the common good) *or mediately* (as when things are regulated [ordinantur] by the legislator *as being relevant to the good education* [pertinentia ad bonam disciplinam] *by which citizens are brought up to preserve the common good of justice and peace*).[33]

In this passage Aquinas clearly affirms that within a state there are "private goods" (of individuals and small groups, e.g., of friends) whose good (e.g., whose right) is not part of the common good specific to the state— is not, I shall say, part of the specifically political common good.

That is only one of the ways in which Aquinas makes plain his view that, notwithstanding the "completeness" of political communities, their specific common good is limited. Another important limitation can be indicated without taking up the question of religious liberty. The specifically political common good does not include the common good of another community in which the state's members will do well to participate, the community—also *perfecta*[34]—of the Church. Moreover, the common good of the political community does not, as such, include certain important human goods which essentially pertain to individuals in themselves, such as the good of religious faith and worship; the fact that such individual goods are goods for many people, or for everyone, does not convert them into the good of community:

> In human affairs there is a certain [type of] common good, the good of the *civitas* or people (gentis). . . . There is also a [type of] human good which— [though it] benefits not merely one person alone but many people—does not consist in community but pertains to one [as an individual] in oneself (humanum bonum quod non in communitate consistit sed ad unum aliquem

pertinet secundum seipsum), e.g., the things which everyone ought to believe and practice, such as matters of faith and divine worship, and other
things of that sort.[35]

Aquinas's clearest name for this limited common good, specific to the
political community, is *public good* (bonum publicum). It is distinct from
the private good of individuals and the private common good of families
and households, even though the political community (in Aquinas's most
usual account) is comprised precisely of individuals and families. As the
public good, the elements of the specifically political common good are
not all-round virtue but goods (and virtues) which are intrinsically interpersonal, other-directed (ad alterum),[36] person to person (hominum ad
adinvicem):[37] justice and peace.[38]

"Peace," of course, should not be understood thinly. In its fullest
sense, peace (pax), involves not only concord (absence of dissension,
especially on fundamentals) and willing agreement between one person
or group and another, but also harmony (unio) among each individual's
own desires.[39] And Aquinas will make related observations: "the principal
intention of human law is to secure friendship between people (ut faciat
amicitiam hominum ad invicem),"[40] and efforts to maintain peace by
laying down precepts of justice will be insufficient without foundations
in mutual friendship or love (dilectio).[41] But in the context of the passages
about public good, it is clear that "peace" refers directly only to (1) absence
of words and deeds immorally opposed to peace, such as disorderly
contentiousness,[42] quarrelsome fighting,[43] sedition,[44] or war;[45] (2) concord,
that is, the "tranquillity of order"[46] between persons and groups which
is made possible by love of neighbor as oneself,[47] along with the avoidance
of collisions (e.g., in road traffic) and dissensions such as can occur without
personal fault; and perhaps also (3) a sufficiency of at least the necessities
of life.[48] In short, it is the peaceful condition needed to get the benefit(s)
(utilitas) of social life and avoid the burdens of contention.[49] It is a peace
that falls short of the complete justice which true virtue requires of each
of us; so legislatures can reasonably, *in the interests of peace*, provide that
adverse possession for a length of time gives a good title even to squatters
who took possession in bad faith—but a squatter who acted in bad faith
never becomes morally entitled, in good conscience, to rely on this title.[50]

Even when all that is taken into account, Aquinas's position remains
firmly outlined: vices of disposition and conduct that have no real relationship, direct or indirect, to justice and peace are not the concern of state

government or law.[51] The position is not readily distinguishable from the "grand simple principle" (itself open to interpretation and diverse applications) of John Stuart Mill's *On Liberty*.

III

But can this reading of Aquinas be reconciled with his treatment of the question in *De Regno*,[52] or with his frequent assertion that inculcating virtue is a primary and proper rationale of law and state, with the "completeness" of the political community, and with the primacy of *politica* among the parts of *moralis philosophia*?

The *De Regno*, an openly theological little treatise written in a style unlike Aquinas's academic works in philosophy and theology,[53] but very probably authentic,[54] includes some main elements of Aristotle's position that states are appropriately organized, and legally regulated, with a view to making their citizens truly good. Early in the *De Regno*'s exposition of the common good, or ultimate end, for which a king is responsible, we hear unmistakable echoes of *Politics* III.5 on the object of the *polis*, echoes inflected by the Christian understanding of history's point. Civil society (congregatio civilis) is gathered together not simply to live but to live *well* (ad bene vivendum) and *in virtue* (vivere secundum virtutem); its ultimate end and good—*beatitudo perfecta*, as Aquinas elsewhere calls it[55]— is beyond the reach of human virtue but attainable by divine power (virtus). Since reaching this most ultimate end is the subject matter of a set of governing arrangements (regimen) not human but divine,[56] kings must regard themselves as subjects to that divine *regimen*—a *regimen* administered by priests[57] concerned with spiritual (spiritualia) not earthly or temporal matters (terrena; temporalia bona).[58] That being said, "it belongs to the authority and responsibility (officium) of a king to promote (procurare) the good life of the group in such a way that it is in line with the pursuit of heavenly fulfillment (congruit ad celestem beatitudinem consequendam); so the king may *prescribe* (praecipiat) *whatever things lead to such fulfillment* and forbid, as far as possible, the contraries of those things."[59] And Aquinas's advice on this question concludes:

> Therefore a threefold responsibility (cura) lies on the king. [i] First, in relation to the replacement of those who hold various offices: just as divine rule preserves the integrity of the universe by arranging that corruptible, transient things are replaced by new ones generated to take their place, so the king should be concerned to preserve the good of the group subject to him

(subiectae multitudinis) by conscientiously arranging how new officials are to succeed those who fail or drop out. [ii] Second, *by his laws and decrees, punishments and rewards, the king is to restrain his subjects from immorality and lead them to virtuous action* (ab iniquitate coerceat, et ad opera virtuosa inducat), thereby following the example of God, who gave us law and who requites with reward those who follow and with punishments those who violate it. [iii] Third, the king is responsible for keeping the group subject to him safe against enemies; there would be no point in avoiding internal dangers, if the group were defenseless against external dangers.[60]

Don't the statements here italicized clearly propose an ambitious purpose for state rule, and acknowledge no limit on the inherent scope of that purpose?

No. The immediate context of each of the passages quoted shows that Aquinas has several restrictions in mind. Take first the passage about the king's triple responsibilities, (i) supervising succession of offices, (ii) restraining immorality and leading subjects to virtue, and (iii) defense. As its opening "therefore" signals, it is the conclusion of a wider argument. That argument develops a careful parallel between what is needed for an individual's good life and what is needed for a community's. What an individual's good life (bona unius hominis vita) requires, above all, is virtue-in-action (operatio secundum virtutem); secondary and quasi-instrumental requirements are the bodily goods necessary for action. So, too, a group's good life requires that the group act well. But there is a precondition for acting well: the unity of the acting being's parts. In individual human beings this precondition is secured by nature. But in communities the needed unity of life, the unity called "peace" (pax), has to be procured by government (per regentis industriam). So the community counterparts to individual virtue-in-action as primary element in an individual's good life are (i) the constituting of the community in the unity of peace, and (ii) the directing of the peacefully united group toward well-doing (ad bene agendum). The king's next (consequens) problem is to maintain and preserve these two primary elements of the group's good life.

At precisely this point, Aquinas shifts from group "good life" (bona vita in multitudine constituta) to "public good" (bonum publicum), treating them as synonymous. The *De Regno*'s treatment of our questions will be misunderstood unless one notices the effortlessness of this shift, and the synonymity and equivalence thus signalled.

There are, Aquinas is saying, three things incompatible with lasting public good, with that group good life whose primary elements are peace and acting well (tria quibus bonum publicum permanere non sinitur). And the triple responsibility (cura) whose second element—"restraining subjects from immorality and leading them to virtuous action"—is our present concern, is simply the appropriate response to these three "things incompatible with lasting public good." The first thing is unsuitable public officials; the third is the incursions of enemies. The second, which, like the first, is "an internal impediment *to preserving the public good*, is perversity of people's wills—their laziness in doing *what the public weal requires* (ad ea peragenda quae requirit res publica), or again their harmfulness to the group's peace, their *disturbance of others' peace* by their violations of justice."[61] So the second concern or responsibility (cura) of rulers, a responsibility proposed by Aquinas precisely as the appropriate response to *these* just-mentioned "things incompatible with lasting public good," is not: to lead people to the *fullness* of virtue by coercively restraining them from *every* immorality. It is no more than: to lead people to *those* virtuous actions which are required if the public weal is not to be neglected, and to uphold peace against unjust violations.

What about the passage stating that rulers have the duty to promote heavenly fulfillment? This, too, should be taken to assert much less than appears on a first, noncontextual glance. For it too rests on the distinction between individual and group "good life." Promoting the *group's* good life is the king's concern. But Aquinas never supposes that such groups can attain perfect, that is, heavenly fulfillment. What he says here is this: the group's—the political community's—good life is to be in line with (congruit) the "pursuing of heavenly fulfillment (coelestem beatitudi-nem)"; by promoting group good life in that way, rulers are like sword-smiths or house builders, whose role is to make an instrument suitable for others to put to their own good purposes. Thus the good life for which rulers are responsible is a *public* good, the justice and peace (rooted in citizens' characters rather than merely in fear of royal troops and judges) that in turn facilitate the domestically and ecclesially fostered individual virtue which is the human contribution to perfect *beatitudo*. The statement that rulers are to "prescribe those things that lead to [perfect] fulfillment" (and "to forbid their contraries *so far as is possible*") must be read as asserting a responsibility and authority no wider than the responsibility and authority for which Aquinas argues in the complex and carefully thought-out paragraphs by which the statement is flanked. And those paragraphs, as is now clear, deny rather than assert that a ruler should impose on individuals a legal duty to pursue their ultimate happiness or to abstain from choices which block that ultimate happiness without violating peace and justice. That denial will, as we have seen, be made much firmer and more explicit by the *Summa Theologiae*'s repeated differentiation of scope between divine governance and human governments' limited responsibility for their subjects' virtue.

IV

Still, how should one understand those many texts throughout Aquinas's work[62] which flatly say that law and state have among their essential purposes and characteristics the inculcation of virtue by coercively requiring (within the limits of practicability) abstention from acts of vice?

The answer seems to be this. Human law must inculcate virtues because it will only work well as a guarantor of justice and peace if its subjects internalize its norms and requirements and—more important—adopt its purpose of promoting and preserving justice. The public good cannot be well preserved if people are untrustworthy, vengeful, willing to evade their taxes and other civic duties, biased in jury service, and so forth. So the preservation of public good needs people to have the *virtue*, the inner dispositions, of justice.

This objective of inculcating virtue for the sake of peace and just conduct is coherent with Aquinas's constant teaching[63] that government or law, while rightly demanding of subjects that they do what is just and abstain from doing what is unjust, cannot rightly demand of them that they do so with a just mind and will, cannot require that they be just in the central, character-related sense of "be a just person." For just acts and forbearances are distinctly less likely to be chosen in the absence of a just character (habitus). So it is a legitimate hope and important aim (finis) of government and law that citizens will come to have the virtue of justice and act out of that particular excellence of character.[64]

And if that is a legitimate purpose, then it must be at least a legitimate interest of government that citizens have other virtues too. For there is no doubt that practical reasonableness is essentially all of a piece;[65] those who violate or neglect its directiveness in "private" choices are thereby weakened in their rational motives for following its directiveness in "public," other-affecting choices. Moreover, it seems clear that government and law—though Aquinas scarcely affirms this directly and clearly[66]—can rightly, for reasons ultimately of justice and peace, require and enforce a *public* morality going wider than issues of justice and peace. For parents have a primary educative responsibility to their children, and this responsibility—which, unlike public authority, includes a responsibility not only for peace and justice[67] but also for seeing to the all-round character of the children[68]—may well be frustrated unless it is given some assistance and support by state government if only so that the educative responsibility of families to their children will not be frustrated. Those who corrupt children (e.g., drugs, sex, lying, greed, or sloth) do them a great injustice. So does anyone who neglects the child's nutrition, nurture, and education; making provision for such matters therefore falls within the responsibility of government (ad eum qui regit rempublicam).[69] But even in seeking to promote justice-related virtues by requiring patterns of conduct which should habituate its subjects to the acts of these virtues,[70] the law cannot rightly require that people acquire, or be motivated by, these virtuous states of character or disposition. As Aquinas reiterates, the law's requirements (though not its legitimate objectives) are exhausted by "external" compliance.[71]

Aquinas's thesis that state law is in these ways restricted in legitimate jurisdiction helps explain the disconcertingly formal character of his treatment of two questions to which he gives some prominence: whether law seeks to make its subjects good,[72] and whether a good citizen must be a good person.[73] One expects something richer than Aquinas's answers, which are (i) even wicked laws and rulers seek to make their subjects good (so that they be not merely obedient but readily obedient [bene obedientes] and thus good *as* subjects[74] and relative to the purposes of *that* regime);[75] and (ii) in bad states a good citizen need not be a good person (though in all states a ruler, to be a good ruler, *should* be a good person). These answers make reasonable sense if Aquinas is taking the usual question about law and virtue to be one about the conditions for securing justice and peace by sufficient coordination of social life through law. The nonformal, substantive question, whether the point of such coordination is to make people *really* good persons *all-round*, is simply not the issue in these passages.

V

One may still wonder how far all this can be reconciled with the Aristotelean critique of social-contract and mutual-insurance conceptions of the state, a critique which the De Regno puts thus:

> The ultimate purpose (ultimus finis) of a community (multitudo) gathered together (congregatae) is to live in accordance with virtue; for *people gather*

together (congregantur) to *live well*, which someone living alone cannot attain; but *good life* is life in accordance with virtue, and so *virtuous life is the purpose of human gathering-together* (congregationis). . . . The only people who are counted as a community are those who, under the same laws and the same governing arrangements (regimen), are directed toward living well (diriguntur ad bene vivendum).[76]

Are such statements about the purpose of political community (statements often parallelled in Aquinas's other works)[77] really consistent with the idea that governments' or law-makers' responsibility to promote virtue does not authorize them to require more than the actions and forbearances necessary, directly or indirectly, for maintaining public and interpersonal good? I shall argue that they are, and that Aquinas's differentiation of three diverse kinds of practical reasonableness (prudentia), individual, domestic, and political, helps make clear his whole, complex thought about the state's virtue-promoting responsibility and authority.

If one is a reasonable individual, one wants to "gather together" into political community, and is willing to direct oneself by laws, for the sake of the help this community, this *congregatio* can give one in one's own unrestricted purposes: *beatitudo* at least *imperfecta*, involving "general justice" and love of God and neighbor as oneself. If one is a reasonable parent, one wants one's family to participate in the political community so that the family may flourish in every practicable way and its members cooperate with a view to that same *beatitudo*. If one is a reasonable citizen-voter or other participant in state government, one wants the law and the government to fulfill—that is, to act in a way that advances and does not fall short of—these purposes of individuals and families. Thus there is an important sense in which the common good of the political community is all-inclusive, nothing short of the *beatitudo* of its members and the fulfillment of their families. This all-inclusive common good of the state includes the all-round virtue of every member of the state.

But it simply does not follow that lawmakers and other participants in state government are responsible for directing and commanding all the choices that need to be made if this all-inclusive good is to be attained. It may well be that their responsibility is more limited, leaving families and individuals with a range of responsibilities that they must carry out within the requirements of justice and peace, but without the direction of government and law. If so, the goods that define the range of lawmakers' and other rulers' responsibility—say, the goods of peace and justice—can be called the common good of, specific to, the political community or state. This is the common good of, or specific to, a type of community which includes individuals and families, but whose successful organization, while assisting individuals and families to attain fulfillment, does not supersede their responsibility to make good choices and actions on the basis of their own deliberation and judgments. These choices and actions are "private"; the political community does not make, perform, or even stipulate them; they can be constitutive of *beatitudo imperfecta* more directly and immediately than any action by or on behalf of the political community can be (precisely as public, political action). There is, then, a specifically political common good whose content is understood in knowing what exactly the political community, organization, government, and law can properly contribute toward the *beatitudo* of the state's members.

Accordingly, the reasonable pursuit of the "all-inclusive" common good is stratified into three distinct specializations of responsibility. Individual practical reasonableness (*prudentia*, without trace of selfishness), domestic practical reasonableness, and political practical reasonableness are three irreducibly distinct (diversi) species of *prudentia*,[78] three distinct "parts" of moral practical reasonableness.[79] *Each* of these species of *prudentia*, unlike military prudence,[80] is concerned not with some special project which can be finished off but with "the whole of life (tota vita)."[81] The specifically political *prudentia* which is paradigmatically and principally, though not exclusively, the viewpoint of legislators[82] neither absorbs the other two nor includes, directly, the whole of their content. Although rulers are in many respects in charge of their subjects, their direct concern as rulers is only, as we have seen, the promotion of *public good*. Public good is a part or aspect of the all-inclusive common good, the part that provides an indispensable context and support for, and thus supplements, subserves, and supervises, those parts or aspects of the common good which are private (especially individual and familial good). And here we may add Aquinas's partial anticipation of the principle of subsidiarity: "it is contrary to the proper character of the state's government (contra rationem gubernationis [civitatis]) to impede people from acting according to their responsibilities (officia)—except in emergencies."[83]

Still, the justice and peace which rulers must maintain *are* for the sake of individual and familial well-being and cannot be identified and pursued without a sound conception of individual and domestic responsibilities.[84] The *politica* which is the highest (principalior, principalissima) practical knowledge[85] must be *politica* in the sense that it includes, along with the specifically political, the considerations called by Aquinas *oeco-*

nomica and *monostica*—the last being the *Ethics* which precedes the *Politics*.[86] Because the *prudentia* of rulers must comprehend, though without replacing, the *prudentia* of individuals and families, it is the most complete (perfectissima),[87] and though people who are not good persons can be good citizens (qua *subjects*), they cannot be good rulers.[88] The immediate and direct measure of individual and parental responsibility remains the practical reasonableness of individuals and parents, respectively.

In sum: The common good attainable in political community is thus a complex good attainable only if the state's rulers, its families, and its individual citizens all perform their proper, specialized and stratified roles and responsibilities. This common good, which is in a sense *the* common good of the political community, is *unlimited* (the common good of the whole of human life). But there is also a common good which is "political" in the more specific sense that it is (i) the good of using government and law to assist individuals and families do well what they should be doing, together with (ii) the good(s) that sound action by and on behalf of the political community can add to the good attainable by individuals and families as such (including the good of repelling and overcoming harms and deficiencies that individuals, families and other "private" groupings cannot adequately handle). This, and only this, specifically political common good is what the state's rulers are responsible for securing and should, by legislation and lawful judicial and administrative actions, require their subjects to respect and support. This specifically political common good is *limited* and in a sense *instrumental*.[89] It is what Aquinas, as we have seen, calls public good.

VI

Aquinas's treatment can thus be understood as coherent. But there remains the challenge of principle. Are there good grounds for judging that the state's specific common good is this limited, public good of justice and peace? If a government or legislature should, as Aquinas certainly thinks, ascertain and adhere to the truth about human fulfillment and morality, why shouldn't it use its public powers, and law's coercive pedagogy, to require of all citizens the acts and forbearances which will advance their fulfillment and complete virtue? Aren't rulers obliged to do so by *moralis philosophia*'s master principle, general justice or love of neighbor as oneself? Of course, if bad side-effects are too serious—if blowing one's nose too hard draws blood[90]—the effort should doubtless be made more gradual and perhaps indirect. But why judge the effort wrong in principle, an abuse of public power, *ultra vires* because it is directed to an end which state government and law do not truly have?

Aquinas's answers to such demands for justification are not as clear as we may wish. (When Kant and Mill announced positions similar to Aquinas's, their attempted justifications were at bottom, at least as sketchy.) Responding to the question whether there are limits (of subject matter) to what can be required of subjects by their rulers, Aquinas denies that human law and government can have some obligation-imposing authority over "matters which concern the inner life of the will (in his quae pertinent ad interiorem motum voluntatis)."[91] In such matters we are subject only to God.[92] Ground for this denial perhaps emerges in the next sentences, where Aquinas further denies that one can be morally obliged to obey human rulers in relation to certain matters of actual bodily behavior, namely those which pertain to the nature of one's body (ea quae pertinent ad naturam corporis).[93] In such matters, too, we are subject only to God—and this time a reason is assigned, the fundamental equality of human persons: "for we are all, by [or: in our] nature, on a par (quia omnes homines natura sunt pares)."[94] The matters thus outside state power include those (e.g., whether and whom to marry) which elsewhere he says are beyond the power of even the highest authority in a *perfecta communitas*[95] because in them "one is so much a free and independent person (ita liber sui)."[96] And Aquinas mentions other such matters.[97]

Sometimes Aquinas identifies them compendiously as "matters that concern one's person—one's bodily self (ea quae pertinent ad suam personam)."[98] It is no coincidence that the status of freedom, self-possession, and equality—the metaphysical reality and normative entitlement which he is appealing to—is the status of *persons*.[99] This is the status which Aquinas seems to be taking for granted when he puts forward the arguments to which we now turn, arguments that concern the competence of government.

The first argument points to the inability of state rulers to *succeed* in supervising movements of the human spirit that are quite beyond their knowledge.[100] We can often reasonably judge the proximate intention with which someone is acting, but can rarely know the further and deeper intentions and dipositions with which that proximate intention was formed;[101] the lack of competence (capacity) is ground for denial of competence (jurisdiction, authority, right): God, not any human ruler, is the judge of secrets.[102] The rulers or directors of human communities, for example, a religious congregation or state, have absolutely[103] no right or authority to require anyone to disclose a secret sin which does not affect that community's public well-being. Only the effect on public well-being is the concern of human judges. A secret immorality may have this effect either intrinsically (e.g., plotting to betray the state to its enemies)[104] or extrinsically, as when it has become a matter of public notoriety (infamia) or of formal and responsible accusations.[105] Only in cases thus stamped with a public character may a judge or other ruler override the legitimate privacy of wrongdoers or those who know their secrets, and require disclosure.

This line of thought assumes that judges and lawmakers appropriately have only limited responsibility and authority. This assumption is elaborated in a second argument, which develops more broadly the positions sketched in the preceding section, about the different viewpoints, responsibilities, and strata of the common good. Fully developed, the argument would go well beyond this essay to consider Aquinas's theories of moral limits (exceptionless moral norms, absolute human rights) and of property. But this argument can be suggested in outline, as it is in the remaining portion of this essay. It asks the questioner to go behind the proposition that states are complete communities, and to consider the grounds for that assertion, on the tacit assumption that the institutions which give this community its completeness—law and government— need justification in the face of the natural equality and freedom of persons, and need to show just why and when their authority overrides the responsibility of parents and the self-possession[106] of free persons above the age of puberty.[107]

The state is not an organism, but an order of cooperative action for some purpose.[108] But what is that purpose, and why does it differ in *kind* from the purposes of other groups which might be constituted for far-reaching economic, educational, or defensive purposes? What makes the political community "complete," rather than merely higher on a scale of increasingly inclusive membership and extensive objectives?

Prior to or independent of any politically organized community, there can exist individuals and families and indeed groups of neighboring families. Any such groups of families are contingent in their size, interactions, and common purposes and activities, if any. Families, in their central form, are not in that way contingent.

No doubt families are contingent in the sense that each is formed by free choices—in the central case, by the free choice of a man and a woman to enter upon that sort of reproductive and educative partnership, which is also the "closest form of friendship."[109] But families are noncontingent in the sense that they directly instantiate a basic human good[110]—

the good probably best described as marriage itself.[111] And, for a lengthy period in the life of all human infants, families are the direct and practically indispensable means of instantiating the basic good of life and health and, almost as directly and indispensably, the goods of knowledge, friendship (*societas*), and practical reasonableness, at least in their beginnings. No one is born without a mother and a father; the nurture without which no one survives cannot be more perceptively, lovingly, and fittingly provided than by a virtuous and capable mother and father, this mother and this father.[112] Love of neighbor as oneself has its perhaps most immediate and far-reaching demands right here, in the nurture of children to the point where they become what the parents were when they made by free choice the commitment of marriage: truly self-standing, each a *liber* or *libera sui*, a *dominus* or *domina sui actus*.

"Human beings are by nature more conjugal than political."[113] The family, essentially husband, wife, and children, is antecedent to, and more necessary than political society (because oriented around [ordinatur ad] acts of procreation and nurture necessary for life itself).[114] The complementarity of man and woman in domestic life is the basis for an exclusive and fully committed friendship which (with good fortune) is not only useful and sexually enjoyable but also delightful simply as a friendship of virtue, a sharing of life and human goods (*communicatio*) which, Aquinas indicates, makes good sense even if children fail to be born or do not survive.[115] The life of the family and its household (*domus*) has such a far-reaching sufficiency of independent ends and such stability in patterns of effective means that it is the subject of a distinct discipline or practical science, *oeconomica*.

Aquinas knows that one can detach resource management from the household in order to make it simply the art of accumulating wealth on a scale as wide as the *civitas*, or wider.[116] He knows of economists who do this, "thinking that their function is the same as that of money-dealers (who seek cash [denarios] for its own sake), conserving and multiplying cash *in infinitum*.[117] But in a reasonable conception of economics, accumulated money-wealth is merely instrumental to the good of persons— primarily and directly, of households,[118] the good of the *totum bene vivere* in shared domestic life (secundum domesticam conversationem).[119] (The wealth of a household is properly held and administered for the common good of the household and thus for the benefit of the family members,[120] primarily and directly for spouse, children, and other members of the family, secondarily and indirectly for the benefit also of the person responsible for this administration and distribution.)[121] Even if, unlike Aquinas,

one envisages economics as an understanding of capital formation, pro-
duction, and consumption on a scale as wide as the political community,
if not of regional and worldwide markets, Aquinas's household-oriented
conception of the basic human purpose of economic activity can reasonably be sustained.

So Aquinas reaches the concept of "complete community" only by
attending to the deficiencies of such a community's elements or "parts"—
fundamentally, individuals and families. These parts are prior to the
complete community not historically but in a more important way: in
their immediate and irreplaceable instantiation of basic human goods.
The need which individuals have for the political community is not that
it instantiates an otherwise unavailable basic good. By contrast, the lives
of individuals and families directly instantiate basic goods, and can even
provide means and context for instantiating all the other basic goods, for
example, education, friends, marriage, and virtue. As for the *non*basic
goods needed to support life and other basic goods—notably the instrumental goods of produce and exchange—Aquinas regards them as goods
which, at least primarily and directly, are appropriately within the control
of *private* persons and groups (potestati privatarum personarum sub-
duntur res possessae),[122] dealing sometimes "in public"[123] and sometimes
in private. Their instrumentality is essentially in the service of households.
As we shall see, a state's government and law can protect and greatly
enhance the utility of these instrumental goods. Law and government
thereby serve basic human goods which in other ways they serve more
directly and immediately. The justice they can restore by "private law"
reparatio or *restitutio* and "public law" *retributio* is doubtless an aspect of
the basic good of *societas*, and in that respect one can say that the specifically political common good is more than merely instrumental. In all
other respects, however, the *specifically* political common good which is
interdefined with the responsibilities of state government and law seems
indeed to be an instrumental good or set of goods, albeit of preeminent
complexity, scope, and dignity among instruments.

VII

Contrary to what is often supposed, Aquinas's many statements that we
are "naturally political animals" have nothing particularly to do with
political community.[124] So they cannot be pressed into service as implying
that the state or its common good is the object of a natural inclination or
an intrinsic and basic good. Strikingly, they do no more than assert our

social not solitary nature,[125] our need to have interpersonal relationships for acquiring necessities such as food and clothing,[126] for speech,[127] and in general for getting along together (convivere);[128] or the need for various social but not peculiarly political virtues, such as good faith in promising and testifying, and so forth.[129] On the other hand, Aquinas accepts Aristotle's opinion that we are "naturally civil animals" because we are *naturally* parts of a *civitas*,[130] which stands to other natural communities[131] as an end.[132]

In human affairs that are matters of deliberation and choice, what is natural is settled by asking what is intelligent and reasonable.[133] That in turn is settled by looking to the first principles of practical reason, to the basic human goods.[134] So the *civitas* could be called "natural" if participation in it (a) instantiates in itself a basic human good, or (b) is a rationally required component in, or indispensable means to instantiating, one or more basic human goods. Aquinas's opinion, rather clearly, is that it is the latter. At the relevant point in his lists of basic human goods he mentions nothing more specific than living in fellowship (in societate vivere)[135]—something that is done with parents and children and spouse and friends and other people in various more or less temporary and specialized groups (of pilgrims, of students, of sailors, of merchants, and so forth).[136] The thought that we cannot live reasonably and well apart from a *civitas*[137] is consistent with the proposition that the common good specific to the *civitas* as such—the public good—is not basic but, rather, instrumental to securing human goods which are basic (including other forms of community or association, especially domestic and religious associations) and none of which is in itself political. If that proposition needs qualification, the qualification concerns the restoration of justice by the irreparable modes of punishment reserved to state government.

Consider both the proposition and the possible qualification. What is it that solitary individuals, families, and groups of families inevitably cannot do well? In what way are they inevitably "incomplete"? In their inability (i) to secure themselves *well* against violence (including invasion), theft, and fraud,[138] and (ii) to maintain a fair and stable system of distributing, exploiting, and exchanging the natural resources which, Aquinas thinks,[139] are in reason and fairness—"naturally" (not merely "initially")—things common to all. That is to say, individuals and families cannot well secure and maintain the elements that make up the *public good* of justice and peace—a good which, with good fortune, also includes prosperity.[140] And so their realization of basic goods is less secure and full than if public justice and peace are maintained by law and other specifically political institutions and activities, in a way no individual or private group can appropriately undertake or match. The need which individuals and groups have for political community is *that* need, and the political community's specific common good[141] is, accordingly, that *public* good.

Suppose nobody was badly disposed, unjust, recalcitrant. Would there be need for states with their governments and laws? Aquinas is clear that in such a paradise there would still be need for "government and direction of free people," since social life requires some unity of social action and, where there are many intelligent and good people, there are many competing ideas about what actions should be done for the sake of the common good.[142] But he does not say that in such a state of affairs there would be need for specifically *political, state* government or law, and his discussion, important and clarifying as it is in some respects, does not really carry further the question why we need states, political government, and state law.

Consider that question in the context of, say, violence within the household. Why can't this be dealt with by paternal power? Is it merely that the son may grow stronger than his parents, or outrun them? That is perhaps a relevant consideration.[143] But why does Aquinas say that neither the father nor any other nonpublic person can rightly threaten or impose penalties that are fully coercive?[144] Why can there be no law, in the focal sense,[145] within families or neighborhood groups of families?

Aquinas here does not explain as much as we may wish. He is insistent about distinguishing public from private. He does so in many contexts: self-defense, war, resistance to tyranny, intrafamilial discipline, ecclesiastical order, forms of justice, correction of wrongdoers, and so on. But he treats it rather as if axiomatic.[146] Still, if we bear in mind the content or force of the distinction, we may discern its purpose just below the surface of his texts.

What is matter for public authority is matter for law: the sword and the balance. It is matter for judgments, with often irreparable finality of outcome, given by impartial judges representing the *princeps*[147] before whom all who seek justice are equal.[148] None of us can rightly be simultaneously prosecutor, judge, and witness.[149] Private persons and bodies are not equipped for *judgment*, especially judgment according to publicly established *law*,[150] and so cannot rightly impose the irreparable measures which may be needed to restore justice and peace. So they are incomplete, *imperfecta*, and in need of completion by the order of public justice. When a society not only has individuals flourishing in families and other private associations and dealings but also is equipped for public justice, it is in principle complete, *perfecta*.

The irreparability of various measures often needed to restore justice plays a large part in the argument. The family or household (including domestic servants) is an *imperfecta communitas* and within it there is an *imperfecta potestas coercendi*, a limited authority or right (not in any way delegated by the state) of imposing relatively light penalties, "penalties, such as a beating, which do no irreparable harm."[151] But irreparable penalties are different. The point is made vivid by Aquinas's discussion of the law which in certain states in his day (as in various countries today) allowed a husband who found his wife committing adultery to kill her then and there, "on account of the unsurpassable provocation." Aquinas denies that this legal provision can justify or even excuse the grave wickedness (reatus poenae aeternae) of such a killing. He notes the law's inequity between the sexes: husband and wife are properly judged on the same basis (vir et uxor ad paria judicantur).[152] But what concerns him more is that "no man is his wife's *judge*."[153] As family head he could chastise the wife with a view to reforming her.[154] But no penalty going beyond such a limited measure of reformative correction can rightly be imposed, under any circumstances, by any private person (even as head of a family). For such persons are not judges. They lack the detachment which becomes possible in principle when the *persona publica* is differentiated from the *persona privata*.

That differentiation of *personae*, of roles, impressed Aquinas very greatly. It is the basis, for example, of his rigorous teaching (rejected by distinguished colleagues) that judges, because they act as *personae publicae*, must in all cases proceed only on evidence legally admissible before them, and never on their private knowledge, even when that is certain and would entitle someone accused of a capital offense to be acquitted.[155] And the differentiation is also, for Aquinas, a principal component in the "rule of law which is not the rule of men."[156] Not that Aquinas thinks the rule of law is *ultimately* a matter of institutional arrangements; rather, it is a matter of doing what can be done to see that the state is ruled by *"reason*, i.e. by law which is a prescription of reason (dictamen rationis), or by somebody who acts according to reason" (rather than by "men, i.e. according to whim and passion").[157] Still, there must be judges, people appointed to adjudicate, especially when the facts disputed and/or the dispute about them are issues of justice affecting the peace of the community. But Aquinas's principal appeal to the Aristotelian "rule (governance) of law" is for the purpose of arguing that as far as possible there should be laws to determine in advance what the judges are to decide; the fewest possible matters (paucissima) should be left to judicial discretion.[158]

Indeed, one can say that for Aquinas the whole construction of a strictly "public" realm is *by* law and *for* law. Both when working in the Platonic/Aristotelian paradigm of the *civitas*, as the civil and "complete community,"[159] and when shifting to the Jewish and perhaps Roman equivalent, the *populus*, Aquinas forcefully affirms the centrality of law in the political: "it belongs to the very notion of a *people* (ad rationem populi) that people's [the members'] dealings with each other be regulated by just precepts of law."[160]

And as we have seen, law—the central case of coercive law made and enforced by persons with public responsibility—appropriately requires of its subjects, not that they be or become persons of all-round virtue, but that they respect and uphold justice and peace. The justice and peace which the state's law rightly seeks to secure are, of course, often violated in private, within families or between the parties to private dealings. The public good of justice is not restricted to "public spaces" or the transaction of public business. It can be desirable to get the rule of law into some private relationships which otherwise will become the occasion of injustice, of wrong done by one person to another.

"Public good prevails over private good,"[161] and private good should be "related (ordinari) to public good as if (sicut) to an end."[162] Such statements about the relationship between private and public or common good are frequent in Aquinas's work.[163] But they must be understood with precision, and read as compatible with what we have seen him clearly asserting: that there are private goods that prevail over public or other common good; the state's rulers cannot intervene in private relationships and transactions to secure purposes other than justice and peace; the individual good, the common good of a family, and the common good of the state are irreducibly diverse; and private persons need not regard their lives as lived for the sake of the state and its purposes.[164]

The human common good—now understanding that phrase without restriction to the state's or political community's good—is promoted, and love of neighbor is intelligently put into practice, when the common good that specifies the jurisdiction of state government and law is acknowledged to be neither all-inclusive nor (with one qualification) basic, but limited and (except perhaps for restorative justice) instrumental. We should not deny that this is made clearer by the Church's teaching during this century, teaching expounded with fresh clarity by Grisez in *Living a*

Christian Life. But we may add, as a historical footnote, that amid very different, obfuscating circumstances and concerns, St. Thomas had reached the same *sententia*.

NOTES

1.   Germain Grisez, *The Way of the Lord Jesus* vol. 2 *Living a Christian Life* (Quincy, Illinois: Franciscan Press, 1993), 850.

2.   As to "religious liberty," however, I shall in this essay leave aside altogether both "recent Church teaching" and Aquinas's position. Each is quite complex.

3.   Ibid., 836.

4.   Thus Grisez uses "government" where Leo Strauss would say "regime," and vice versa.

5.   So *civitas* in the treatise on law is treated as synonymous with *gens* (e.g., S.T. I–II q.105 a.1c) and *populus* (q.96 a.1c with q.98 a.6 ad 2).

6.   S.T. I–II q.21 a.4 ad 3; In Eth. V.2 n.4 [903]; In Pol. I.1 n.3 [11]; III.6 n.5 [395]; likewise *societas politica*: Contra Impug. II c. 2c.

7.   S.T. I–II q.100 a.2c; In Pol. I.1 n.33 [41]; II.8 n.6 [259]. Likewise *communitas civilis*: In Eth. VIII.12 n.19 [1720].

8.   What Grisez calls the state and Aquinas the *civitas* or *societas/communitas civilis/politica* is called by Maritain the body politic; what Grisez calls government and Aquinas *princeps/principatus*, *praelatus/praelatio*, etc., Maritain calls the State, that *part* of the body politic which specializes in the interests of the whole, a set of institutions entitled to use coercion, and so forth: Jacques Maritain, *Man and the State* ([1951] London: Hollis & Carter, 1954), 8–11; *Oeuvres Complètes* vol. IX (Fribourg & Paris, 1990), 490–95. Much the same distinctions are being drawn by the three writers, but, precisely in terms of those distinctions, the word "state" is used in opposing senses (each rooted in common speech) by Grisez and Maritain. I here follow Grisez's usage (as also in ignoring Maritain's distinction between "individual" and "person").

9.   Aquinas calls these, too, *civitates*; only the context shows that in such cases he does not mean a "complete community."

10.   He speaks, for example, of quasi-federal arrangements whereby a single king rules over a number of different *civitates* each of which is ruled by different laws and ministers: S.T. I q.108 a.1c.

11.   De Reg. II c.5 [123, 126]; In Pol. II.4 n.1; In Meta. II.5 n.3.

12.   So in the treatise on law *civitas* is treated as synonymous with *gens* (e.g., S.T. I–II q.105 a.1c) and *populus* (q.96 a.1c with q.98 a.6 ad 2).

13.   Though treating the state very much as if it were the only politically organized people in the world, Aquinas's account also holds that the statewide common good which the state's laws are to promote and protect is but part of a wider common good. For this community is but part of a wider whole (see In

Eth. I.2 n.12 [30] and ultimately of the whole community of the universe (tota communitas universi) (S.T. I–II q.91 a.1c). Law makers' *prudentia*, justice, and fully reasonable directiveness towards the common good of their own *communitas perfecta* must be informed by, and consistent with, the law of a universal community—a law which as understood and shared in by us is called the natural law (lex naturalis; lex naturae; ius naturale). What the organization of that universal community really is remains, philosophically speaking, to be determined. But it must extend at least as wide as the whole of humanity, present and future. That is not to say that Aquinas is articulating a duty to future generations, or envisaging an international law, or an actually worldwide government; nor that any or all of these would exhaust the significance of the open-endedness of the common good even of a community stipulated to be "complete."

14. Aquinas's methodological decision is not, of course, a decision to regard the *civitas* as internally static or as free from external enemies. Revolutions and wars, flourishing, corruption, and decay, are firmly on the agenda, but not the question which people are or are entitled to be a *civitas*.

15. See S.T. I–II q.5 a.5c: 'the imperfect *beatitudo* attainable in this life can be acquired with natural human capacities, in the way that people can acquire virtue, in whose working out in action it [imperfect *beatitudo*] consists [virtus, in cuius operatione consistit]; likewise q.4 a.6c, a.7c & a.8c; In Eth. I.13 nn.4–7 [157–160].

16. See S.T. I–II q.90 a.2c: "perfecta communitas civitas est"; q.90 a.3 ad 3; II–II q.65 a.2 ad 2; De Reg. I.2 [14]; In Pol. I.1 n.23 [31]: "civitas est communitas perfecta"; see also S.T. II–II q.50 a. 1c: "communita[s] perfecta[] civitatis vel regni."

17. Aquinas's implicit procedure hereabouts is similar to his explicit procedure in relation to *beatitudo* (see S.T. I–II q.3 a.2 ad 2; q.5 a.3c & 8c; see also II Sent. d.38 q.1 a.2 ad 2; IV Sent. d.49 q.1 a.3c; SCG IV c.95 n.7): give first a merely formal description, a *communis ratio*, a general or formal idea; then find the appropriate *specialis ratio*, the critically defensible, morally substantive account attainable by attending to the human goods at stake and their directiveness.

18. See S.T. II–II q.58 a.5c.

19. I–II q.91 a.4c.

20. I–II q.96 a.2 ad 2.

21. I–II q.93 a.3 ad 3.

22. Politics III.5: 1280b11–14 (Aquinas's commentary stops at 1280a6, but see In Pol. prol. n.4; I.1 n.23 [31] and, more clearly, De Reg. II c.3 {I,14] [106] (at n.76)). See also VII.12:1332a28–b12; Nicomachean Ethics X.9:1179b32–1180a5; Fred. D. Miller, *Nature, Justice, and Rights in Aristotle's* Politics (Oxford University Press, 1995), 225, 360; Robert P. George, *Making Men Moral* (Oxford University Press, 1993), 21–28.

23. Politics III.5:1280b33–35, 1281a1–4.

24. S.T. I–II q.90 a.3 ad 2. See Nic. Eth. X.9:1179b31–1180a22; In Eth. X. 14 nn.13–18 [2149–2154]. Other passages affirming that the point of law is to use its coerciveness in the promotion of virtue: In Eth. I.14 n.10 [174]; II.1 n.7 [251]. Passages making the same sort of point without special reference to the coercive power of law: In Eth. I.19 n.2 [225]; V.2 n.5 [904]; V.3 nn.12–13 [924–5].

25. In Eth. X.14 n.17 [2153].

26. In *Eth*. X.15 n.4 [2158] & n. 5 [2159]: "this is the only difference, that a parental precept {sermo} does not have the full coercive authority of a royal [or other *public*] precept {sermo}."

27. S.T. I–II q.98 a.1c. This important thesis was elaborately and clearly set out by Aquinas in his first version of SCG III c.121, one of about nine whole chapters which he later decided to eliminate from his draft treatment of divine law and government in SCG III. Among the material suppressed was a triplet of chapters *contrasting divine law* with the rule of tyrants, *with the rule of just kings*, and (less sharply) with the rule of human fathers. The chapter stating the disanalogy with just "kings" (i.e., with the very idea of state government) ran as follows (the emphases here as elsewhere in this essay are mine):

> *God's law does not require merely that one behave well in relation to other people (sit bene ordinatus ad alios), as the laws of just kings do.*
>
> It is not merely that divine rule is dissimilar to the rule of tyrants who for their own advantage exploit those subject to them. Rather, *divine rule also greatly differs from the rule of kings who intend their subjects' advantage.* For kings are constituted *to preserve interpersonal social life* (ad socialem vitam inter homines conservandam); that is why they are called "public persons," as if to say promoters or guardians of *public good*. And for that reason, the laws they make direct people *in their relationships with other people* (secundum quod ad alios ordinantur). *Those things*, therefore, *which neither advance nor damage the common good are neither prohibited nor commanded* by *human* laws.
>
> God, however, is concerned not only with ruling the human multitude, but also with what is in itself good for each person individually. For he is the creator and governor of nature, and the good of nature is realized not simply in the multitude but also in persons in themselves—each one. And so *God* commands and prohibits *not only those things by which one human being is related* (ordinatur) *to another*, but also those things according to which human persons are, in themselves (secundum se), disposed well or badly. Here what St Paul says is relevant: "The will of God is that you be made *holy* {sanctificatio}."
>
> In this way we exclude the error of those who say that only what harms or corrupts one's neighbor {quibus proximus aut offenditur aut scandalizatur} is sinful. (*Opera Omnia* [Leonine ed.], vol. 14, 46* col. 1).

The passage clearly affirmed that just state law does not prescribe or prohibit thoughts, dispositions, intentions, choices, or actions which affect only the person whose will or deed they are. State law does not properly have as its responsibility the preservation or promotion of the all-round virtue, let alone the sanctification, of the individual subject, precisely as such. Its role is only to preserve and promote the common good, understood not as every true good in which human beings can share, but as the *public* good—a matter of interpersonal dealings, of specifically *social* life.

Although Aquinas eventually excised the (carefully revised) chapters which include this text, every part of the striking political thesis it articulates appears in the *Summa Theologiae*, if not always as clearly. The complex story of the composition of this part of SCG III is recounted in *Opera Omnia* (Leonine) vol. 14, Preface pp. viii–xxi, and Appendix pp. 3*, 42*–44*. The critical editor who analyzed the intricate series of changes judges that Aquinas's motive was concern for the internal logic of this *Summa* as a whole: see esp. pp. xi–xii. (The revision's goal was a treatment more economical and more tightly aligned with the general themes of the work as a whole. Divine law would now be explained, not by comparing and contrasting it with human law and government—which are nowhere discussed in SCG—but by appeal to other theological themes.) The shift in strategy affects material now mostly (but not entirely) found distributed from c.110 to c.139.

28. S.T. I–II q.98 a.1c; the passage continues: "The purpose of divine law is to lead one to the end (finis) of eternal fulfillment (felicitas), an end which is blocked by any sin, and not merely by external acts but also by interior ones. And so what suffices for the perfection of human law, viz., that it prohibit wrongdoing (peccata) and impose punishments, does not suffice for the perfection of divine law; what that needs is that one be made completely ready for participation in eternal fulfilment." SCG III c.121 n.3 argues that divine law can rightly regulate our internal dispositions (interiores affectiones) as well as our external acts and dealings: "Any law rightly made induces to virtue. But virtue consists in the rational regulation not only of external acts but also of internal dispositions. Therefore . . . ." Since the *Summa contra Gentiles* as a whole steers well clear of political questions, one need not take this argument as seriously offering a proposition—"*any and every* just law seeks to *regulate* the internal disposition of its subjects"—which in relation to human law is unambiguously and repeatedly rejected by the *Summa Theologiae*: see I–II q.91 a.4c; q.98 a.1c (just quoted), and q.100 aa.2c & 9c. Rather, SCG III c.121 n.3 is employing a rapid theological argument: law is always in some way directed to virtue; but real, complete virtue—the sort that God wills people to have—involves internal dispositions; therefore . . . .

29. As the deleted SCG passage (see note 27) put it: "kings are constituted to preserve *interpersonal social life* (ad socialem vitam inter homines conservandam) . . . For that reason the laws they make direct people [*only*, unlike divine government] *in their relationships with other people* (secundum quod ad alios ordinantur).

30. So it is unlike divine government, which, as the deleted SCG passage stated, "commands and prohibits not only those things by which one human being is related (homo ad alium ordinatur) to another, but also those things according to which human persons are each, in themselves, disposed well or badly " (see fn. 27 above).

31. S.T. I–II q.100 a.2c. Aquinas here appeals to Nic. Eth. V, perhaps (as the Leonine editors suggest) V.1:1129b14–25, but more likely V.2:1130b25 (and see In Eth. V.2 n.5 [904]; V.3 nn.12–13 [924–5]), though nowhere does Aristotle make with any clarity the points which Aquinas is here concerned to assert about law's *restricted* purpose and content. At any event, the point was equally clear to Aquinas in his early writings: see e.g., III Sent. d.37 q.1 a.2 sol.2c: "civil law's precepts direct people in communications and dealings (communicationibus) which are other-directed (ad alterum), in accord with the character of political life which can only be of one human person to another (secundum vitam politicam, quae quidem non potest esse nisi hominis ad hominem)" [i.e., which cannot reach into our *societas* with God]. See likewise S.T. I–II q.99 a.5 ad 1; q.104 a.1 ad 1 & ad 3.

32. "Practical reasonableness": the virtue of *prudentia*, the instantiating of the good of reason(ableness), the *bonum rationis*: see e.g. III Sent. d.33 q.1 a.1 sol.1c & sol.2 ad 1; S.T. I–II q.94 a.3c.

33. S.T. I–II q.96 a.3c. *Disciplina*, moral education, is at least principally a matter of the young (minores): II–II q.16 a.2 ad 2. What sort Aquinas has in mind is indicated, for example, in I-II q.105 a.2 ad 1: law should seek to accustom people to getting along together easily (assuefacere ut facile sibi invicem sua communicarent), which involves give and take (not being too concerned if someone passing through one's vineyard eats some of the grapes); people who are well brought up, *disciplinati*, are not disturbed by this sort of thing; indeed their *amicitia* with their fellow-citizens is strengthened by it, and getting along together easily (facilis communicatio) is thereby confirmed and encouraged. It goes without saying that the *disciplina* includes many negative elements, such as the vigorous discouragement of acts such as homicide, theft, and so forth, which prejudice the maintenance of any decent *societas humana* (I–II q.96 a.2c) unless both prohibited and discouraged.

34. Aquinas treats *ecclesia* and *respublica* in parallel: S.T. II–II q.31 a.3 ad 3; q.43 a.8c; Contra Impug. II c.2 ad 10 [67]; III Sent. d.9 q.2 a.3 ad 3. The Church resembles the political rather than the domestic (oeconomica) community (ecclesia similatur congegationi politicae): IV Sent. d.20 q.1 a.4 sol.1c.

35. SCG III c.80 nn.14, 15: "in rebus humanis est aliquod bonum commune, quod quidem est bonum civitatis vel gentis. . . . Est etiam aliquod bonum quod non in communitate consistit, sed ad unumquemque pertinet secundum seipsum; non tamen uni soli est utile, sed multis; sicut quae sunt ab omnibus et singulis credenda et servanda, sicut ea quae sunt fidei et cultus divinus et alia huiusmodi." And see S.T. q. 99a.3c.

36. III Sent. d.37 q.1 a.2 sol.2c (fn. 31 above).

37. S.T. I–II q.100 a.2c (text at fn. 31 above).

38. On the senses in which justice is and is not for the sake of peace, see SCG III c.34 n.2; c.128 n.6; S.T. II–II q.29 a.3 ad 3.

39. S.T. II–II q.29 a.1c & ad 1; a.2 ad 2.

40. I–II q.99 a.2c.

41. *Opera* vol. 14 Appendix p. 43*.

42. S.T. II–II q.38 a.1c; a serious form of immoral *contentio* is deliberately attacking truth and justice (veritatem iustitiae) in court: ad 3.

43. II–II q.41 a.1c & ad 3.

44. II–II q.42 a.1.

45. II–II q.40 a.1.

46. II–II q.29 a.1 ad 1; q.45 a.6c.

47. II–II q.29 a.3c: for "this [neighbor love] involves being willing to do one's neighbor's will even as one's own."

48. The state's rulers (politici) have a responsibility for providing their *civitas* with these economic necessities, though the provision itself will normally be by traders (negotiatores) who act not because they have a duty but for profit (propter lucrum quaerendum): S.T. II–II q.77 a.4c.

49. De Reg. I c.2 [17]. It is a peace which is compatible with even tyranny: De Reg. I c.6 [44].

50. Quodlibet XI q.15 a.2: intendit civilis legislator . . . pacem servare et stare inter cives . . . ; a.3 ad 1: although wrongfully dispossessed owners have no action at civil law, they do have according to divine law "whose purpose is the salvation of souls."

51. S.T. I–II q.96 a.3c (fn. 33 above); see also q.99 a.5 ad 1; In Eth. V.3 n.13 [925].

52. See George, *Making Men Moral* 28–31; Grisez, note 1; Finnis, "Liberalism and Natural Law Theory," *Mercer Law Rev.* 45 (1994): 687 at 695.

53. See De Reg. prol. [1]; this dedication to the King of Cyprus states that the exposition will be "according to the *authority of the holy scriptures* and the teachings of philosophers, as well as the practice of worthy princes" and will rely throughout on the help of God who is King of Kings, etc.

54. "Inachevé, peut-être accidenté, . . . cet opuscule se présente dans des conditions un peu difficiles; elles imposent prudence et discrétion dans le recours à son texte comme expression de la pensée de l'auteur': Dondaine in Aquinas, *Opera Omnia* vol. 42 (1979), 424. See also Eschmann in Aquinas, *On Kingship* (Pontifical Institute of Mediaeval Studies, Toronto, 1949), p. xxx (dating the work to 1260–1265); pp. xxii–xxvi (holding that *De Regno* is a posthumously edited collection of unrevised and somewhat jumbled pages). Eschmann himself later rejected Aquinas's authorship of the work, though perhaps rather equivocally; see Eschmann "St. Thomas Aquinas on the Two Powers," Mediaeval Studies 20 (1958), 195–6; Weisheipl, *Friar Thomas D'Aquino* Catholic University of America Press, Washington, DC, (1983), 434 n. 6; Dondaine (op. cit.), 423. The later Leonine editor (Dondaine, 421–424) plausibly concludes that it is substantially by Aquinas, and favors a later date before 1268.

55. For example, IV Sent. d.49 q.1 a.2 sol.2 ad 4; I–II q.3 a.2 ad 4 & a.3.

56. De Reg. II c.3 [I, 14] [106–109].

57. Ibid. [110 (primacy of the Pope in administering this regimen); 111]; II c.4 [I, 15] c.16 [15] [114].

58. De Reg. II c.3 [I, 14] [110, 111].

59. De Reg. II c.4 [I, 15] [115].

60. Ibid. [120].

61. De Reg. II c.4 [I, 15] [119].

62. S.T. I–II q.95 a.1c; SCG III c.121 n.3 (note 28); In Eth. II.1 n.7 [251]; V.3 n.12 [924].

63. IV Sent. d.15 q.3 a.4 sol.1 ad 3; S.T. I–II q.96 a.3 ad 2; q.100 a.9 ad 1.

64. S.T. I–II q.96 a.3 ad 2; q.100 a.9 ad 2; II Sent. 28 q.1 a.3c & ad 3; IV Sent. 15 q.3 a.4 sol.4 ad 3; Eth. II.1 n.7 [251].

65. On the unity or connectedness (interdependence) of the virtues, see especially S.T. I–II q.65 a.1; De Virt. q.5 a.2; III Sent. d.36 q.1 a.1c.

66. A clear statement, though directly concerned with ecclesiastical jurisdiction, is In I Tim. c.5.3 ad v.20 [221]: "The role of judges is public (iudex gerit personam publicam), and so they ought to have as their goal the common good (intendere bonum commune), which is harmed by public wrongdoing—because many people are corrupted (scandalizantur) by the example this gives. And so

ecclesiastical judges ought to impose public punishments of a kind that will instruct and encourage others (ut alii aedificentur)." Aquinas's constant references to conduct which is corruptive of character ("scandalizes" in the theologian's sense of that word), not least the reference at the end of the excised SCG text quoted at note 27, now the final sentence of SCG III c.121, suggest this, though falling short of proving it.

67.   State law can rightly prohibit conduct which is an *occasion* of evils: see IV Sent. d.15 q.3 a.1 sol.4c.

68.   See, for example, the chapter on paternal authority in the deleted section of SCG II: *Opera* vol. 14 Appendix pp. 46*–48*. Here Aquinas argued that, *unlike* the rule of just kings, paternal rule over and responsibility for children extends "not only to matters in which the child relates to other people but also to matters which pertain to the child as such (pater curam habet de filio non solum quantum ad ea in quibus ordinatur ad alios, sicut rex, sed etiam quantum ad ea quae pertinent ad ipsum secundum se)" (pp. 46*–47*). Parental rule is still restricted (unlike divine rule) to what is externally apparent, since hearts remain hidden from human beings, even parents, though some aspects of the child's dispositions will doubtless be externally expressed and parents can be concerned with these (quatenus per exteriores actus interior dispositio explicatur).

69.   Contra Impug. II c.2 ad 10 [68]; In Eth. X. 14 n.13 [2149]; IV Sent. d.15 q.3 a.1 sol.4c.

70.   S.T. I–II q.95 a.1c.

71.   I–II q.96 a.3 ad 3; q.100 a.9; IV Sent. d.15 q.3 a.4 sol.1 ad 3.

72.   For example, S.T. I–II q.92 a.1; In Eth. I. 19 n.2 [225];

73.   For example, In Eth. V. 3 n.14 [926]; In Pol. III.3.

74.   S.T. I–II q.92 a.1c: inducere subiectos ad propriam *ipsorum* virtutem.

75.   ibid.: non bonos . . . simpliciter, sed secundum quid, scilicet in ordine ad tale regimen.

76.   De Reg. II c.3 (I, 14) [106]. The next paragraph [107] looks beyond the imperfect beatitude of living virtuously and concludes that the ultimate end of the community, which is the same as the ultimate end of an individual, is to attain the fruition of perfect beatitude (per virtuosam vitam pervenire ad fruitionem divinam).

77.   E.G. S.T. I–II q.107 a.2c: "the purpose of any law is that people become just and people of virtue (iusti et virtuosi)"; II Sent. d.44 q.1 ad 3c: "a [third] purpose of government (praelatio) is the rectification of conduct (corrigendum mores), as when bad people are punished and coercively brought to acts of virtue" (the first two functions of governance being to give people direction in their activities, and to make up for weaknesses [as when peoples are defended by kings]).

78.   Cf. the similar use of *diversi* in respect of the irreducibly distinct types of *ordo* and *scientia* discussed in In Eth. I.1 n.1 [1–2]: "secundum hos diversos ordines . . . sunt diversae scientiae" [2]. *Diversa* may differ in their very nature (essentia) (I q.31 a.2c & ad 1) and/or in their way of originating (Cred. 4).

79.   S.T. II–II q.48 a.1c; q.47 a.11 ("the good of individuals, the good of families, and the good of *civitas* or realm are different ends (diversi fines); so there

are necessarily different species of *prudentia* corresponding to this difference in their respective ends: (i) *prudentia* without qualification (simpliciter dicta), which is directed (ordinat[ur]) toward one's own good; (ii) domestic prudence directed toward the common good of household or family, and (iii) political prudence directed toward the common good of state or realm"); q.50 a.1c (the form of political prudence which is proper to state rulers is the most perfect form of prudence because it extends to more things and attains a further end than the other species of prudence).

    80.   S.T. II–II q.48 a.1c; q.50 a.4. If military prudence deserves its place as a fourth species of *prudentia*, it is because it shares in the open-endedness of political prudence—is, so to speak, the extension of political prudence into the external hazard of war in which the whole life of the *civitas* and its elements is at stake: see II–II q.50 a.4 ad 1 & ad 2.

    81.   II–II q.48 a.1c; "tota vita" is short for "the common end of the whole of human life" (communis finis totius humanae vitae) and "the good of the whole of life" (bonum totius vitae): q.47 a.13c & ad 3.

    82.   II–II q.50 a.2 (note that in the preamble to this *quaestio*, the prudence of rulers (regnativa) is called the prudence involved in law-making [legispositiva]).

    83.   SCG III c.71 n.4. What are these responsibilities? Marriage is one natural responsibility (officium naturae humanae) with which human law is rightly concerned (IV Sent. d.27 q.1 a.3 sol.1 ad 1; d.31 q.1 a.2c & a.3 sed contra 2; d.39 q.1 a.2 ad 3) and is a community responsibility (in officium communitatis) (d.34 q.1 a.1 ad 4).

    84.   In leaving unprohibited the acts of certain vices (e.g., selling at unfair prices; or sex between unmarried adults), government does not approve them: S.T. I–II q.93 a.3 ad 3; II–II q.77 a.1 ad 1.

    85.   In Eth. I.2 n.12–13 [30–31]; In Pol. prol. n.7 [7].

    86.   See IV Sent. d.2 q.1 a.3 ad 3.

    87.   S.T. II–II q.50 a.2 ad 1; see also In Eth. VI.7 n.7 [1201].

    88.   S.T. I–II q.92 a.1 ad 3.

    89.   In other contexts, too, Aquinas will use the term "common good" to refer to some good which falls short of, and is instrumental to, a more ultimate common good. Thus he will say that "the army's leader intends the common good, that is to say [not peace and the state's common weal, nor even victory, but rather] the whole army's order (intendit bonum commune, scilicet ordinem totius exercitus)": S.T. I–II q.9 a.1c.

    90.   S.T. I–II q.96 a.2 ad 2, citing Proverbs 30:33, and arguing that human law is to bring people to virtue gradually, lest, being pushed too hard, they break out into worse wrongdoing.

    91.   S.T. II–II q.104 a.5.

    92.   He appeals, ibid. to Seneca's teaching that even the servitude of the Roman slave does not rightly include the better part (melior pars) of the human being; one's mind (mens), which is in charge of and responsible for itself (sui iuris).

    93.   S.T. II–II q.104 a.5c; he mentions the preservation (sustenantatio) of one's body, and propagation. See also IV Sent. d.36 q.1 a.2c: servants/serfs (servi) are not subject to their masters in any way that would restrict their freedom to eat, sleep and "do other things like that, pertaining to the body's needs"—or their freedom to marry.

94. Ibid. For this proposition see also S.T. I q.113 a.2 ad 3; II Sent. d.44 q.1 a.3 ad 1 (natura omnes homines aequales in libertate fecit); and likewise De Ver. 11 a.3c; In Rom. 9.3 ad v. 14 [766].

95. Among the matters in which one's freedom can rightfully prevail over all human commands are the decision not to marry someone: ibid. Of course, marriage necessarily concerns justice, not least because it is likely to result in children; so state laws can regulate the general conditions of marriage (De Malo q.15 a.2 ad 12; IV Sent. d.39 q.1 a.2 ad 3)—minimal age, incest bounds, and so forth—if they do so with fairness and humanity and in ways genuinely related to the true "political good" (SCG IV c.78 n.2). But even if doing so would advance some public policy or the well-being of a family or church or state, neither the state's officials nor any domestic or religious authorities can rightly compel anyone to marry, or to marry this person, or forbid the marriage of two consenting adults who are not within the classes of persons reasonably disqualified or forbidden to marry (S.T. II–II q.104 a.5c; IV Sent. d.29 q.1 a.4; d.36 q.1 a.2).

96. IV Sent. d.38 q.1 a.4 sol.1c.

97. Another matter outside the rightful power of state government and law is the decision to take religious vows, for example, of virginity; here "private good" is more weighty (potius) than, preferable (excellentior) to, public or common good, because it belongs (Aquinas judges) to a different, higher genus than the common good of continued bodily propagation of the human species (S.T. II–II q.152 a.4 ad 3).

98. S.T. II–II q.88 a.8 ad 2; IV Sent. q.1 sol.3 ad 2.

99. Those who can "freely dispose of their own persons (libere de sua persona disponere)" (S.T. II–II q.189 a.6 ad 2); a daughter is not her father's maid-servant (ancilla), and he has no power over her body (and so from the age of puberty [II–II q.88 a.8 ad 2], she can make her own decisions, for example, enter religious life without parental consent) "because she is a free person" (IV Sent. d.28 q.1 a.3 ad 1).

100. For example, I–II q.100 a.9c: "it does not belong to human beings to judge any save external acts, for 'human beings see [only] those things which show' (1 Kings 16:7)." So even parental rule, which resembles divine government more closely than state rule does (because unlike state rule it can rightly concern itself with its subjects not merely as citizens but as what they are [secundum quod in sua natura subsist(unt)]), is restricted to "those things which are externally evidenced about someone (illa . . . quae in homine apparent exterius)" (*Opera* vol. 14 p. 47*, excised from SCG III after c.121.

101. See e.g. De Malo q.16 a.8c.

102. S.T. II–II q.33 a.7 ad 5; De Secreto 2 [1217].

103. See De Secreto 1–3 [1216].

104. S.T. II–II q.33 a.7c: "those secret sins which are physically or spiritually harmful to one's neighbors. . . ." De Secreto 6 [1222] instances theft or arson in a [communal] house. Aquinas's six colleagues on the 1269 Dominican consultative commission were less willing than him to regard the public interest as overriding the entitlement to keep secrets private. See also S.T. II–II q.68 a.1 ad 3.

105.   S.T. II–II q.33 a.7 ad 5; Quodl. IV q.8 a.1c; De Secreto 4 & 5 [1219, 1221].

106.   S.T. II–II q.88 a.8 ad 2 (suae potestatis); q. 189 a.5c (propriae potestatis); a.6 ad 2.

107.   Puberty (usually about age 14 in males, 12 in females) is significant for these purposes as being the age by which most people can make proper use of reason in deliberation (debitum usum rationis): II–II q.189 a.5c.

108.   In Eth. 1 n.2 [5]; S.T. I–II q.17 a.4c; III q.8 a.1 ad 2; in De Malo q.4 a.1c note the *quasi*.

109.   SCG III c.123 n.6 [2964]: between husband and wife there is evidently the greatest friendship (maxima amicitia).

110.   That is, one of the human goods (bona humana) directed to by the first principles of human action (prima principia operum humanorum): S.T. I–II q.94 a.1 ad 2; a.2c; also II–II q.47 a.6c; q.56 a.1c; De Ver. q.5 a.1c.

111.   As in IV Sent. d.26 q.1 a.1c; also in S.T. I–II q.94 a.2c read with (i) its reference to Justinian's Digest I.1.1 as read in IV Sent. d.26 q.1 a.1 sed contra and implicitly in In Eth. V.12 n.4 [1019], and (ii) In Matt. c.19 ad vv.4, 5; SCG III c.123 n.7 [2965]. Also IV Sent. d.26 q.1 a.3 ad 4.

112.   Critique of alternatives to marriage and family: In Pol II.1 n.7 [175]–.5 n.2 [208].

113.   In Eth. VIII.12 n.19 [1720]; also n.18 [1719]; Nic. Eth. VIII.12: 1162a17–18.

114.   In Eth. VIII.12 n. 19 [1720].

115.   Ibid. nn.22–25 [1721–24]; IV Sent. d.34 q.1 a.2 ad 3.

116.   De Reg. II c.3 [I,14] [106]: "if the ultimate end [of the human multitude] were abundance of wealth (divitiarum affluentia), the economist (economus) would be king."

117.   In Pol. I.8 n.4 [125].

118.   S.T. II–II q.50 a.3 ad 2; In Eth. I.1 n.15 [15]; In I Tim. c.3.2 ad v.5 [104]: "wealth is not the end of economics but an instrument."

119.   S.T. II–II q.50 a.3 ad 2.

120.   So the other and more basic meaning of "economist" (oeconomus) is "a family's *procurator* and *dispensator*," the person who nurtures and distributes the family's goods: In Pol. I.1 n.5 [13]. "The one in charge of a family (gubernator) is called a *dispensator* as being the one who with due weight and in due measure distributes to each member of the family the tasks and necessities of [their common] life": S.T. I–II q.97 a.4c.

121.   In Pol. III.5 n.5 [388].

122.   S.T. I–II q.105 a.2c: " . . . and so private persons can have voluntary dealings with each other in relation to these possessions, for example, buying, selling, making gifts, and other things of that sort." The article proceeds to explain the need for state law to remedy the difficulties that arise in connexion with such dealings. Thus, as q. 104 a.1 ad 1 says, "rulers (princ[ipes]) have authority not only to regulate (ordinare) matters in dispute but also the voluntary contracts which people make, and indeed everything which pertains to a people's *communita[s] et regimen*."

123.   Thus a large trade fair or market is a public association (albeit temporary) of traders: Contra Impug. II c.2 [57] note 146.

124. The only seeming exceptions to this are texts in which his commentary tracks Aristotle's argument that we are more naturally conjugal *than political*. Here "political" does refer to the political whole of which marital communities are parts: In Eth. VIII.12 nn.18–19 [1719–20].

125. S.T. I–II q.72 a.4c; IV Sent. d.26 q.1 a.1c.

126. SCG III c.85 n.11.

127. In Periherm. I.2 n.2.

128. In Eth. IX. 10 n.7 [1891]; see also De Reg. I c.1 [4–8].

129. S.T. I–II q.61 a.5c (and see ad4); In Trin. II q.3 a.1 sed contra 3.

130. Outside the commentary on the *Politics*, the notion that individuals and/or households are (naturally) parts of the *civitas* is stated at S.T. I–II q.90 a.2c; a.3 ad 3; q.92 a.1 ad 3; II–II q.47 a.11 ad 2; q.50 a.3c; q.59 a.3 ad 2; Contra Impug. II c.2 ad 3. The subjunctive conditional in S.T. I–II q.60 a.5c casts doubt on the appropriateness of calling people *naturally* parts of a particular *civitas*.

131. At the relevant point in In Pol. I.1 n.20 [28], the neighborhood community is judged natural, alongside (or between) the family and the *civitas*.

132. "*Animal naturaliter civile*" translates the same Greek phrase as "*animal naturaliter politicum*." It is used only in In Eth. I.9 n.10 [112]; In Pol. I.1 nn.24,26,28,29 [32,34,36,37]. The naturalness of the *civitas* is stated in In Pol. I.1 nn.23,24,29,32 (which also states that we have within us a natural *impetus* to political community [communitas civitatis] as we have to the virtues).

133. See e.g. S.T. I–II q.71 a.2c; q.94 a.3 ad 2.

134. See note 110.

135. S.T. I–II q.94 a.2c. See also Contra Impug. II c.2c: "societas nihil aliud esse videatur quam adunatio hominum ad unum aliquid communiter agendum. . . . adunatio hominum ad aliquid unum perficiendum . . . divers[ae] communicationes . . . nihil aliud sunt quam societates quaedam . . . [or] amiciti[ae]."

136. In Eth. I.9 n.10 [112].

137. So the whole complex of human goods can be called our "civil and natural good (bonum civile at naturale hominis)," to which our will (i.e., our response to *understood* goods) has a natural, premoral inclination: III Sent. d.33 q.2 a.4 sol.3c. Now *civilis* in this sense is a common thirteenth theological term for "secular", referring to this world as distinct from our heavenly *patria*. Still, as q.1 a.4c makes clear, Aquinas welcomes the "political" connotation of *civilis* even in this sort of context; for in one's spiritual life one is *civis civitatis Dei*, citizen in a realm which, unlike our earthly *civilitas*, will not be left behind (evacuabitur) but rather perfected.

138. The paternal power (authority) of admonition is inadequate in the face of rebels and contumacious offenders: S.T. I–II q.105 a.4 ad 5.

139. S.T. II–II q.66 aa.2 & 3.

140. See De Reg. I c.2 [20]: the fruits of good government are peace, justice, and *affluentia rerum*; and note 48. For the sake of economic benefits (commoditates), government and law can rightly permit (though never promote) certain economic injuries (e.g., unjust transactions such as usurious loans): Mal. q.13 a.4 ad 6; S.T. II–II q.78 a.1 ad 3.

141. Sometimes called the civil good (bonum civile); see, for example, De Virt. q.5 a.4 ad 4: the purpose of legislation (and of the military art) is the preservation of the civil good (conservatio boni civilis est finis et terminus militaris et legis positivae).

142. S.T. I q.96 a.4; cf. II Sent. d.44 q.1 ad 5 (omitting this reason for *dominium* and *praelatio* in paradise).

143. See In Eth. I.1 n.2 [4].

144. In Eth. X.14 n.17 [2153]; S.T. I–II q.67 a.1c; q.90 a.3 ad 2 (persona privata non . . . habet vim coactivam; quam debet habere lex). Note that a leader of the domestic community (an *imperfecta communitas*) has the "incomplete" coercive power of imposing rather light penalties, penalties which do no irreparable harm (beating): I–II q.87 a.8 ad 3; II–II q.65 a.2 ad 2; IV Sent. d.37 q.2 a.1 ad 4. But fundamentally, paternal discipline is by admonition (monitiones; potestas admonendi): S.T. I–II q.95 a.1c; q.100 a.11 ad 3; q.105 a.4 ad 5; see also In I Tim. c.1.3 ad v.9 [23].

145. In a secondary sense of "law," the household or family is governed by the order imposed by its leader's "law and precept (ordo per legem et praeceptum)" (Meta. XII.12 n.8), "precepts or standing orders (praecepta vel statuta)" which [because not fully coercive] do not strictly speaking (proprie) have the character (ratio) of law (I–II q.90 a.3 ad 2 & ad 3).

146. Since "public" and "private" are analogous rather than univocal terms, the line between them can be drawn in other ways in other contexts. So, for example, in Impug. II c.2, where the context is the admission of monks and friars to universities hitherto composed of other sorts of clerics, Aquinas undertakes a sketch of the difference between public and private: public societies (societates; communicationes) include the *civitas* or *regnum* (perpetual), traders foregathering at large trade fairs or markets (temporary), and the university (studium generale); private societies include families (perpetual), two friends or associates in a hostel (temporary), and colleges within the university. But his definitions of "public" and "private," in terms of the type of matters with which they are respectively concerned (*respublica* versus *negotium privatum*) are unhelpfully circular. So the issue in the texts in question is not to be settled by attending to the words "public" and "private," taken out of their context in the questions about coercion and adjudication.

147. The *custodia iustitiae*, as a response to wrongdoing, is a *commune bonum* which is committed to a ruler (praelatus) as *persona publica*: IV Sent. d.19 q.2 a.1 ad 6.

148. II Sent. d.44 q.2 a.1c.

149. S.T. II–II q.67 a.3 ad 3: homo non potest esse simul accusator, iudex, et testis.

150. See II–II q.60 a.6c & ad 1.

151. S.T. II–II q.65 a.2 ad 2; in the household the father has, not full governmental authority (perfecta potestas regiminis), but a rulership analogous to (similitudo) the government of a realm (regii principatus): q. 50 a3 ad 3.

152. IV Sent. d.37 q.2 a.1 sed contra. Aquinas uses exactly the same phrase to state that husband and wife are equals in their right to marital intercourse (In Cor. VII.1 ad v.3 [321]) and in their right to marital separation (IV Sent. d.35 q.1 a.4c).

153. IV Sent. d. 37q.2 a.1ad 1. The point is dramatized by Aquinas's view

that the husband in such a case can rightly lay a charge against the adulterous wife in the state's courts, and that he can even seek her execution, if such is the legal penalty and he does so "only out of concern for justice and without being moved by any vindictive ill-will or by hatred" (d.37 q.2 a.1c).

154. IV Sent. d.37 q.2 a.1 ad 4.

155. S.T. II–II q.67 a.2; q.64 a.6 ad 3: the judge in such a case should make exceptional efforts to obtain admissible evidence entitling the accused to be acquitted.

156. On "the rule of law and not of men," see In Eth. V.11 n.10 [1009].

157. Ibid. *Dictamen* in Aquinas signifies the content of rational (even if mistaken) practical judgment (sententia vel dictamen rationis) (e.g. II Sent. 24 q.2 a.4c), and is thus frequently used by him to refer (i) to the content of one's conscience (e.g. "conscience is a *dictamen* of reason": II Sent. 24 q.2 a.4c; likewise I–II q.19 a.5c; "the judgment (iudicium) or *dictamen* of reason, the judgment which is conscience": II Sent. 39 q.3 a.3c), and (ii) to the requirements of natural moral law and of "natural reason" (naturalis ratio): "moral precepts are in accord with human nature because they are the requirements/prescriptions (de dictamine) of natural reason": IV Sent. 2 q.1 a.4 sol.1 ad 2; likewise I–II q.99 a.4c; q.100 a.11c; q.104 a.1c.

158. S.T. I–II q.95 a.1 ad 2: for it is easier to find the relatively few people of practical reasonableness (sapientes) needed to enact decent laws (rectae leges) than the many people needed to reach sound judgments (ad recte iudicandum) in court; legislation can be long-mediated, but many judgments have to be given in circumstances of some urgency (subito); and legislative judgments, being concerned with matters both general and future, are less likely to be corrupted by affection, ill-will, or some other desire arising in relation to present and pressing litigants and circumstances. Few people left to assess the justice of a case without close direction by law can be trusted to give a just judgment (iustitia animata iudicis non invenitur in multis).

159. To earlier references, add S.T. II–II q.161 a.1 ad 5: "civil life (vita civilis), in which the subjection of one person to another is determined according to the legal order (secundum legis ordinem)."

160. I–II q. 105 a.2c: " . . . ut communicatio hominum ad invicem iustis praeceptis legis ordinetur." Similarly II–II q.42 a.2c: the unity [of a people, whether state or kingdom] attacked by desertion is a unity of law and common welfare (iuris et communis utilitatis). When commenting on Aristotle's characterization of the "complete community" (koinônia teleios) as one arranged to secure sufficiency in the necessities of life and, beyond that, in such a way that people live in a morally good way, Aquinas adds a restrictive qualification: "*insofar as* people's lives are directed toward virtues *through state laws* (inquantum per leges civitatis ordinatur vita hominum ad virtutes)": In Pol. I.1 n.23 [31].

161. S.T. II–II q.117 a.6c.

162. IV Sent. d.19 q.2 a.1 ad 6.

163. See, for example, III Sent. d.30 q.1 a.1 ad 4; IV Sent. d.38 q.1 a.4 sol.1 ad 3.

164. Even when one recognizes that one's spouse or child has been sentenced by law justly and for the common good, one has no duty to stop wanting the punishment not to be imposed; one is fully entitled to hope that one's family's private common good will prevail in this way. In this precise sense, one can rightly *prefer* the private good of spouse, child, self, and family to the public and political common good: S.T. I–II q.19 a.10c; III q.18 a.6c: the preference does not contradict the public common good, and should not extend to willing to *impede* the public good. (It is not the sort of preference one shows in choosing one option rather than another available option which one also regards as acceptable, still less is it the sort of preference one shows in ranking two commensurables.)

PART FOUR

A Reply by Germain Grisez and Joseph M. Boyle

Response to Our Critics and Our Collaborators

GERMAIN GRISEZ AND JOSEPH BOYLE

I. AN OVERVIEW WITH A FEW CRITICISMS IN PASSING

In Grisez's Ph.D. dissertation on logical theory, he explained how St. Thomas avoids both the view that logic is a science of the general features of reality and the view that logic is the art of constructing cognitive complexes, such as sciences. The first confuses logic with metaphysics; the second, with a technique for using concepts and language to achieve a particular goal. Rather than assuming that those confused views exhaust the possibilities and embracing one of them, Thomas holds that logic bears upon an order that reason considers and, by that very consideration, makes in its own acts. Logic thus studies an order distinct from the order of nature (which reason in no way makes) and that of technique (which reason brings about outside the intellect and the will). This understanding of logic is not only consistent with, but necessary for, both a realistic metaphysics and a theory of scientific knowledge that avoids the errors of empiricism and pragmatism.

Having thus learned that reality cannot be divided adequately into what already exists independently of human thought and action, and what results from them, Grisez was not surprised, when he began working on moral philosophy in 1959, to find that some philosophers and theologians confuse the principles of ethics with theoretical knowledge of the essential features of human beings, others with the starting points of a technique for achieving some end or set of ends, and still others with various unstable combinations of the two. Grisez at once began exploring the alternative St. Thomas suggests: moral philosophy studies an order that reason, by its consideration, makes in the operations of the will—an order irreducible to the orders of nature, logic, and technique, just as they are irreducible to one another. Following up that suggestion required two inquiries: one into the volitions, especially the free choices, that are ordered by morally practical reasoning; the other into such reasoning's starting points, which are irreducible to theoretical, logical, and technical knowledge.

Of course, as Ralph McInerny, following Aristotle and St. Thomas, points out, the ultimate end or ends of practical reasoning are given by nature, and what is thus given *considered as given* can be known only theoretically. In other words, human knowledge about the natural order, the order that reason in no way makes, includes both the *knowledge that* there are irreducible starting points of morally practical knowledge, acts of the will specified by them, and free choices; and *knowledge identifying* these principles and elements of the moral order. Moreover, knowledge about these matters throws light on human capacities, and so on human nature. Consequently, much of the theoretical work done by us and our collaborators has been in philosophical anthropology. Some, of course, has been in metaphysics, including our defense of the proposition that the first principles of morality cannot be truths of philosophical anthropology or metaphysics, or be deducible from such theoretical truths.

Besides this philosophical work, in chapters thirteen through thirty-four of *Christian Moral Principles* Grisez presents a theological anthropology of sinful and redeemed human persons. In that treatise he shows how the truths of faith and the sacraments call for and shape a specifically Christian way of life, whose moral norms guide each of Jesus' followers in finding and fulfilling his or her personal vocation.

What we have just said makes it clear that various critics, including Benedict M. Ashley, O.P., misunderstand our work when they claim that we have avoided or neglected philosophical or Christian anthropology, because, they allege, we have been overly influenced by the dictum of analytic philosophy that "ought" cannot be reduced to "is." Despite its misuse by empiricists, the dictum is true: it expresses the irreducibility, already pointed out by St. Thomas, of the moral order to the other three orders. And taking this truth into account, far from leading us to avoid or neglect philosophical and Christian anthropology, has led us to set aside theoretical questions irrelevant to ethics and Christian life, and focus on relevant ones, not least the question of free choice and determinism.

During the past two or three centuries many moral theorists, including both utilitarians and Marxists, have regarded ethical-political thought as an architectonic technology for reforming society and shaping individuals' lives. Such thought focuses, not on the act of free choice, but on determinants of outward behavior, and evaluates possible courses of action as more or less efficient means that might be used to bring about states of affairs, including specific patterns of behavior by others, that are assumed to be desirable.

In studying such thought, Grisez noticed that it often combines two things: (1) the proposal that moral judgments be made by some sort of cost-benefit analysis, and (2) psychological determinism—the view that, though people really do make their own choices, they necessarily choose the option they think will better (or best) serve their purposes. But this sort of determinism is falsified by the experience of making any morally significant choice: no option appears unqualifiedly better or best; rather, interesting options offer and threaten diverse and incommensurable benefits and harms. And just as it falsifies psychological determinism, the incommensurability of benefits and harms precludes morally evaluating options for choice by comparing them with respect to prospective benefits and harms so as to determine which is likely to bring about the better or best (or less bad or least bad) overall results.

Grisez reached this position by 1963, around the time some Catholics, without denying freedom of choice, were implicitly embarking on a similar reduction of morality to technique by adopting—though initially only *ad hoc* in the contraception debate—what they later called proportionalism. As Edward C. Vacek, S.J., makes clear, part of proportionalists' difficulty with Grisez is that he focuses ethics on the operations of the will rather than on outward performances, and focuses on what individuals and groups of people do to themselves in choosing rather than on the effectiveness of their behavior considered as a means of bringing about a desired state of affairs.

Against these Catholic reductionists, we deployed the following argument: their attempt to justify exceptions to received moral norms assumes that options for choice can be morally evaluated by determining what benefits and harms they offer and threaten, measuring (or estimating) their values and/or disvalues, and comparing these measurements; but *this* commensurability is incompatible with the incommensurability presupposed by a free choice. The proportionalists responded by pointing out three things: (1) that there is a hierarchy of values, (2) that various commensurations of goods and bads are possible, often made, and even required by the older moral theology and our own theory, and (3) that people *can* make reasonable choices between (or among) alternatives that offer diverse goods and threaten diverse harms.

That response, however, missed the point. (1) Values of various *kinds* are graded in several ways, but none of their hierarchies make it possible to commensurate the diverse prospective *concrete* values and disvalues in options available for choice. (2) The commensurations of goods and bads that are compatible with free choice do not establish that one eligible option is unqualifiedly better (or less bad) than the (or any) other, but only that one option is better (or less bad) than the (or any) other in some respect. (3) People make reasonable choices between (or among) alternatives that offer diverse goods and threaten diverse harms, not by measuring (or estimating) and comparing those benefits and harms, as proportionalism proposes, but in the light of moral truths, including the Golden Rule and exceptionless norms that protect the fundamental goods of persons. (Of course, people who consider the diverse goods offered and harms threatened by two or more available options sometimes willfully ignore or set aside relevant moral truths, discern which option they feel more comfortable or less uncomfortable with, and unreasonably choose that option; in doing that, they are likely to tell themselves and others that the factors that motivated them gave good reason—a proportionate reason—for their choice, or even that those factors left no alternative to choosing as they did.)

Pressed hard to show how the diverse benefits and harms in options for choice can be commensurated, Catholic proportionalists, like the non-believing utilitarians who preceded them along the same path, retreated from their initial efforts to provide some rational way of determining proportions and fell back upon spontaneous and instinctive judgments. They had set out to show that good reasons required exceptions to the moral absolutes that the Church has taught constantly and most firmly; they ended, without intending or admitting it, in subjectivism disguised as intuitionism.

As the preceding paragraphs make clear, our controversies with certain philosophical positions and with theological proportionalism have turned on a metaphysical thesis: the moral order is irreducible to other orders of reality. Since the multiplicity of the orders of reality is not logically necessary, that thesis must be defended, and its defense requires a cogent philosophical argument that people can make free choices.

The mere experience of making choices that seem free is not enough to establish that they really are free. However, a practical principle, *Truth is to be sought*, directs people to engage in inquiry, and moral norms guide their choices about how to think and judge when neither evident truths nor logical deductions settle a question. One can, of course, deliberately violate these norms. In doing so, one is unreasonable without being irrational, as would be a person who deliberately tried to maintain a logically inconsistent position or who continued trying to do something after it became clear that the effort was futile. Thus, there is an ethics of inquiry, which scholars engaging in debate often invoke and always at least pretend to follow.

This ethics presupposes that inquirers can freely commit themselves to pursuing truth rather than choose to do something else, such as rationalizing unexamined commitments or supporting politically correct or theologically "mainstream" positions, which may or may not be true. Consequently, any attempt to defend the proposition that no one can make a free choice undercuts itself precisely by eliminating morality, including the various inquiry-guiding norms to which determinists appeal in arguing for their view. On this basis, Olaf Tollefsen and we showed that, though the freedom of particular choices can be called into question by contrary evidence, the ability of normal human adults to make free choices cannot reasonably be denied.

Though individuals make choices, two or more persons, in and by their individual choices, can make unified choices, and some things can be chosen only in this way. For example, an unconditional choice to marry or to join a covenant community can be made only by the parties' mutual commitments. Still, for simplicity's sake, we usually speak of choices by individuals.

Free choice cannot be *separated* from action: one chooses to do something, and if one carries out the choice, it and its execution together constitute a human act in the central sense. However, choices must be *distinguished* from particular performances that come and go, one after another. Though a bodily person makes and carries out free choices, they are not transient, bodily functions or processes. Rather, like acts of intellectual knowing, they are spiritual and lasting. They endure as elements of one's character unless and until one makes a new choice which is inconsistent with them—which may just be the choice to choose differently if faced with relevantly similar options again.

Some choices are bigger than others. A choice to write a book or direct a dissertation is carried out by intermittent behavior and usually implemented by many other, subordinate choices. People not only sometimes choose even larger projects but occasionally make a choice that commits them to a particular role and responsibilities: the choices involved in marrying or making vows or receiving holy orders, in undertaking a profession or enlisting in the military, and so on.

Because free choices last, they are self-determining. Choosing for or against a basic human good actualizes and limits the self in respect to that good. For example, choosing to sin puts one in a state of sin. This state simply is the unrepented sin which persists until one makes a choice incompatible with it—a more or less explicit act of repentance. Thus, contrary to what Kevin Flannery, S.J., thinks, a "moment of decision" is necessary in *making* any choice, though, as he rightly points out, freedom (of previously made, persisting, sinful choices) often shapes wicked acts without requiring any fresh deliberation and new choice to sin.

By the same token, a harmonious group of good commitments, made to implement one's act of faith in response to God's calling, sets one's heart upon intimacy with God and all the other basic human goods, whose realization in the kingdom is an essential part of the hoped-for fruit of living the faith in love (see Vatican II, *Gaudium et spes*, 38–39). Consistently implementing and faithfully carrying out such a group of vocational commitments—which presupposes the gift of charity—involves and integrates one's thoughts, emotions, and behavior. Increasingly, a person is able to put his or her whole self into every action he or she does; deeds flowing from a sound conscience and an upright will are less and less marked by residual wayward feelings and inappropriate behavioral habits. Thus Christian character develops.

Various aspects of saintly character—the different Christian moral virtues—can be distinguished and described by theoretical reflection, just as different slices through a living organism can be made by magnetic resonance imaging (MRI). But unlike an MRI, which can be useful for health care, a theory of moral virtues has no obvious use in overcoming sin and discerning, accepting, and faithfully carrying out God's will. That is why Grisez devoted a great deal of time in the first two volumes of *The Way of the Lord Jesus* to personal vocation but "almost no time," as Ashley points out, "to the definition or classification of virtues." Like other proponents of virtue ethics, Ashley commends it for viewing moral life as a whole. But an ethics of personal vocation more intelligibly and fruitfully views Christian life as an ordered whole. So, where Ashley says, "The New Testament Torah shifts the emphasis on the legal norms of morality, to the formation of the Christian in view of eternal life, and thus on the development of character through the virtues," we would say: "The New Testament Torah shifts the emphasis from the legal norms of morality to following Jesus, seeking his kingdom and righteousness, and helping to carry on his saving work, by exercising the gifts of faith, hope, and love in discerning, accepting, and faithfully carrying out all the elements of one's personal vocation." And we think the New Testament as a whole, not merely a few proof texts, supports our thesis better than Ashley's.

While we have not spent much time on St. Thomas's various treatises on the moral virtues, John Finnis and we have tried hard for the past twenty years or so not only to understand Thomas's theory of action but to refine and develop it. Ordinary language talks of and classifies human acts in many ways: as pieces of behavior (things in the world, including sneezing and stubbing one's toe, along with thunderstorms, flies buzzing around the room, and so on); as technical performances that bring about specific results by art much as animals do by instinct (such as construction workers building buildings as birds build nests, lumberjacks cutting trees as beavers down trees); as described by laws or other rules; and so forth. But none of these ways of talking and classifying picks out acts precisely insofar as they are moral. To identify an act as moral one must refer to what the moral order orders, namely, operations of the will. So, moral acts can be understood and classified, and their instances can be identified, only by including intention in their very definition. (We use *intention* here in the sense in which it includes not only willing an end but choosing a means.)

This focus on choice is misunderstood if it is contrasted, as it is by Vacek, with what is chosen rather than, as it is by us, with outward behavior and technical performances considered in abstraction from any choice they carry out. As we said before, when one makes a choice, one chooses to do something, and one's action is the unified whole: one's choice and what one chooses to do. In the 1970s, Grisez began using communal decision making to clarify the point: a deliberative body chooses by adopting a motion, and the proposal that it adopts defines the community's action. Just so, precisely what an individual intends in choosing to do something defines his or her action, and we call what is intended *the content of the proposal adopted by choice.* Considered precisely as intended, the content of the proposal is not a state of affairs outside the moral order. Rather, it includes both what one chooses to do and the good (benefit, end) or goods (benefits, ends) that provide the decisive reason or reasons for choosing to do that. Thus, every moral act is essentially determined both by the intention of its specifying object and of the good or goods hoped for in choosing that object. Still, somewhat as natural things have qualities, quantities, relationships, and so on in addition to their substance, a moral act includes modifications in addition to its essential determinants. Among the most important of these are the act's relationships to prior moral acts and the foreseen effects, not included in the proposal, of carrying it out. Not only the essential determinants but all the other modifications must be considered in the light of relevant moral norms to see whether a prospective act will be morally good.

These points can be clarified with simple examples. If Sam chooses to play tennis as a way of getting exercise, he adopts a proposal to play tennis. In being chosen, that object is the specifying intention of his act of tennis playing. But the proposal also includes as essential determinants the intention of exercise, implicit in which is the intention of health—the good that provides the reason to choose to exercise by playing tennis. At the same time, Sam foresees that he will put wear on his tennis shoes, leave his wife to manage things at home while he plays tennis, be tempted to flirt with the young lady who manages the club where he plays tennis, and so on. These are not essential determinants of Sam's act of tennis playing. Rather, they are foreseen but unintended modifications. Notice, however, that the morality of what Sam is doing cannot be evaluated without taking such things into account, since *bonum ex integra causa, malum ex quocumque defectu* (the moral goodness of an act comes from the goodness of the whole set of factors that contribute to its reality; the moral badness of an act can come from a defect in even one of those factors). Thus, perhaps Sam mortally sins by playing tennis, despite the moral acceptability of all that he *intends*, for he may be gravely failing in his duty to stay home and help his wife or rashly risking a sin of adultery in the heart.

If Jane also chooses to play tennis, but as a professional, the object of her act is the same as Sam's, but the proposal as a whole is not. For Jane, the exercise she gets in playing may well be no more than a foreseen effect that she only reluctantly accepts and in no way intends. Jane has a different reason for choosing to play tennis—say, making money to support herself, including large expenses for, and payments to, younger women with whom Jane engages in sexual activities. The true goods displaced by the merely apparent good (of apparent one-flesh communion) that is one of the decisive reasons for Jane's tennis playing makes what she is doing morally bad, since *bonum ex integra causa*.

If Sally also chooses to play tennis as a professional, to support herself and her aged parents, the object of her act is the same as Sam's and Jane's. But, again, the proposal as a whole differs, since Sally intends to earn money which, in turn, is a means to the benefits for life and health that money helps sustain, protect, and/or promote. Suppose Sally, one day, needing extra money for life-saving surgery for her mother, chooses to throw a match for a Mafia bribe. The object of her act has changed.

Sally does not simply play tennis; rather, she plays tennis *badly*. That violates the good of play, which is enough to make it morally evil, even if not gravely so. But foreseen factors outside the proposal, such as the act's contribution to the syndicate's fraud, make her playing badly gravely wrong. Once more, moral evaluation must take everything into account, since *bonum ex integra causa*. And that includes even the consequence that Sally's mother could die for want of the surgery if Sally refuses the bribe and plays well. Sally surely should not ignore her mother's plight. Rather, though refusing to pervert her own skill and participate in fraud, Sally must do what she uprightly can to meet her mother's needs—say, negotiate a loan, or, perhaps, accept the bribe (assuming she can do so without lying), pay for the surgery, play well, and help the public authorities bring to justice the gangsters who paid the bribe.

The preceding explanation and examples only begin to sketch the fruit of the work Finnis and we have been doing on action theory. But they are enough to suggest four things: (1) why we think intention *always* functions in objective morality (not *often*, as Vacek thinks), (2) that this theory of action is not constructivism or subjectivism (as Vacek suggests), (3) that a moral agent's behavior can be the object essentially determining his or her act only insofar as that behavior carries out a choice (contrary to Vacek's suggestion that technical effectiveness as such is a moral determinant), and (4) that our theory appropriately takes into account everything bearing on the morality of human acts (contrary to Vacek's claim that only proportionalism does so).

Moreover, just insofar as arguments about how to identify and analyze morally significant human acts are not merely philosophical controversies but disagreements about what tends toward salvation and damnation, the Church's *magisterium* can speak authoritatively about them. Thus, theologians should pay attention to the confirmation by the papal *magisterium* of the heart of St. Thomas's theory of action, which our work accepts and develops. John Paul II teaches:

> *The morality of the human act depends primarily and fundamentally on the "object" rationally chosen by the deliberate will,* as is borne out by the insightful analysis, still valid today, made by Saint Thomas (cf. *Summa Theologiae*, I–II, q. 18, a. 6). In order to be able to grasp the object of an act which specifies that act morally, it is therefore necessary to place oneself *in the perspective of the acting person*. The object of the act of willing is in fact a freely chosen kind of behaviour. To the extent that it is in conformity with the order of reason, it is the cause of the goodness of the will; it perfects us morally,

and disposes us to recognize our ultimate end in the perfect good, primordial love. By the object of a given moral act, then, one cannot mean a process or an event of the merely physical order, to be assessed on the basis of its ability to bring about a given state of affairs in the outside world. Rather, that object is the proximate end of a deliberate decision which determines the act of willing on the part of the acting person (*Veritatis splendor*, 78).

This analysis makes it clear that the exceptionless moral norms that the Church teaches (and we defend) are not the "merely behavioral norms" that proportionalists posit as the target of their attack on moral absolutes.

II. SOME COMMENTS ON EACH OF THE EIGHT PAPERS

Since the eight papers differ greatly from one another in subject matter, method, and purpose, and each of them deals with an important and interesting topic, we shall be able in the space allotted us to comment only on a few points that seem rather urgent. Our silence about points we pass over should not be taken to mean that we agree with everything else our collaborators say or concede everything else our critics assert and assume.

William E. May's "Germain Grisez on Moral Principles and Moral Norms: Natural and Christian" describes two central elements of the fundamental moral theology presented in *Christian Moral Principles*, defends them against certain criticisms, and suggests that Grisez's positions on those matters have been confirmed by John Paul II's teaching in *Veritatis splendor*. And in the endnotes to his paper, May extends his defense to several related positions. Though May mentions the collaboration of Finnis and Boyle in Grisez's theoretical work, with characteristic modesty he leaves unmentioned his own smaller but real contribution to it. May also has in fact contributed greatly—as with the present essay—to the dissemination and defense of the fruits of our common effort.

John Finnis's "Public Good: The Specifically Political Common Good in Aquinas" corrects Grisez's interpretation of certain texts of St. Thomas. Finnis shows that Thomas anticipated positions that Grisez, in *Living a Christian Life*, said had been clarified only by recent Church teaching. This paper contributes to a discussion of political theory between Finnis and us that began when we published *Life and Death with Liberty and Justice* in 1979 and he published *Natural Law and Natural Rights* the following year. Our treatment of political theory was subordinate to our effort to sketch out an effective strategy for prolife opposition to euthanasia, and we conceded somewhat too much to political theories that are prevalent in the United States. As Finnis and we discussed these matters while we worked together on *Nuclear Deterrence, Morality and Realism*, both he and we reconsidered our positions and moved toward the views that Grisez subsequently incorporated in the political theology proposed in chapter eleven of *Living a Christian Life*. It now appears that those views are more Thomistic than Grisez thought, and the consensus among the three of us on these matters is complete or almost so.

Sometimes someone asks, and we suppose many people wonder, how Finnis and we collaborate as closely and agree as extensively as we do. Our ongoing and partly public discussion of political theory shows how. Unlike writing fiction or poetry, doing philosophy and theology is inquiring into a subject matter. When we find ourselves disagreeing, we go back to the subject matter, try hard to communicate with one another, learn from one another, and generally arrive at a common position.

Gerard V. Bradley's "No Intentional Killing Whatsoever: The Case of Capital Punishment" argues that the *Catechism of the Catholic Church* and John Paul II's encyclical *Evangelium vitae* are best understood as saying that capital punishment can be morally acceptable only if it can be imposed and carried out without intentionally killing the convicted criminal. Though we find Bradley's interpretation of the documents plausible, we think they are too opaque to establish his view. Moreover, Bradley's argument includes the claim that public authority could (under certain conditions) use capital punishment without intending to kill—could "impose death without choosing it." Though public authorities, like private citizens, certainly sometimes can do things they know will cause someone's death without intending to kill, we fail to see how they can *impose* death on anyone without choosing, among other things, to kill him or her.

On this issue, Bradley agrees with the view Finnis has defended. In writing *Nuclear Deterrence*, Finnis and we could not agree whether capital punishment necessarily involves intentional killing. So we agreed to disagree frankly, while noting that our disagreement is not over fundamentals but only over the analysis of the specific act of capital punishment: What must public officials include in the proposal to impose capital punishment and/or to execute criminals? We still think that capital punishment is an act whose precise object includes killing the condemned person, even if that is ordered to the morally good purpose of just retribution. Nevertheless, we do think that, without choosing to kill violent individuals, some societies that lack adequate resources to deal with them less destructively could take measures necessary to stop them even if those measures were sure to result in their death. For instance, a nomadic tribe perhaps justifiably drove out habitual and violent troublemakers, fully expecting them to die, but without choosing to kill them. Taking such measures, however, probably was done on the same basis, and may well have been equally justifiable, even if the violent individual was insane—in which case it would not have been *punishment*.

The disagreement between Finnis and us regarding capital punishment indicates that we still have work to do on action theory. However, Finnis and we do not disagree about how intention affects objective morality (as Vacek mistakenly suggests). Applying the theory of action that we sketched out in the first part of this response, one can easily distinguish in most cases between what is included in a proposal and what is not— that is, between what is intended as an end or as a means, on the one hand, and, on the other, what is accepted as a side effect. Sometimes, however, it is hard to tell whether a good immediately instantiated by carrying out a choice can be regarded as the object of the act. Can doing justice be the object of the act (rather than an intended end distinct from the object) when a court's decree (or a supposed divine command) is carried out by hanging a convicted criminal until he or she *dies*, or by stoning *to death* someone who has violated a precept carrying that sanction?

Somewhat similarly, identifying the object of a deliberate omission is not always easy, even if one adopts, as one should, the perspective of the acting person. Thus, though Finnis, May, and we are convinced that couples can practice periodic abstinence to regulate births without precisely intending to impede conception, not only Vacek and others who hold that contracepting often is morally acceptable, but some who hold that it never is, maintain that the two do not differ as we think they do. So, additional clarifications of the distinction between what is and is not intended are needed and, we are confident, can be made without affecting the main lines of the action theory, which St. Thomas already proposed and *Veritatis splendor* confirms.

Patrick Lee's "Human Beings Are Animals" provides fresh arguments in support of the antidualist thesis that is central to many of our works. The support is welcome; as long ago as 1977, when we worked together on *Life and Death with Liberty and Justice*, we realized that our rejection of person-body dualism called for a more adequate treatment than we provided. However, Grisez's 1974 paper, "Dualism and the New Morality," had already criticized the dualism implicit in the 1966 arguments of the majority of Pope Paul VI's Commission on Population, Family, and Birthrate, and, for whatever reasons, dualism seemed to subside after that, at least among Catholics. However, it now is resurgent, as many authors dealing with life-and-death questions assume some sort of dualism in treating the supposedly *merely* biological life of human beings as an instrumental good, rather than as fundamental.

Lee's main thesis is that dualism is false, and biological life is an essential, intrinsic aspect of the human person. We think the first nine sections of his paper soundly support that thesis and respond effectively to objections. In section ten, "The Intrinsic Value of the Bodily Person," Lee proceeds from the falsity of dualism and other assumptions to sketch out an argument for the ethically significant proposition that bodily life is not only intrinsic to human persons but part of their perfection, that is, a basic human good. (Of course, since first practical principles ground moral judgments only when those principles are supplemented with other propositions, the proposition for which Lee is arguing, though it is ethically significant in the sense that it is a principle of some moral truths, is not itself a moral truth.)

We do not doubt that bodily life is a basic human good, but we think Lee's argument needs development. He only sketches, rather than fully articulates, the conceptual connections among the ideas of (1) what are ultimate reasons for action, (2) what fulfills potentialities, and (3) what is intrinsic to persons. So we are not sure his argument is sound; it at least *appears* to beg the question. Moreover, Lee's move from what is intrinsic to persons and what are ultimate reasons for action to the intrinsic goodness of human life *appears* to be an instance of something he and we agree is impossible: the demonstration of a first practical principle from theoretical premises. Further clarification, not to be found in anything we or any of our collaborators have so far done, plainly is needed.

Ralph McInerny's "Portia's Lament: Reflections on Practical Reason," mining some relevant texts of Aristotle and St. Thomas, begins to articulate a theory of practical reason and its relationship with theoretical reason. Since McInerny irenically stops short of invading the fields where we have been working and engaging us in battle, we can only applaud his effort and offer a few constructive suggestions for extending it in ways that will forestall future conflict.

McInerny says that practical intellect "takes its rise from the good desired." That is unqualifiedly true of technically practical reasoning: when it comes to bringing something into being by human work—building houses, making chicken soup, and so forth—nobody begins thinking about means without having a goal in mind and wanting to achieve it. But it is true of morally practical reasoning only in a certain respect. Since acts of the will always are specified by intellectual knowledge, the first principles of practical reasoning cannot presuppose volitional desires for goods but must themselves present to the will what is to be desired.

The principles of practical reasoning are not, however, practical reasoning; at least one more premise is needed. One of that premise's terms must refer to a possible option for choice, and possible options for choice presuppose sensory desire. Thus, along with the propositional principles of practical reasoning and the volitions corresponding to them, sensory desire is a principle of practical reasoning. Of course, Aristotle either fails to distinguish sensory desire from willing, or he is unclear about their distinction. Not surprisingly, St. Thomas's commentaries on Aristotle also leave such matters unclear. So, closely following Aristotle's text and Thomas's commentary on it, McInerny characterizes choice as "desire's acceptance of what has been deliberated," which plainly is inadequate to distinguish *free* choice from a response of sensory appetite to technical means for pursuing some concrete goal. Therefore, we suggest that, in extending his present study, McInerny distinguish more carefully than he has in this paper between technical reasoning and moral reasoning, and between volition and the acts of sensory appetite.

Again, in discussing practical truth toward the end of his paper, McInerny cites texts that refer to ultimate practical judgments and ignores their irrelevance to the first principles of practical reason. Since the initial acts of the will are specified by first practical principles, the truth of those principles cannot consist in any conformity to right appetite. So, when Aristotle and St. Thomas say that practical truth is such conformity, they obviously must not be understood as referring to the truth of practical principles. Rather, they are referring to the truth of conclusions, reached by practical reasoning, that direct action morally (whether rightly or wrongly) and/or technically (whether successfully or not).

If McInerny, rather than being content to be—as he puts it—a mendicant worm munching his way through St. Thomas's *Opera omnia*, had ambitions like ours, we would suppose that he is developing a theory of his own that would reduce the moral order to nature and technical performance: a theory identifying the end determined by nature and articulating a technique to direct behavior toward that end. If he were to articulate such a reduction, we would criticize it by developing a point we made in the first part of this response: the ultimate ends are given by nature precisely insofar as the first principles of practical reason are known naturally. One can know by theoretical reflection that there are such practical principles and what they are, and such reflection pertains to philosophical anthropology. But first practical principles cannot themselves be theoretical truths.

Kevin Flannery, S.J.'s "Practical Reason and Concrete Acts" attempts a dialectical defense of the first principle of practical reason similar to Aristotle's vindication of the principle of noncontradiction, discusses the notion of "practical matter" in St. Thomas's theory of action, and criticizes the central argument in Tollefsen's and our book on free choice. We shall comment on Flannery's first and third topics.

Anyone who rejects the principle of noncontradiction implicitly uses it in stating the rejection. So the act of denying the principle uses it in stating its denial. Therefore, the denying either falsifies what the person says, or what that person says makes the denying something other than a logical denial. And so, anyone wishing to deny the principle of noncontradiction must remain silent in order to avoid running afoul of the position he or she wishes to hold. Deprived of language, such a person might as well be a vegetable, as Aristotle says. Flannery's intuition is that denying the first principle of practical reason runs into a similar difficulty. We never thought of trying to make that point, and we consider the idea appealing. Still, the details of Flannery's attempt to work it out seem to us questionable.

He apparently regards *Good is to be done and pursued; evil is to be avoided* as if it were equivalent to "a straightforward statement about human nature and its general orientation," namely, the theoretical proposition that explicates the intelligibility of good as "that which all things seek after." We deny that equivalence: the first principle of practical reason is *founded on* the intelligibility of good ("primum principium in ratione practica est quod fundatur supra rationem boni" [St. Thomas, *S.t.* 1–2.q.94a.2.c.]), but the two are not identical, just as the principle of noncontradiction is founded on the intelligibilities of being and nonbeing but is not identical with them.

Moreover, though we are not sure we understand Flannery's elenchic argument, it does not seem to run parallel to Aristotle's. In particular, does the action on which Flannery's argument turns include the precise act of affirming what Antipraxis is trying to deny? Also, we are unsure what Flannery takes to be the contradictory of the first practical principle. An empiricism like Hume's maintains that the intelligibility of good, if any, has no power to ground anything normative or prescriptive (the to-be-done character of a possible action judged to be good). Does Flannery think the contradictory of the first practical principle is implied by such an empiricism? If so, we will have to disagree with him about several propositions he asserts.

We have still greater difficulties with Flannery's criticism of the central argument of our *Free Choice: A Self-Referential Argument*. He asserts, but does not try to prove, that our argument shows—or that a better argument would show—that the no-free-choice position is logically incoherent. But philosophical positions such as determinism are neither offered as logical truths nor commended as the only possible alternative to a self-contradictory position. Besides, by contrast with a world including square circles and the like, the world depicted by determinists surely is possible, for instance, as a created universe without any rational creature sufficiently mature to make free choices. Furthermore, since a logically incoherent expression cannot refer to anything definite, we fail to see how an argument to show that a position is self-refuting due to some aspect of its *self-reference* could demonstrate the position in question to be logically *incoherent*.

Our argument that the no-free-choice position is self-refuting turns on the fact that affirming this position appeals to a norm that cannot be in force unless someone can make a free choice. We hold that the self-refutation would not work if the determinist appealed to no norms other than the rules of logic (as would be the case if determinists maintained that the free-choice position is self-contradictory). Flannery disagrees. His disagreement rests on two things: his claim that a free choice need not be between open alternatives and his rejection of the distinction we point out between the norms of strict logic and rationality norms. But the quest for truth, about free choice and everything else, is not really an option unless one at least can choose to commit oneself to it or refuse to do so; and arguments for determinism, as we show, regularly assume norms of reasonable inquiry and judgment that unreasonable people can deny without violating any rule of logic.

Edward C. Vacek, S.J.'s "Contraception Again—A Conclusion in Search of Convincing Arguments: One Proportionalist's [Mis?]Understanding of a Text" is a critique of thirteen pages of *Living a Christian Life* in which Grisez articulates a particular way of understanding the truth of the Church's teaching on contraception—by proposing and explaining the argument that contraception is always wrong precisely by being contralife.

In our view, the great merit of Vacek's contribution is that, though narrowly focused on one argument about one kind of moral act, it exhibits very clearly the nature and extent of the disagreement between proportionalists and us. As Grisez's mentor, Richard McKeon, powerfully demonstrated, sound interpretations of philosophical opponents' positions often are impeded—and attempts to criticize their seemingly obvious errors often are vitiated—by the theoretical gulf between views that radically differ in their principles and methods. Surprising as it may seem that such differences also exist in Catholic theology, we think Vacek's paper makes it clear that they do.

There are in Vacek's paper some mistakes of the sort that characterize almost any instance of polemical argument. For example, when he attempts an "internal critique" of Grisez's explanation of the distinction between natural family planning and contraception, he omits from his formulation of the latter choice the intention to impede conception and *thereby* to prevent the entire state of affairs which, by hypothesis, both those who contracept and those who practice periodic abstinence may rightly desire to forestall—and may even be morally forbidden to bring about. But more important, Vacek's criticisms often beg the question against Grisez's position by presupposing—or even, occasionally, explicitly but gratuitously asserting—assumptions about human action and the nature of morality that Grisez has never held and need not accept. These many points deserve fuller discussion than is possible in this response.

So, if the issues between Vacek and us were exclusively philosophical, we would respond generally by saying that his central objections to Grisez's argument against contraception are not sufficiently dialectical—that is, that they seldom are so precisely to the point and within the framework of our principles and method as to trouble us much. For example, in part III of his paper, Vacek criticizes Grisez's answers to a series of objections, but uniformly misses their point by mistakenly treating each of those answers as if it were an independent argument that contraception is contralife. More radically, objecting to our account of moral action, in which volition is central, Vacek makes it clear that he prefers a different account, but never clearly articulates it and provides no reasons for others to share his preference. Similarly, attributing moral significance to acts as performances considered in abstraction from any volition, Vacek makes it clear that he does not understand the moral order as we do, but by no means shows either that our account is mistaken or that any coherent alternative is available.

This gulf that separates Vacek's view and ours (perhaps together with our own lack of nuance and/or incompleteness in stating our view), leads to one of Vacek's chief misunderstandings: that defining human acts by the agent's intention entails ethically excluding something, or even everything, else about them. We hold, on the contrary, that, though a choice and its execution together constitute a human act in the central sense, everything a person knows or should know about such an act can be ethically evaluated and must measure up if the act is to be morally good—*bonum ex integra causa*. Philosophically, then, most of Vacek's shots either are blank shells or tear into positions we do not hold.

The differences between Vacek and us, however, are not merely philosophical. In the pages Vacek criticizes, Grisez offers a theological account of the Church's constant and most firm teaching on contraception. It is part of this tradition that contraception is contralife, and as such is gravely wrong outside marriage as well as within it. Nothing in the twentieth-century *magisterium* has repudiated this element of tradition, though recent Church teaching has focused increasingly on the incompatibility between contraception and the *marital* character of a married couple's sexual intercourse—a distinct reason why it is evil that Grisez explains in a later passage, which Vacek, for brevity's sake, leaves uncriticized. Moreover, in *Humanae vitae*, Pope Paul VI characterizes the third of three kinds of morally unacceptable, birth-regulating activity precisely by the intention to impede conception, rather than by listing techniques, describing performances, or puzzling over possible ordinary-language meanings of *contraception*—a word that does not even appear in Pope Paul's central, operative sentence. As a Catholic theologian, Vacek should regard every one of these considerations as crucial, not ignore, evade, or dismiss them.

More generally, insofar as Catholic tradition and the recent *magisterium* have addressed issues on which Vacek and we disagree, those theological sources are relevant for settling the disagreements. Though we criticize many things in the *theological* tradition, including some aspects of the account of human action common in the manualists, we build on the longer and deeper *Catholic* tradition. For instance, as we showed at the end of the first part of this response, our understanding of moral action is rooted in St. Thomas and has been confirmed by John Paul II in *Veritatis splendor*. And behind those sources is our Lord's own word that morality is a matter of the heart: one who intends to commit adultery but fails—whether through lack of opportunity or mistaken identity— does nevertheless commit it (see Matt 5:27–29). Here, a revealed truth is illuminated by an account of moral action that focuses on self-determining choices but becomes unintelligible when considered by an account that reduces action to a performance that brings about a result.

Similarly, the Catholic tradition developed and increasingly clarified the distinction between what some manualists called *objective morality* and *subjective morality*. We follow the tradition in drawing what we think is the relevant distinction. Moral acts are *objectively* constituted by what people think they are doing. *Subjective* morality is in the possibility of a person's confusion and/or error about the moral goodness or badness of his or her act, and in the possibility that a person's freedom to choose is blocked or impeded. Vacek, by contrast, tries to correlate the distinction between subjective and objective with that between three moments— intending, attempting, and performing. That correlation might make sense for a utilitarian, for whom actually making the best of a situation is the objective fulfillment of merely subjective good-heartedness. But why a Catholic theologian should hold such a view is a mystery to us. In short, we are confident that a full, scholarly discussion would show that on the issues that divide Vacek and us, our positions consistently develop Catholic tradition while Vacek's echo alien sources.

Yet Vacek's detailed commentary on Grisez's explanation of why contraception is contralife has caused us to have second thoughts about some things we have said on this subject.

First, Vacek finds it perplexing "that Grisez claims to know what contraceptors necessarily have in their minds," and he strongly presses this line of criticism. Indeed, he presses it too far by extending it to instances in which Grisez, rather than articulating an agent's intention as an essential step in an argument, is only clarifying the attitude compatible with a choice by formulating what someone who made it *could* say. Still, with respect to the formulation of the contraceptor's intention, we must make a concession: Grisez—and Finnis, May, and Boyle with him in the earlier article that Grisez is reworking and summarizing in the section Vacek is dealing with—misleadingly used two words, *imagine* and *effectively* (and Grisez made matters worse by replacing the latter with *efficaciously*—in this unwisely imitating the manualists' use of *efficax voluntas*). Rather than saying that someone choosing to contracept must *imagine* the baby who might come to be, we should have said: must *foresee* that a baby might come to be. And rather than saying the contraceptor *efficaciously wills* that the prospective person never be, Grisez should have said simply: choose to do something precisely *in order to* make it less likely that the unwanted baby come to be. The misleading expressions corrected, Grisez would have said: contraceptors necessarily foresee that a baby might come to be, they want that foreseen baby not to come to be, and they choose to do something in order to make it less likely that he or she will be.

Second, Vacek's challenge to our understanding of the relationship between natural family planning and contraception has compelled us to reflect and detect an important mistake. We have said that a couple who have chosen to contracept could carry out that choice by adopting natural family planning as their technique. That is not true, we now see, though a couple who are willing to contracept can decide for merely technical reasons to practice periodic abstinence instead. So, though natural family planning can be chosen with a contraceptive mentality, as John Paul II also makes clear, the two kinds of acts differ precisely in the object "rationally chosen by the deliberate will": the choice to practice natural family planning is a choice to abstain from acts in which a baby would become a real possibility; the choice to contracept, presupposing the intention to engage in such acts, is a choice to try to prevent the baby who might result from them.

We thank Vacek for provoking us to reflect and make these corrections, and even more for the clear light his paper sheds on the controversy between proportionalists and ourselves. And we hope that this exchange will initiate a continuing dialogue that will further clarify both their positions and ours.

Benedict M. Ashley, O.P.'s "The Scriptural Basis of Grisez's Revision of Moral Theology" criticizes Grisez's effort to ground moral theology in Scripture and proposes a different program. In considering the following reflections, readers should bear in mind that, though Ashley's criticisms are about to receive an appropriate response, he and Grisez agree on theological issues more important than those on which they disagree, and have been friends since 1950, when Grisez was beginning and Ashley completing graduate studies at the Dominican House of Studies in River Forest, Illinois.

Ashley rightly notes that Grisez pays little attention in *The Way of the Lord Jesus* "to the question how, even in principle, the biblical data as established by modern biblical scholarship are to be employed as the *norma normans* of Christian ethics." Part of the explanation is that Grisez, following St. Thomas's example in the *Summa theologiae*, decided to treat methodological issues as briefly as possible, in order to avoid burdening students with questions not essential to a basic course in moral theology. And Ashley overlooks the bit of attention Grisez gives the question that interests him:

> In attempting to carry out this project, I see a chief obstacle in the transitory and provisional character of current theology, which the Holy See notes. The present flux in thinking about central doctrines on Jesus, original sin, the last things, grace, and so on is especially disconcerting, for I must touch on all of these matters, but can hardly become expert in every one of these fields.

> To try to overcome this obstacle, I undertake to expound doctrinal points not so much in a subtle as in an accurate way, for the most part taking for granted positions commonly held by Catholic theologians until recent years. Fresh reflection upon the implications of faith for living the Christian life cannot wait for the settling of all other theological questions.
>
> Also, because this work is intended as an essay at fulfilling the mandate of Vatican II, I must make extensive use of sacred Scripture and other witnesses of faith. Much of what I have just said about the present situation in systematic theology applies analogously to the situation in Scripture scholarship and positive theology in general. While I shall do my best not to abuse Scripture and other witnesses of faith by distorting their meanings, I cannot pretend to handle these materials with the competence of a Scripture scholar. I shall strive only to use Scripture and other witnesses as the Church uses them in her teaching—for example, as they are used in the documents of Vatican II (*Christian Moral Principles*, 24).

Thinking that no new doctrinal definitions were needed, John XXIII directed Vatican II to expound the truths of the ancient deposit of faith in a fresh and more effective way, while taking care to keep intact the meaning and truth claims of Catholic doctrine. The task of restating truths of faith pertains to theology. Thus, though Vatican II's teaching is a collegial exercise of the Church's *magisterium*, it also is theology, through and through. Therefore, Grisez reasonably assumed that the Council's use of Scripture can serve as an appropriate model for carrying out its mandate about using Scripture in moral theology.

Ashley thinks Vatican II called for "a biblically based systematic moral theology," apparently meaning by that a system whose core would be drawn immediately from Scripture. Grisez willingly concedes that doing that would be ideal. But Vatican II's documents, such as *Gaudium et spes*, much of which pertains to moral theology, do not attempt it, and while some of John Paul II's documents move in that direction, even they hardly fulfill the ideal. For example, while there are some logical links between the first and second parts of *Veritatis splendor*, the first part provides only a small fraction of the second's biblical basis, most of which is supplied by using Scripture much as Grisez does.

Moreover, to base systematic theology immediately in Scripture, one would have to be able to identify the propositions in the Bible that could be used as premises, namely, those asserted by the sacred writers and the Holy Spirit (see Vatican II, *Dei Verbum*, 11). One might be able to do that with some confidence if Scripture scholars followed Vatican II's mandate for interpreting the Bible (see *Dei Verbum*, 12): (1) to use every available scholarly technique to try to determine what propositions each sacred writer is asserting; (2) to correlate the evidence regarding possibly asserted propositions in each of the Bible's books (and its parts) with that regarding them in the others, and in the living tradition of the whole Church regarding all the elements of faith; in order (3) to reach confident judgments as to precisely what truths the Holy Spirit intended to communicate to us through the Bible as a whole. Unfortunately, however, the Council's hermeneutical project does not seem to have attracted the interest of many contemporary Scripture scholars; few of them even consider whether any proposition is asserted in the Bible except when one of them tries to show that a sacred writer *did not assert* a particular proposition that might be decisive evidence in some theological controversy. So, for the foreseeable future, at least, Ashley's ideal cannot be fulfilled.

Consequently, Grisez's understanding of Vatican II's mandate to nourish the basis of moral theology with scriptural teaching is different from Ashley's. Moreover, Ashley fails to appreciate the relevance of what Grisez actually attempts. As a result, Ashley finds relevant to the problem only the brief passage he quotes (on the Ten Commandments and the Beatitudes), notes that Grisez sometimes refers to biblical scholars, and concludes: "Yet Grisez himself goes no further in exploring this topic than to attempt a correlation between the 'eight modes of responsibility' which are a characteristic feature of his system and the eight Beatitudes." Grisez, by contrast, thought that chapters thirteen through thirty-four of *Christian Moral Principles* as a whole rooted his moral theology firmly and profoundly in Scripture, not so much by the many Scripture texts he quotes or cites, or by his references to Scripture scholars, but by his drawing out the implications for Christian life from all the central truths of faith, which are themselves rooted in Scripture.

This approach to Scripture is relevant for evaluating Ashley's characterization—"an arbitrary and even fanciful accommodation"—of Grisez's arguments that the modes of responsibility correspond to the Beatitudes, which can be reformulated as modes of Christian response. Ashley asks: "Is it really plausible that Jesus (or Matthew) promulgated the New Law by a series of Beatitudes corresponding to Grisez's modes of responsibility and in just that order?" We answer: Obviously, Grisez's thought did not influence Jesus, but Grisez's philosophical thinking was informed from the start by his faith, and we, intent upon grounding moral theology in Scripture, rethought all Grisez's previous philosophical ideas as we worked out the outline for *Christian Moral Principles*. In doing that, we noticed a striking affinity and partial correspondence between the modes of responsibility and the Beatitudes, and rethought and developed the modes so that they would correspond to the Beatitudes. However, in presenting the results of our inquiries in his book, Grisez first expounded the common principles of morality, including the modes of responsibility, and then explained how those principles are transformed by faith and grace in the specifically Christian moral lives of Jesus' followers.

Ashley, however, faults Grisez who, he says: "devotes almost no time to the definition or classification of virtues and tends to reduce them all to modes of Christian response understood as aspects of the single virtue of charity." But Grisez does not, in fact, understand the modes of Christian response as aspects of the single virtue of charity. Rather, he holds something quite different: that the modes of Christian response are the modes of responsibility transformed by charity into inclinations to live one's whole life as cooperation with Jesus' redemptive act. On this view, by God's grace Jesus does for Christians what the old law and its ceremonial practices failed to do for the Jews, and what wisdom and virtue failed to do for the Greeks, so that, as St. Paul says: God "is the source of your life in Christ Jesus, whom God made our wisdom, our righteousness and sanctification and redemption" (1 Cor 1:30). Thus, according to Grisez, in Jesus the virtues are transformed: "Wisdom and justice (righteousness) take on a new depth and meaning. Self-control yields to sanctification and fortitude to redemption, as limited goods are embraced by the prospect of glory and human evils are overcome by the might of God's intervention" (*Christian Moral Principles*, 621).

Misunderstandings aside, Ashley, following St. Thomas, thinks that treatises on the moral virtues should be central in moral theology, and here the disagreement between him and us is real, though it is quite limited. Like Ashley, we hold that the moral virtues are essential for a morally good *life*. Christians acquire them as they undertake to discern God's will for each aspect of their lives, commit themselves to doing it, and, with the help of grace, faithfully carry out their commitments. We also hold that the other virtues are necessary conditions for prudence, without which one cannot consistently make the moral judgments that will shape a good and holy life. But unlike Ashley, we do not think detailed *analyses* of the moral virtues, in general and/or in particular, deserve an important place in moral theology. We have three reasons for holding this view.

First, we know of no evidence that detailed analyses of the moral virtues and prudence help people to be good and holy. Many saints certainly knew nothing of such analyses. Would Maria Goretti have been better off in any way by knowing that chastity is a virtue, a special rather than a general virtue, a part of temperance distinct from abstinence, and a virtue to which modesty specially belongs? More important, analyses of the virtues are no help to people who lack them, even those who are well-disposed, such as children who wish to be good.

Second, not being propositional, the virtues cannot serve as premises for normative judgments. That should be clear to anyone who studies the second part of the *Summa theologiae*: the general theory of virtues and the treatises on the various virtues have virtually nothing to do with the norms articulated in the second part of the second part. There, rather than anything that has been said about the virtues, more or less general propositional moral principles are used to ground and clarify more or less specific moral norms. To see this point, one need only compare what St. Thomas says about the virtues in general and in particular with what he says about specific sorts of acts, such as killing in self-defense and sodomy.

Third, virtue ethics is a singularly unpromising framework for a renewed moral theology nourished by sacred Scripture. Ashley admits that Thomas derived his list of virtues from Aristotle rather than from the Bible—he might have mentioned other pagan sources, including Cicero. Yet he claims that the moral virtues are *rightly* central in Thomas's "reformulation of revealed data on moral life in the New Testament." Central indeed they are, but, we think, not rightly. That is why Grisez, rather than imposing a theoretical construct from nonbiblical sources on the revealed data, tries to explain their moral implications in terms of cooperating with Jesus and imitating his exemplification of the Beatitudes in fulfilling one's personal vocation.

At this point, we think our response is long enough—at least for now. But Grisez wishes to add one more point, not in response to anyone in particular:

Whenever I come back to my favorite airport, Baltimore-Washington International, I pass under an official message of the State of Maryland: "Welcome to Maryland! Enjoy your visit!" and my heart is warmed by the reminder that, though Jeannette and I reside permanently in Maryland, we will not live there forever. Despite the danger that the U.S. Supreme Court will find Maryland's welcome inconsistent with the First Amendment, this State, at least, officially reminds its returning citizens that Maryland is not their real home, that we are only visiting and can look forward to a better, a heavenly home. I have tried to keep this thought at the center of my theology, and have striven to tie my treatment of specific issues tightly to hope for heaven. My ultimate criticism of alternative approaches to moral theology is that they do not do this very well, if at all, and so are not helpful in guiding and encouraging people to seek God's kingdom. But in the end nothing else matters for theology or, what is more important, for any of us struggling through this vale of tears.

Afterword

Pioneering the Renewal
in Moral Theology

RUSSELL SHAW

I.

Leaning back behind the desk in his high-ceilinged, book-lined office, Germain Grisez tells how his mother handled the experience of attending an elementary school run by a Protestant minister who did not like Catholics: "Her revenge was to learn the faith very well so she could argue with people."

As Grisez no doubt is aware, the description also fits him. His monumental labors over the past four decades have earned him a reputation for prodigious scholarship and disputatious readiness to defend the truth as he sees it. "Grisez's work in fundamental moral theory," says one admirer, "represents the most important advance in this field at least since the Christian humanist movement and scholastic revival of the sixteenth century."[1] Yet in the politicized world of contemporary Catholic moral thought, Grisez's achievement suffers an apparently calculated silent treatment from opponents on the left, even as conservative Catholic scholars fault him for deviations from the thought of Thomas Aquinas and other sins. Whatever judgment history ultimately renders on him and his work, however, Germain Gabriel Grisez is an imposing, even dominant, figure whose influence on serious thinking about human behavior and morality seems likely to grow.

Since the late 1970s Grisez has been engaged in a project whose purpose is to reshape Catholic moral theology in light of the prescription of the Second Vatican Council—the composition of a vast four-volume treatment of moral theology under the overall title *The Way of the Lord Jesus*. In an interview some years ago I asked him what he meant in saying he sought to carry forward the renewal of moral theology according to the mind of Vatican II, and he gave an answer that sheds considerable light on the intentions underlying his *magnum opus*:

> It [the Council] called for a renewal of moral theology which is Scripturally based, related to the basic truths of faith, and Christocentric, and which

241

strikes a proper balance between two ways of viewing Christian life—as oriented to fulfillment in heaven and as oriented to the betterment of this world. . . . The renewal of moral theology which Vatican II is asking for is really very new. What the Council wants just hasn't been done before.[2]

After nearly two decades, two volumes have been published in pursuit of this ambitious vision, *Christian Moral Principles* and *Living a Christian Life*; and a third is well along (its tentative title is *200*—or possibly *201* or *202*—*Difficult Moral Questions*). Completion of the entire work plainly lies somewhere in the third millennium.

On this particular warm, hazy day in May I am encouraging Grisez to take an overview of his career and work, and once again I ask him what he has in mind in writing *The Way of the Lord Jesus*. He says, "Essentially, what I'm doing is trying to do moral theology the way I think it ought to be done." Hasn't moral theology up to now *ever* been done as it should? "No, it hasn't ever been very adequate," he replies. (This habit of saying what he thinks is one reason Grisez is controversial in some circles.) The inadequacy of moral theology, he continues, is "not too desperately important when you have a community of faith that accepts and transmits moral truth. Then the morality is part of the community, it's 'the way we do things.'" For a long time this was pretty much the situation of the Catholic community in most places: "A group of people could kind of live by themselves. You didn't have television and newspapers; you didn't have the *Washington Post* and CBS. Generally through history it's been that way."

Today, by contrast, Catholics live surrounded by a secular culture in which the whole idea of Revelation and a way of life based upon it is dismissed out of hand, and believers have no "insulation" against the intrusive witness of nonbelief. "Christian morality isn't 'the way we do things' in any substantial group of *we*, although it may be the way I and my family try to do things. In this context we really need to understand who we are as Christians and what the Christian life is and how to live it, and to be very self-conscious about this in a way that's never been necessary before."

Grisez considers Catholic moral theology before the Second Vatican Council (1962–1965) to have been in conspicuously bad shape, shot through with poor arguments and pervaded by a legalistic spirit carrying over into bad pastoral practice. The unarticulated assumption appeared to be that the Church's moral teaching was not so much a body of moral truth as it was a legal code, susceptible to being interpreted, modified, temporarily set aside by "dispensations," or even changed entirely at the discretion of the authorities. While the elaborate casuistry that had grown up over the centuries had its value and its justifications, it tended to lend tacit support to such attitudes.

Vatican Council II called for something far different and better. In its *Decree on the Training of Priests* the Council said theology in general should be clearly Christocentric and grounded in Revelation. The document continues:

> Special care should be given to the perfecting of moral theology. Its scientific presentation should draw more fully on the teaching of holy Scripture and should throw light upon the exalted vocation of the faithful in Christ and their obligation to bring forth fruit in charity for the life of the world.[3]

These indications, although sketchy, have provided the outlines for Grisez's huge undertaking.

Spurring him on is acute distaste for what in fact has been occurring in Catholic moral theology since Vatican II. Instead of a renewal according to the conciliar prescription, he holds, these years have witnessed the institutionalization of theological dissent from the Magisterium. While this has been true of Catholic theology generally, the phenomenon has been particularly evident in the moral field, where proportionalism now appears to be the dominant school among Catholic moralists in the United States and countries like it. As many people see it, not the least significant contribution of volume one of *The Way of the Lord Jesus* is Grisez's devastating critique of proportionalism ("rationally unworkable") and of theological dissent in general.[4] It has not, needless to say, endeared him to those who are its targets.

While Grisez ultimately is writing for the entire community of believers, Catholic seminarians are the immediate intended audience of *The Way of the Lord Jesus*. His decision to live and work at Mount Saint Mary's College and teach in the seminary there was a deliberate part of his plan. Situated on the edge of rolling foothills midway between Frederick, Maryland (of Barbara Fritchie fame), and Gettysburg, Pennsylvania, and lying on the outskirts of the town of Emmitsburg, Maryland, where St. Elizabeth Seton and her Daughters of Charity labored more than a century and a half ago, the college, founded in 1808, is the second oldest Catholic institution of higher learning in the United States (Georgetown University in Washington, D.C., claims 1789 as its founding date). Overlooking the bucolic campus from a nearby hill is a towering gilded statue of the

Blessed Virgin Mary under the title of the Immaculate Conception, her hands extended in a benevolent, protective gesture.

Across the highway from the main campus—a road once officially described as being among the most dangerous in the nation but now considerably less threatening as a result of improvements—Germain and Jeannette Grisez live in a compact split-foyer house that could serve as a kind of metaphor of their relationship: close-knit, unassumingly comfortable, extremely well-organized. For several years after coming to Mount Saint Mary's the Grisezs had a campus apartment, where they were driven to distraction by the undergraduates' all-hours racket; besides saving their sanity, the house, built by the college to their specifications, probably has helped keep them where they are.

Grisez in his mid-60s is a stocky, ruddy-faced man whose dark hair is going silver-gray. His ample waistline testifies to Jeannette's skills as a cook, but he keeps in reasonably good shape by walking the campus and using an exercycle that occupies a prominent place in the family room. Other items there suggest unspectacular recreational tastes. The bookshelves hold popular paperback novels; there is a "Forrest Gump" videocassette next to the TV. On one of my earlier visits several years ago Grisez made a point of taping a Washington Redskins' football game and playing the tape after dinner, fast-forwarding to skip the commercials. One set of shelves is for mementos, including the Grisezs' Pro Ecclesia et Pontifice Medals, papal honors bestowed in 1972 at the request of their great friend and patron Cardinal Patrick O'Boyle of Washington.

Up a short flight of stairs with a dogleg turn at the front door, the living room is simply but comfortably furnished, with a stereo set and bookshelves containing Germain's works and books by friends. A corkboard on the dining room wall holds a revolving exhibit of Grisez family photos: sometimes grandchildren, sometimes Germain's and Jeannette's trips. Nova Scotia is featured on this occasion. The Grisezs attend Mass together almost every day, and say the Liturgy of the Hours together at home, Germain often leading from the dining room table while Jeannette gives the responses from the kitchen. It is, taken as a whole, an orderly, sequestered, very nearly monastic way of life.

Many of their waking hours are spent on the main campus in a two-room office suite just off the college's human resources department at the second floor rear of the administration building. The rooms look out on wooded hillside; there is a sense of isolation and tranquillity. There are ceiling-high bookshelves crammed with works in philosophy and theology, file cabinets, desks, tables, chairs. There also is a good deal of state-of-the-art computer equipment, since the Grisezs have learned to put technology at the service of scholarship and now operate a kind of late twentieth century scriptorium—a computerized version of the monastery room where medieval monks labored over their manuscripts. Here *The Way of the Lord Jesus* has been taking shape for almost two decades.

Published in 1983, the first volume, *Christian Moral Principles*, runs to just over a thousand pages while the second, *Living a Christian Life*, is just under. *Christian Moral Principles* in particular is considered a daunting read. Reviewing volume two in the British magazine *New Blackfriars*, a writer called its predecessor one of "the greatest books since Vatican II NOT reviewed by this journal." According to this source, "Legend tells that the prospective reader was simply overwhelmed by it."[5] The book is a forbidding thicket that includes a table of contents running twenty pages, a nine-page "User's Guide and Preface," large-type passages with frequent bold face (meant to highlight the main thread of the argument), copious and detailed footnotes, chapter summaries, scores of chapter appendixes that in many cases are small monographs (e.g., "Immanuel Kant's theory of moral principles," "The notion of the 'common good'," "Charity as one of three theological virtues"), a glossary of terms, and a comprehensive index. The apparatus is supposed to make the book user-friendly, but, initially at least, it probably discourages some.

Still, persevering readers find the book uncommonly illuminating: not only a deeply serious probing of the Christian moral life in its many dimensions but an introduction to the entire vast terrain of Catholic theology, considered in relation to the lives of Christians. What is the book actually about? "The implications of Christian faith as a whole for Christian living," Grisez explains. This requires examining not just moral theology as it is narrowly (and traditionally) understood but also such things as dogma, the sacraments and liturgy, and prayer in relation to Christian life.

"I try to do all that in volume one," Grisez says, along with providing a detailed critique of "old-fashioned moral"—Catholic moral theology prior to Vatican Council II—and of the dissenting moral theology that has succeeded it in the postconciliar years. John R. Connery called the result "a monumental work."[6] Benedict M. Ashley said the full four-volume treatise "promises to be the most important work in the field (at least in English) to appear since Vatican II." But Ashley also sounded a cautionary note: "There is danger it will be misunderstood and slighted because it challenges so many received opinions which now dominate the teaching of Christian ethics in American Catholic seminaries and theological schools."[7] The full implications of these two volumes remain a long way from sinking in and producing the impact they are likely eventually to have.

While volume two, *Living a Christian Life*, is as massive as its predecessor, Grisez regards it as being, in genre at least, a less innovative work
("very clearly what anybody would call moral theology"). Drawing on
principles laid out in the first volume, its eleven chapters are largely self-
contained treatises on common obligations shared by Christians, (e.g.,
"Faith, Religious Assent, and Reverence for God," "Hope, Apostolate, and
Personal Vocation," "Charity, the Eucharist, and Church Membership,"
among others). Yet within this framework, the book contains numerous
surprises and controversial novelties: for example, the identification and
analysis of a basic human good called marriage,[8] and the argument (with
important pastoral implications, if true) that there are such things as
"imperfect" marriages that "both are and are not marriages."[9] In fact, the
book is dotted with passages of striking originality. For example, an
explanation of why prizefighting "cannot be justified and should not be
supported" is followed by a two-page exposition of why "others' space
and mobility should be respected"; a close discussion of Christian responsibility toward the subhuman world is succeeded by a crushing refutation
of the case for animal rights—along with a careful explanation of why
people should treat animals kindly.[10] In the light of volume two as it
actually is, a hostile reviewer's assertion that Grisez is "engaged in a
personal crusade to reinstate the theology of the preconciliar handbooks,
all based upon a single, simple reading of natural law"[11] seems merely ec-
centric.

As for volume three, a work in progress at this time, Grisez says it
will correspond to the "old-fashioned case books" of pre-Vatican II moral
theology. The work is organized in the form of answers to questions
drawn from work and the professions, family life, and other practical
contexts. Some questions come from Grisez's reading in the literature
of various fields; others are composites, but many are actual dilemmas
presented to him by real people. In developing the book, Grisez engaged
in a consultative process that involved inviting questions through letters
placed in Catholic journals as well as face-to-face discussions with individuals and groups.

The results are as uncompromising as his views on moral obligation
generally are, but it would miss the point to call them—as some critics
very likely will—products of the ivory tower. Taking *The Way of the Lord
Jesus* as a whole, Grisez says, the aim of volume three is to show how
the principles laid out in volume one apply to various special fields of
endeavor and particular life situations. Working with the second and
third volumes, he contends, other scholars with a solid grasp of his moral

theory would have no difficulty developing courses or even writing books on such matters as medical ethics, legal ethics, and the ethics of business and commerce. (Volume four—whenever in the third millennium it finally makes its appearance—will deal with the special responsibilities of clergy and religious.)

Not long after *Christian Moral Principles* was published in 1983, I asked Grisez what sort of reception he expected. "From certain points of view, the book is very vulnerable," he said.

> For one thing, it takes a tough view of theological dissent and consistently defends the Church's teaching. So it is likely to get bad reviews from dissenting theologians and those who sympathize with them. Also, it is very ambitious—necessarily so, in view of what Vatican II is asking for. But what the Council asks literally can't be done by one person, since he'd have to be expert in Scripture, dogma, Thomism, pastoral experience, contemporary theology, ethical theory, and a good deal else. Thus the book is open to criticism in detail by specialists in various fields, and the danger is that it can be torn to pieces without its being made clear what the book as a whole is trying to do. Nevertheless I am hopeful that it will be read and taken seriously by a lot of people who are interested in the subject matter. If that happens, I believe it could make quite a difference. It might encourage other people to write better books, and it might help further an authentic response to Vatican II's call for renewal.[12]

II.

I ask Grisez for a brief family history. He obliges.

Growing up during the Depression as the youngest in a family of nine children, he ate more seashell macaroni than he likes to remember. "I don't care if I never see another seashell," he says. All the same, one has the impression of a tightly knit family, with a strong sense of identity rooted in shared beliefs and commitments. Two of the sons became religious brothers and one of the daughters became a nun. The Grisez's house in the Cleveland suburb of University Heights was physically isolated from the rest of the neighborhood, and as a small child Germain seldom played with youngsters outside the family, so that, when the time came to go to school, the hurly-burly of classroom and playground struck him at first as an unpleasant change from the well-ordered atmosphere at home.

The forebears of the Grisez clan on the paternal side had come to the United States from France in the 1830s, traveled upriver from New Orleans to Ohio, and settled down to farming southeast of Cleveland.

Germain's father, William Joseph—universally known as "W. J."—worked on the family farm as a child. Trained as a bookkeeper, he went to work as a bookkeeper-accountant with a firm in Alliance, Ohio, and remained there some twenty years. In the 1920s, when the family moved to Cleveland so that the children could attend Catholic schools, W. J. became the wholesale credit manager for a manufacturer of major appliances. The family lived at first in East Cleveland, then in 1929 moved into a newly built house in University Heights. On September 30, 1929, their youngest son was born, and on October 29 the stock market crashed. The appliance manufacturer struggled on until 1933 but eventually the firm failed. One of Grisez's earliest memories is of his father coming home from his last day there.

Thereafter W. J. Grisez, like many other men in the Depression, took whatever work he could get to support his family—part-time bookkeeping for a succession of business establishments, door-to-door vacuum cleaner sales, peddling a mineral water from Toledo. All in all, he made a go of it. "My dad was a good salesman," Grisez says. "He was quiet and not pushy, not at all aggressive. He was an effective salesman because people liked him and trusted him. He was very straightforward. He was just what he seemed. He didn't talk much, and when he said anything, he really meant it." These traits carried over to W. J.'s approach to parenting. "He was really completely unselfish in his whole approach to family life. He would never, never do anything or propose to get anything for his own benefit."

On January 9, 1905, back in Alliance, W. J. Grisez had married Mary Catherine Lindesmith, whose family was of German-Swiss stock. Her education in the school run by a minister with a dim view of Catholics ended after eighth grade. Her father, a railroad switchman, had died in an accident, and thereafter the fourteen-year-old girl was needed at home to help with the younger children.

By current standards, Mary Catherine Lindesmith Grisez was not a highly educated woman; but, according to her son, "she read so much that she was really quite well educated." This reading included standard Catholic authors of the day—Newman, Chesterton, Belloc—as well as the Bible, which she knew much better than most Catholics. Her belief in learning is reflected in the fact that, although the family was hardly well-off and had no tradition of extensive schooling, much less scholarship, in its background, the Grisez children received as much education—college in most cases, graduate degrees in several—as they could use.

Germain attended a parochial school where he was taught by nuns and Cathedral Latin School, conducted by the Brothers of Mary, and in both places found at least some able instructors. ("Most schools have a few good teachers," he observes, "and it doesn't matter too much where you go if you can find the one or two teachers who are good for you and get what they can give you.") At fourteen he began working after school in the East Cleveland public library, a job that expanded to full-time in the summers. That established a pattern of working while attending school that would continue through his graduate years at the University of Chicago, when he held a full-time clerical job at night at the Federal Reserve Bank.

Graduating from high school in 1947, Grisez entered Cleveland's John Carroll University, run by the Jesuits. It was there that, intellectually speaking, significant things started happening for the young man.

In his sophomore year he encountered a youthful philosophy professor, Marshall Boarman, who had studied for his master's degree under Etienne Gilson at the University of Toronto and become an ardent Thomist. Boarman was eager to share his enthusiasm not only in the classroom but outside. He organized an informal Aquinas seminar for his better students that convened weekly in the basement of a nearby pub. There, over beer and potato chips, Germain began reading St. Thomas.

It was an eye-opening experience. "I had three or four years of accumulated curiosity from the time I was sixteen or seventeen, and Aquinas was very satisfying. Where my mother's ability to answer questions gave out, he took up. I discovered that he was very smart and that he had a lot of answers to a lot of questions I'd been wondering about." He became a philosophy major.

Senior year brought one of those vocational epiphanies that often come to serious-minded young people. Until then, Grisez had been mulling a career in journalism or law. He had also attended philosophical gatherings outside the sheltering Catholic environment of John Carroll and had encountered a largely negative attitude toward Catholic philosophy; and he was doing research for a bachelor's thesis on "Art and Beauty in Aquinas"—in fact, he was skimming widely in St. Thomas. On Christmas morning of 1949, while he was sitting quietly in the family living room, things came together:

> I had been going through the four books of the *Commentary on the Sentences of Peter Lombard*. The end of the fourth book is on the Last Things. Aquinas

has quite a good imaginative description of heaven there. I was very taken by this, and I came to the conclusion that it would be a good thing to go ahead and do philosophy—be a professional philosopher and try to teach in a state university or a non-Catholic university. A place where many Catholics go but don't have a chance to get much of what I was getting and where there are many non-Catholics who don't have anybody to argue with them about their faith or lack of it. You could do some good in a place like that. I thought it would be a worthwhile thing to do.

But first he would face the long slog of becoming a scholar. Aware that he had a great deal to learn about his revered model, Thomas Aquinas, Grisez concluded that the best place to start learning would be at the house of studies conducted in River Forest, Illinois, by the saint's brother Dominicans, many of them contributors to a new three-volume translation with commentary of the *Summa Theologiae* prepared under Dominican auspices. Today it is common for lay people to study in Catholic seminaries, but it was virtually unheard of then. How did he manage it? He supposes his application to River Forest was accepted because the Dominican reviewing it assumed that, sooner or later, the applicant would end up in the Order. Whether for that reason or simply out of a generous spirit (they are mendicants, too), the Dominicans charged him nothing. "They accepted what I was up to, and I didn't have much money," he says. Thus, in 1950–51 Grisez was a nonresident student at the Dominican College of St. Thomas Aquinas, receiving in due course both a Master of Arts and a Pontifical Licentiate in Philosophy, *summa cum laude*.

The teachers at River Forest proved to be an accomplished lot who knew their Aquinas. Particularly able was the prior, Father Edmund Marr, O.P., known as "Bunny" for his ears. Marr taught a two-semester, five-day-a-week course in the *Summa*—"probably the best course I had there," Grisez says. "He was a very solid citizen and always available—a good priest. He never bought into the idea that I was going to become a Dominican. He wasn't a clericalist nearly as much as most priests."

One day, departing from custom, the prior asked the young layman to lunch in the refectory. Rising at the end of the meal, the priest announced to the community, "This is the first case in which a student in the *studium* has announced he was getting married and remained a student in the *studium*." Says Grisez, "I think he invited me to lunch so he could make that joke."

Germain had met Jeannette Selby two years earlier, in the spring of 1949, at a parish dance. Soon they were dating regularly, and by the summer of 1950 they knew they wanted to marry; but the Korean war was on by then, Germain expected to be drafted, and River Forest lay ahead even if the Army did not. They decided to wait. In the year that followed, living in a boarding house and attending school, Germain was intensely lonely. Perhaps Jeannette was, too. On June 9, 1951, "despite everything"—no money, years of graduate school ahead, and a distinct lack of enthusiasm for the marriage on the part of both families—they were married. Germain was twenty-one.

As everyone who knows the Grisezs realizes, theirs is an exceptionally close relationship in which the ideal of complementarity—on each side a set of skills, attitudes, and personality traits that balances and meshes harmoniously with the other party's—is realized to an unusual degree. Besides successfully carrying off her roles as wife, mother, meticulous housekeeper, and admirable cook, Jeannette acts as Germain's secretary, sounding board, and commonsense critic. God alone—literally—knows how much she has contributed to his work, both directly and indirectly, over the years.

Germain once took a stab at it.

> She began helping me with my work even in the years when we had young children at home. . . . She does secretarial work, research assistance, handles correspondence and record-keeping. But more than that, it's of great importance that we live and work and pray together daily. We constantly discuss problems together. Jeannette listens, asks questions, makes comments and suggestions from her own experience. I think that for us the reality of Christian marriage as "two-in-one flesh" is carried over into everything we do. We function very much as if we were one person.[13]

As the Grisezs' friends are aware, that is no exaggeration.

Finishing up at River Forest, Grisez was still intent on teaching philosophy in a non-Catholic school. That would require getting a doctorate at such an institution, and the University of Chicago was his choice. I ask why. Because, he explains, it was a renowned institution whose philosophy department contained a lively mix of schools of thought. Given his interests, he gravitated in particular toward Richard McKeon, an eminent scholar of ancient and medieval philosophy who exercised the greatest influence on him among his Chicago professors.

Years ago a conservative Catholic friend cautioned me against Grisez because he had studied under McKeon. Apparently this bit of *ad hominem* wisdom concerned the fact that McKeon was a lapsed Catholic who at this stage of his life was, Grisez says, "just a nonbeliever." (Years later, shortly before his death, Richard McKeon returned to the Catholic

Church.) Grisez dismisses out of hand the notion that he was a bad influence. "McKeon was a nonbeliever, but almost all of the leading people who were teaching there were functionally nonbelievers. You knew that. McKeon was honest, and he wasn't an ideologue. He kept forcing you to think—a very tough teacher. But he wasn't a propagandist. I never found that anything he told me was not true." McKeon's philosophical approach, he adds, was "a subtle kind of relativism, and if you bought into that hook, line and sinker, you would have left the place without any faith. But I didn't go to Chicago to get catechized. I went there having made some effort to prepare myself and conscious that I was going to hear much that I didn't believe. And that's what I wanted; I wanted to learn how to argue with it."

One day in 1953, at the university's Newman center, Grisez met a Japanese student from Nagasaki. The young man told Grisez he had been away from home on the day that an American B-29 had dropped an atomic bomb on his city. He came home to find his school, his neighborhood, and his family gone. "Until then I'd never had any moral qualms about wiping out the enemy," Grisez recalls. The encounter was the genesis of *Nuclear Deterrence, Morality and Realism*, written with John Finnis and Joseph Boyle and published more than three decades later.[14] A reviewer has called this book "the most important contribution so far to the debate over the ethics of nuclear deterrence."[15]

At that time, however, Grisez had no idea of going into ethics. "I thought ethical theory was a vast, swampy area that wasn't philosophically very interesting," he says. With McKeon as mentor, he selected his dissertation topic: "Basic Oppositions in Logical Theory." This involved comparing *The Summary of the Whole of the Logic of Aristotle*, an influential work that once had been incorrectly attributed to Aquinas and that contains an implicit theory of knowledge and metaphysics, with Aquinas's actual views, scattered throughout his writings, and also with William of Ockham's *Summary of Logic*. His aim in pursuing this project was "to figure out how you do metaphysics"—since it was metaphysics in which he was professionally interested.

He was also interested, necessarily, in finding a job. Still planning on a career in a non-Catholic school, he sent off "probably hundreds" of inquiries to such institutions—and ran into "a good deal of resistance to the idea of hiring a Catholic who was a believer." This attitude was demonstrated in a particularly "brutal and grotesque" fashion, Grisez recalls, at a well-known midwestern school. After an apparently successful interview, the philosophy chairman drove him to the airport and there, in the coffee shop, put one more casual yet crucial question about his religious faith: "You don't really believe that stuff?"

"You bet your life I do."

"Then I'm sorry, there's nothing here for you."

Reactions elsewhere were less bluntly expressed, but Grisez got the message. Early in 1957 he sent applications to twenty-five Catholic schools. Five job offers resulted. Georgetown University proposed an assistant professorship at five thousand dollars a year, and Grisez accepted.

III.

By the time Grisez received his Ph.D. from Chicago, he had been teaching at Georgetown for two years and the last of the Grisezs' four sons had been born. Germain was twenty-nine years old. With a doctorate in hand, he was eligible to teach on the graduate level. The only graduate position then open at Georgetown, though, was in ethical theory, and so in 1959 he began working up that subject. Soon he was teaching two graduate courses, one on St. Thomas's moral philosophy, the other on the ethics of Aristotle and Kant. In these years he also read widely in Protestant moral thinkers and dialogued at length with the eminent Princeton ethicist Paul Ramsey, a Methodist, who often participated in summer programs at Georgetown.

Now, too, Grisez was beginning to draw certain conclusions about the version of ethics he found in Aquinas.

> He wasn't primarily interested in philosophy, he was interested in doing theology, and you didn't have to have a tight ethical theory and tight moral arguments in his day because in general the big arguments weren't going on in the area of ethics. So the theory in Aquinas is no more refined and perfected than it needed to be, and it didn't have to be very refined and perfected for his purposes. It's sound as far as it goes and very suggestive, but it's not honed and not worked out carefully. He's a gold mine of a starting-place, he's got a lot of good ideas, but he doesn't have any coherent overall theory of ethics, and he doesn't equip you to argue the issues and solve the problems as they've been posed in modern times.

As for ethical thinking since Thomas: "It's a lot less impressive and a lot less philosophically viable than what you've got in Aquinas."

Grisez began to think he might be able to do something about that. He had been teaching the utilitarians Bentham and Mill in an undergraduate course, and had come to the realization that they were psychological determinists: "What you choose is determined by what looks most appeal-ing." To hold this view, however, places the would-be ethicist in a rather strange position, since if what people choose is determined for them, then they have no freedom of choice. What Bentham and Mill were in fact seeking, Grisez saw, was a "strategy for socially controlling people" so that they would act in society's best interests.

These insights set him musing about why psychological determinism is a false basis for ethics. When making choices, he observed,

> It just isn't the case that one alternative is better or more appealing or seems better to you. That is *not* the experience of choice. The difficult thing about choice is that *both* alternatives are "more appealing" in *different* respects, and you need to choose because the goods and the bads don't commensu-rate—you gain something and lose something from either alternative. So the idea that the right act is the act that's going to have the better payoff is mistaken. You can't know that, and if you could know it, there wouldn't be any free choice. Any kind of ethical theory that tries to derive the rightness or wrongness of action from the calculation of good and bad consequences has got to be wrong.

Around this time, the early 1960s, the birth control debate was heating up in the Catholic Church. To the extent Grisez had given the matter any thought, he supposed that "contraception maybe isn't always wrong." Nevertheless, he read Pius XI's 1930 encyclical *Casti Connubii* in which the Pope unequivocally condemns artificial contraception. "It looks like the Church's teaching is nailed down and cast in concrete on this," he told himself. But what did that mean for the ethical theory he was beginning to conceptualize?

Wrestling with these questions, Grisez drew a diagram representing "different aspects of the well-being of the person." One's attitude of being either for or against these aspects, he had begun to think, was crucial to the moral question. Morality lay in the relationship between choice and action and the good of the human person: to be "for" the different aspects of the well-being and full-being of persons was to be "loving"; to be "against" these human goods was to be "unloving."

In 1963 Louis Dupré, a Georgetown colleague in philosophy and Flemish Belgian who had studied at the University of Louvain, returned from a visit to that important continental center of Catholic thought with the interesting suggestion that contraception is not always wrong. Grisez and Dupré, who later was to teach at Yale, discussed that at lunch one day, and after lunch Grisez invited the other philosopher into his office and showed him the diagram of human goods. "We argued all afternoon," he recalls.

A few months later, Dupré was invited to speak about contraception to a Catholic lay group that met at Georgetown. Grisez was asked to comment, and explained why he considered Dupré's arguments unsound. His remarks drew a "ferociously nasty reaction" from some members of the audience to which his faculty colleagues raised no objection. He recalls the incident as "the beginning of a kind of personal antagonism. I got mad."

In 1963–1964 he had a sabbatical. He also received tenure, was promoted to associate professor, and was awarded a Lilly postdoctoral fellowship. He wrote a long article, "Man, The Natural End of," for the *New Catholic Encyclopedia*,[16] and another long article, "The First Principle of Practical Reason," which appeared in June 1965 in the *Natural Law Forum*.[17] The latter essay he describes as "the first big technical publication where I began laying out the theory in print."

In the spring of 1964 Grisez attended the annual convention of the American Catholic Philosophical Association, in Kansas City. By then the contraception controversy was going strong. Grisez found hardly any Catholic philosophers interested in defending the Church's teaching; it occurred to him that he should further develop his own thinking on the subject and publish an article. But he hesitated. If he went into print defending Catholic teaching on birth control, he could forget about teaching in a non-Catholic school. (This was no idle dream. By now he was acquiring a modest reputation, had taught a graduate course in medieval philosophy for a year at the University of Virginia in Charlottesville, and had received an invitation, which he declined, to be visiting professor at a large university in the Midwest.) "I decided, 'Well, I ought to write the article on contraception.' " After two weeks of concentrated effort in the spring of 1964 he had produced the manuscript of a book. He polished it and, after getting pink slips from other publishers, sent it to the Bruce Publishing Company in Milwaukee, a Catholic house whose principal editor was William E. May, now an eminent theologian, a close friend, and a Grisez enthusiast. The volume was published in January 1965, as *Contraception and the Natural Law*.[18]

Its core was the laying out of Grisez's emerging ethical theory and its application to the question of contraception. In much over-simplified terms: The choice to contracept is a choice against the human good of procreation and as such can never be justified, since it is never morally right to turn one's will against a good of the person, not even for the sake of some other good. The argument was developed meticulously, accompanied by a devastating critique of inadequate "natural law" arguments against contraception (e.g., the "perverted faculty") and a similar critique of the case some Catholic moralists had lately begun to make for the practice (or at least for "the pill"). In the confusion of those days, the new oral contraceptives were sometimes thought to be morally distinguishable from older forms of contraception. The book is dedicated to William Joseph Grisez and Mary Catherine Lindesmith Grisez, "who did not prevent my life."

Canny readers recognized in *Contraception and the Natural Law* a new and potentially important voice, and this was reflected in the reviews. "In the modern controversy [over contraception]," observed the Jesuit moralist John C. Ford, "Grisez's work is the first philosophical attempt I have seen which makes a substantial, constructive contribution to an understanding of the Church's natural-law position."[19] In a long "Special Review" in *The American Ecclesiastical Review*, Jesuit Richard McCormick called the volume "an unusual book," and said "the quality of Grisez's work is a guarantee that we shall profit enormously by his further research in this area."[20] In light of their subsequent careers—Grisez as an innovative defender of received Catholic teaching, McCormick as a major figure in Catholic proportionalist dissent—there is a certain poignancy in the inscription on Grisez's file copy of this review: "To Germain—with affection and admiration. Dick, SJ."

IV.

Pope John XXIII in 1963 had established a Commission for the Study of Problems of the Family, Population, and Birth Rate to advise the Vatican Secretariat of State on positioning the Holy See as a participant in the international discussion of population. In June 1964, Pope Paul VI enlarged the commission and expanded its mandate. As he did, the internal Catholic debate over birth control burst into the open. Was the Pope contemplating a change in the Church's teaching? Might not the pill at least be approved? With change in the air, thanks to the Second Vatican Council then under way, the very existence of the Birth Control Commission (as it became known immediately and forever) seemed to suggest intriguing possibilities.

In the spring of 1965 the expanded commission held its first plenary session in Rome. One of its lay members returned to the United States and shared startling news with a number of interested parties, among them Grisez: about a third of the theologians on the commission held that the Church's position on birth control had to change, another third believed that at least it was subject to change, and the rest argued that the teaching as it stood was true and therefore could not change. Grisez's informant also shared with him the meeting's written report. Having read it, Grisez called John Ford and said, "Let's talk."

Perhaps the most distinguished of the pre-Vatican II American moralists, John C. Ford, S.J., was then teaching at the Catholic University of America. He had read Grisez's contraception manuscript before publication and, as noted, had favorably reviewed the book. In expanding the birth control commission, Pope Paul had named him to it.

From June 1965 on, Grisez collaborated closely with Ford on commission-related work. The collaboration continued after the Pope, in early 1966, reconstituted the body, naming the nonbishops (theologians, physicians, demographers) *periti*—advisors—and restricting membership to sixteen cardinals and bishops. Grisez spent June and early July of that year in Rome working with Father Ford—"drafting stuff, criticizing stuff." (One of the documents they produced was a rebuttal of the document that in time would be called the commission's "majority report" favoring change. Of the commission documents that have been printed, Grisez says dourly that they are "only a small and not very representative part" of the whole—understandably so, since what to publish and what to hold back has been determined by the supporters of contraception.)

All this points to an obvious question, and eventually I ask it: What really was the role of Pope Paul VI? Grisez has no doubt that the Pope believed from the start that contraception is wrong. "What he wasn't sure about was whether the pill is a contraceptive in the traditional, condemned sense." Worried about overpopulation in some areas, Paul thought oral contraception might be a solution, and therefore was "inclined to approve it if possible." Nevertheless, Grisez says, as Vatican II was nearing its end in later 1965:

> Paul VI wanted *Gaudium et Spes* [the Pastoral Constitution on the Church in the Modern World] to say clearly that "contraception is always wrong." That would leave the question about the pill for him to decide. He had Ford and a bishop draft some amendments, and they were sent over to the Council commission around Thanksgiving time. Then there was a big scramble: 'Can we put these in our own words?' By the time they got done doing that, they had changed the meaning of the amendments so that it was no longer clear they were saying contraception is always wrong. So *Gaudium et Spes* came out rather ambiguous in the end.

What the document says, in fact, is that the "sons of the Church" are "forbidden to use methods disapproved by the teaching authority of the Church in its interpretation of the divine law"; a footnote here cites *Casti Connubii* and two allocutions by Pope Pius XII. The footnote adds that "certain questions requiring further and more careful investigation" had been turned over by Paul to a commission, and the Pope would announce his decision in due course. Thus: "With the teaching of the magisterium standing as it is, the Council has no intention of proposing concrete solutions at the moment."[21] Whatever all this was supposed to mean, it naturally had the practical effect of inflaming speculation.

Long before the publication of *Humanae Vitae*, Grisez had concluded that just as contraception had triumphed in secular society, so, practically speaking, it would also triumph—indeed, was already well on its way to triumphing—among Catholics, regardless of what the Pope finally said. He began research for two more books, one on abortion and the other on nuclear deterrence. He was working on the abortion book in the summer of 1968 when *Humanae Vitae* came out. Pope Paul had reached his decision. The condemnation of contraception stood, with no exceptions for the pill or anything else.

Earlier that year, attending an abortion conference at Louvain, Grisez had found the groundwork for theological dissent in the event of such an outcome already laid in Europe. It quickly became clear that dissent in the United States would also be widespread and fierce. For several reasons, the Archdiocese of Washington, D.C., rapidly became a center and focal point for this dissent: it had a concentration of procontraception theologians; a substantial number of archdiocesan priests immediately announced that they intended to set aside the teaching of *Humanae Vitae* in their pastoral practice; and Cardinal Patrick O'Boyle of Washington was a staunch defender of the encyclical. O'Boyle, a crusty Irish-American with a gruff demeanor and a warm heart, took an uncomplicated view of the situation: the Pope had solemnly restated the clear teaching of the Church, and it was his duty as a bishop to uphold that teaching and see that his priests did the same.

O'Boyle called in John Ford to help, and Ford called in Grisez. By the end of the week the two men had a pastoral letter ready to go in the Cardinal's name. It was Friday afternoon. The chancery staff, accustomed to a less frantic pace, maintained that the document could not possibly be issued until the following week. Grisez argued that it needed to be out that weekend. The Cardinal agreed, and the staff suddenly found ways to get the job done. Afterward, the two men were left alone in

O'Boyle's office. Grisez, his voice growing husky, recalls: "He said, 'You'd make a better bishop than I am,' and he put his pectoral cross on me. I handed it back to him and said, 'No, you're the bishop and I'll help.' Then we all went over to the Mayflower Hotel and had dinner."

At O'Boyle's urging, Grisez was given a leave of absence from Georgetown to work full-time for him. Ford having returned to his duties in Massachusetts, Grisez was the principal theological advisor on matters pertaining to the birth control controversy in Washington. His work involved extensive negotiations with the dissenting priests, critiquing the National Conference of Catholic Bishop's collective pastoral letter *Human Life in Our Day*, published in November 1968, in response to *Humanae Vitae*,[22] helping to establish a new national entity, the Human Life Foundation, to foster the understanding and practice of Natural Family Planning, and drafting replies for the Cardinal to the "piles and piles of letters" that poured in. Grisez was able to return to work on the abortion book in the spring of 1969 and to resume teaching at Georgetown in the fall; but he continued part-time work for Cardinal O'Boyle until 1972.

In time, the dissenting Washington priests—those of them, that is, who had elected to remain in active ministry—appealed their case to the Roman Rota, the Church's chief appellate court. Pope Paul removed the case from the Rota and turned it over to the Congregation for the Clergy for what Grisez calls an "administrative-pastoral solution."

Would it be fair, I ask, to say that the rug was pulled out from under Cardinal O'Boyle? Instead of answering directly, Grisez notes that the Washington dispute did not concern theology but centered on "faculties"—under what conditions the dissenting priests, now dwindled in number from fifty-four to a remnant of about fifteen, would be allowed to preach, teach, and hear confessions in the archdiocese. Responses to *Humanae Vitae* on the part of bishops' conferences and individual bishops were now in, and the picture they produced was one of "open, obvious conflict among the bishops about contraception and conscience, the authority of the teaching, and so on," Grisez notes. Instead of risking further, and possibly worse, conflict by confronting this state of affairs, he says, Pope Paul apparently decided to calm things down.

Against this background the Washington case came to its inglorious conclusion. The Congregation for the Clergy apparently was instructed to find a pastoral solution. The result was a statement that seemed to say all the right things but gave the game away by requiring restoration of the faculties if the priests merely agreed to insist that Catholics whom they dealt with in the matter of contraception be "guided by objective moral norms."[23] One night shortly before its publication Grisez argued with Cardinal O'Boyle until well past midnight, urging him to fly to Rome to remonstrate with the Pope and even threaten resignation if need be. "I just can't do that with the Pope," O'Boyle said. Says Grisez: "That was the sad ending of that episode."

V.

Abortion: The Myths, the Realities, and the Arguments was published in December 1970. It confirmed Grisez's reputation as a meticulous scholar and innovative thinker.[24] Wrote one reviewer: "Professor Grisez has exhaustively analyzed the problem in all its significant facets. . . . It is a mine of soundly penetrating ethical analysis."[25] And another: "It is by far the most comprehensive and penetrating discussion of the abortion question."[26] Richard McCormick remarked, "It is impossible to read this book without being enlightened," though he leavened his review in *America* with his emerging proportionalism.[27]

By now Grisez had returned to full-time teaching at Georgetown. His work with Cardinal O'Boyle had made him unpopular with some of his colleagues, but tenure gave him job security, and he had not only lost some friends but also made some new ones. Was it an uncomfortable situation on balance? Not especially, he insists. "I don't feel uncomfortable being in a room full of people all thinking one way and standing up and saying I disagree and why. That doesn't bother me in the least. I feel rather good about it. What some people mistake for courage just comes naturally to me."

But there were problems. Quite apart from the birth control controversy or anything pertaining especially to Grisez, the Georgetown philosophy department was a conflicted place in those years, its members divided over a variety of policy issues, and Georgetown, like other schools, was suffering the ill effects of the campus revolution of the 1960s. Grisez's approach to the hottest issue of all, Vietnam, did not help. "I was against the Vietnam war," he recalls, "but I took the position that if you really thought it was wrong, you should refuse to serve or go to Canada. But to go out and protest and make all kinds of noise and then, if you got drafted, go and kill people—that's outrageous. The students didn't like that position."

At this juncture, Grisez received an offer from Campion College, a Catholic institution within the University of Regina in Regina, Saskatchewan. Though by now he was a full professor at Georgetown, with a sabbatical coming up, the proposal offered a number of advantages: a lighter teaching load, a relaxed atmosphere and more time to write, a way finally to realize his old dream of teaching in a non-Catholic setting. Leaving the two older Grisez sons in Washington by their choice, the family moved to Regina, where Grisez taught at Campion from 1972 to 1978.

He recalls those years as satisfying on the whole. "In general the atmosphere was more friendly and very relaxed." The period also was exceptionally productive for his writing: *Beyond the New Morality: The Responsibilities of Freedom*, coauthored with the present writer and published in 1974;[28] *Beyond the New Theism: A Philosophy of Religion*, a highly creative work published in 1975;[29] with John Finnis, the four chapters on morality in *The Teaching of Christ: A Catholic Catechism for Adults*, a very successful postconciliar catechism first published in 1976 and still selling briskly today;[30] *Free Choice: A Self-Referential Argument*, written with Joseph M. Boyle, Jr., and Olaf Tollefsen, also published in 1976;[31] a 1977 article on "Dualism and the New Morality," which Grisez remarks with satisfaction "has gotten around quite a lot" ("Nobody wants to make the kind of argument the majority were making on the birth control commission after I nailed it");[32] with John Ford, S.J., a long, seminal article "Contraception and the Infallibility of the Ordinary Magisterium," published in *Theological Studies* in 1978;[33] *Life and Death with Liberty and Justice: A Contribution to the Euthanasia Debate*, also written with Boyle and published in 1979.[34]

As this list suggests, collaboration is an important part of Grisez's way of working. Two of these relationships stand out for their importance in the development of his thought, namely, those with Finnis and Boyle. In speaking of the two men, Grisez is at pains to make sure each gets his due.

As a graduate student at Georgetown in the late 1960s Boyle had studied under Grisez, and the two kept in touch after Boyle graduated in 1970 and began teaching philosophy (since 1986 at St. Michael's College, University of Toronto). Soon they were collaborators, working on *Free Choice* and then on what was to be *Life and Death with Liberty and Justice*. Grisez credits Boyle with a major role in the development of the ethical theory as a whole and in the refinement of Grisez's theory of action ("a human act is essentially the carrying-out of a choice, and what the act is, is defined primarily by what you are choosing to do"). Later, in the summer of 1978, Boyle spent weeks working with Grisez on the general plan and outline for the first volume of *The Way of the Lord Jesus*. They have continued to work together since.

Of Boyle's overall contribution to what sometimes is called the New Natural Law Theory, Grisez comments: "A lot of people talk about this as being the Grisez-Finnis theory. Basically, it's the Grisez-Boyle theory through the summer of 1978." In practical terms, he credits the younger man with analytical skills he lacks. "I can't figure out the questions to ask a lot of times. But if he keeps pushing questions at me, I usually come up with answers. Somehow they come out of somewhere."

John Finnis, now a professor of jurisprudence at Oxford and of law at Notre Dame, had read *Contraception and the Natural Law* soon after his conversion to Roman Catholicism, then later read *Abortion* and sent Grisez an appreciative note. Grisez and Finnis met in 1974, when they worked together in Rome on the morals chapters of *The Teaching of Christ*. Five years later, deeply into preparatory work on *The Way of the Lord Jesus*, Grisez spent Easter Week with Finnis at Oxford, digging into the documents of the Second Vatican Council. Thereafter their collaboration—more theological than philosophical, according to Grisez—has been close and continuing, resulting (among other things) in *Nuclear Deterrence, Morality and Realism*, coauthored with Boyle. Grisez also credits Finnis with a significant influence on "the shape of the arguments" in volume two of *The Way*. In 1987, in the *American Journal of Jurisprudence*, the three men published an important article, "Practical Principles, Moral Truth, and Ultimate Ends," carefully laying out their views in response to common misunderstandings by Thomist critics.

Besides influencing the development of Grisez's thought, the association with Finnis, a professor at glamorous Oxford, has brought Grisez more attention—and more criticism. Once Finnis began to publish important work of his own in which he acknowledged a major debt to Grisez's thinking, others working in the natural law tradition were obliged to take note of this upstart theory, allegedly grounded in Aquinas but also departing from him in significant respects.

I asked Grisez what he makes of criticism from these sources. For almost the first time in our conversation, he gives a safe, political answer: "It stimulates you into thinking, forces you to work things out. In that sense, all critics make a contribution." Then combativeness reasserts itself: "Most of the critics haven't really tried to understand the theory. In general, the critics come to your stuff with a very vague idea of what's going on, but they know that they don't like it, that they disagree with it. So they look at it to find the evidence that you are holding these wrong positions—evidence they can use to indict you and convict you and put you down."

VI.

Working on *The Teaching of Christ* in the mid-1970s (besides writing the chapters on morals with Finnis, he also read and commented on two drafts of the entire catechism), Grisez "began to see theology as a unified whole" in a way he had not before. He also began to see something else. "It became clearer and clearer to me that we needed a better moral theology."

But that was somebody else's job. He was a philosopher, not a theologian. Speaking to others, though, he found no one interested in tackling the project he now was sure needed doing. "So I began to think, 'Maybe I need to do this.'" Even at this early stage, it also was clear that, to write a moral theology text, he would have to be at a seminary: the book would be aimed, in the first instance, at men in training to be priests, and he had to teach and work with that audience to have a feel for them. There were also practical considerations such as library resources and access to collaborators. The time was at hand to think of leaving Regina and starting anew.

In the spring of 1977 Grisez began writing to possible sources of support. One of these was Bishop John B. McDowell, Auxiliary of Pittsburgh, to whom, as chairman of an *ad hoc* committee of the National Conference of Catholic Bishops responsible for writing the bishops' 1976 collective pastoral letter on morality, *To Live in Christ Jesus*, he had provided much-appreciated advice. Taking enthusiastically to the idea, McDowell began contacting sources of his own: other bishops, the Knights of Columbus, the De Rance Foundation. Meanwhile Grisez was talking to seminaries. While he was on a February 1978 visit to Mount Saint Mary's, Dr. Robert Wickenheiser, then president, offered him the newly endowed Reverend Harry J. Flynn Chair of Christian Ethics, named for the seminary rector, a supporter of the Grisez project (now Archbishop of St. Paul and Minneapolis). The offer contained a teaching post tailored to his needs and other attractive physical and financial arrangements. Grisez said yes.

At a time when Catholic seminaries typically are scratching for students, "The Mount" is crowded. Many bishops appreciate its reputation for orthodoxy and a sound formation program. This particular morning, before Germain and I started work, he, Jeannette, and I attended Mass in the seminary chapel. The summer break is on; hardly anyone else is there. Walking down one of the old building's long, half-paneled corridors after Mass, we come to a large classroom with a sign over the door saying "Theology Two." The room is crowded with the clutter of students away for the summer: lamps, radios, CD players, boxes of books. "I give my classes here," he says.

Some years ago, in another interview, I asked him what his view of seminaries was. Perhaps the answer reflects something of what he would like to accomplish as a teacher of seminarians.

> Seminaries in their present form are largely the creation of the Council of Trent, and Trent was dealing with the problems of its time when many priests were hardly trained at all. The seminary system instituted by Trent represented a high ideal, but in the centuries since then professional education generally has emerged and developed a great deal. As a result, we need a renewal of seminaries which meets the needs of our times as Trent's renewal did in the sixteenth century. Ideally, I would like to see the seminary program geared much more to developing scholar-priests. Why? Because basically a priest has two jobs to do—administering the sacraments and teaching, through homilies and other means. Of course the objection is that if you look at the priesthood as a kind of "scholarly" profession, you will have very few priests, as you have very few scholars generally. Still, I think priests now are required to spend a great deal of their time on things priests as such don't have to do, such as administration and running various organizations and activities. Furthermore, if people with the aptitude to be scholar-priests were encouraged to see the priesthood in that light, more of them might be attracted to the priesthood.[35]

Although American seminaries undoubtedly turn out some scholarly priests, this vision is far from being generally accepted, much less realized. Indeed, as the shortage of priests becomes more acute, pressure is likely to grow to ordain men simply to plug personnel gaps in parishes and other institutions of the Church. This has implications for what Grisez is doing. Already, one frequently heard criticism of *The Way of the Lord Jesus* is that it is too much for seminarians (as well as for many other people, of course): too long, too complex, too comprehensive, too carefully reasoned and closely argued, too innovative.[36] Grisez continues to pursue his project in his own way.

VII.

Time is running out on our interview. I need to drive back to Washington. Germain wants to attend the college's late-afternoon graduation Mass. I ask him to assess his work. What actually is new about the New Natural Law Theory?

Its "most novel" element, he replies, is the identification and elaboration of those intermediate principles of morality, eight in number, that he calls modes of responsibility. St. Thomas Aquinas pointed to general principles like love of God and neighbor, along with many specific moral norms; the modes lie in between general principles and specific norms, and lead from the one to the other. In *Christian Moral Principles* Grisez writes: "These modes are more definite than the basic principle of morality,[37] yet they are more general than the moral norms regarding specific kinds of acts to which they lead. Each mode excludes a certain unreasonable way of willing, a particular way of acting which is inconsistent with a will toward integral human fulfillment."[38] Here, he holds, is "the most important and original contribution" of the theory.

Also, he continues, "I've got a story about the end of human life"—an account partly philosophical and partly theological—which "theologically is probably the most important element of the theory. If the critics noticed it more, they'd like it less." This, briefly, is a certain understanding of "the kingdom," that state of human persons and the rest of creation, destined to be realized at the end of time yet already incipiently present in history in and through Christ, which will involve both the integral fulfillment of men and women in respect to human goods and also their sharing in a common life with God. Grisez explains: "Created persons have their own created natures, and they are to live richly and fully in accord with those natures. But they also really are to share in the divine nature and to live richly and fully in accord with divine nature with the divine persons." Moreover, the goods of the person, the fundamental human goods, will be part of the kingdom, though in a perfected and fulfilled condition unimaginable by us now.

This insight may contain the key to remedying once and for all the age-old Christian tendency to make a dichotomy between this world and its goods on the one hand and, on the other, the next world and human fulfillment therein. In that dichotomy, inevitably, this world and the goods of the human person come off a poor second—a circumstance not only giving rise to a persistent strain of exaggerated Christian *contemptus mundi* but also, over the last half-millennium or so, contributing not a little to the rise, by way of reaction, of modern secular humanism. Novel as Grisez's approach may seem, its seeds can be found in the teaching of the Second Vatican Council, specifically in sections 38 and 39 of *Gaudium et Spes*: "For after we have promoted on earth, in the Spirit of the Lord and in accord with his command, the goods of human dignity, familial communion, and freedom—that is to say, all the good fruits of our nature and effort—then we shall find them once more, but cleansed of all dirt, lit up, and transformed, when Christ gives back to the Father an eternal and universal kingdom. . . ." Grisez's great contribution has been to take this seriously and begin to explain what it means.[39]

Grisez is still listing contributions, and now it is his action theory and its relevance to a theological understanding of the Redemption and our participation in it. One of the fundamental tenets of his understanding of human acts—moral acts, acts of human free choice—is that they "last," they perdure. So, in the case of the Redemption, he says now, "Jesus' act of dying and rising from the dead lasts, and it is there for our cooperation in the sacraments. That's really original, really a contribution to theology, and hardly anybody has paid attention to it yet."[40]

It is not a long list. Others would add things like his treatment of the fundamental goods of the person, his identification of the modes of Christian response that make Christian morality distinctive,[41] his elaboration of the concept of personal vocation,[42] and of course his arguments regarding specific moral questions from contraception through nuclear deterrence. Taken as a whole, Grisez's work constitutes an exceptionally rich source of ideas and insights waiting to be mined.

Despite that—or possibly because of it—he is surprisingly dismissive regarding his influence. In conversation not long ago a journalist who is a friend of mine, echoing what others have said, referred to Grisez's "vindication" by the Magisterium; others, not at all friendly, claim to see his hand in Pope John Paul II's encyclicals on moral principles *Veritatis splendor* (1993) and on human life *Evangelium vitae* (1995). Grisez does not set much stock in that. *Veritatis splendor* does take the goods of the person as fundamental moral principles—something new for a magisterial document to do—and he supposes that in a general way that reflects the influence of his work and the work of people like Finnis and William May; also, the Pope's treatment of the Beatitudes as setting out a version of the moral life applicable to all Christians without exception resembles his thinking.[43] Otherwise he does not find much of himself there. As for *Evangelium vitae*: "Almost no influence whatsoever."

In the academic world and the Church at large, Grisez appears to have made his presence felt to a real but limited degree up to now. Besides a core of fervent admirers who acknowledge their debt to him and use his thought in their own teaching and writing, there is a more numerous body upon whom Grisez has had at least some effect (one thinks, for instance, of the frequency with which Catholic writing on morality these days speaks of "human goods" and "goods of the person"). Perhaps the only sector of contemporary Catholic moral thought that, with a very few exceptions, systematically ignores Grisez is occupied by dissenters. As for the Church, an admiring former student reviewing *Christian Moral Principles*, once remarked: "If enough of our future priests can be brought to see what is at stake here and are willing to master this book as best they can, its pastoral influence will be great indeed."[44] That may be happening in some places, but if so it is happening slowly indeed.

Grisez is unusually detached—even disengaged—about such matters. Using a formulation that students of his work would recognize as an element of his moral theory, he says: "My overall project isn't that I've got a particular state of affairs in mind that I want to accomplish." It was not always that way. He recalls leaving the May 1968 abortion conference at Louvain deeply discouraged by the evidence of dissent he had found among Catholic intellectuals there not only on birth control but even, to some extent, on abortion. On the way home he stayed overnight with a priest-friend in London. "I woke up very early with the light flooding the room, and I was thinking about this. And it occurred to me, 'Well, the whole thing is providential, and you can't really figure out where what you're doing fits in or what good it's going to do. But that shouldn't really concern you too much. It's all going to come out right in the end.' And beginning to think of things that way made it possible for me to do everything I've done since then."

If that sounds Pollyannish, Grisez's view of the state of the Church is a blunt, harsh corrective. Conditions in Catholicism worldwide, he believes, are very bad, with a kind of "artificial unity" masking confusion and dissent not only on moral questions but on fundamental dogmas like Jesus' bodily resurrection and the real presence of Christ in the Eucharist. The problem extends not only to the simple faithful and the theologians but to people in authority. Much will depend on the next Pope. Grisez's preferred approach would see the Pope summoning the bishops to Rome to discuss some point of dogma—the real presence, the resurrection—so that, having heard various points of view argued by competent theologians, the representatives of the Magisterium might then proceed to consider the question among themselves and come to a decision—"settle it." Says Grisez: "Doing that would transform the situation. It would begin to pull the Church together and would make it clear what it is to be a theologian and what it is to be a bishop. The proper roles of theologians and bishops have not been clear. The role of theologians is pretty much to look at things freely and argue for what they think. But for that to work well, the bishops have to do their job."

Meanwhile the Church is in crisis, and the condition of moral theology is particularly bad. Pope John Paul II, to his credit, is "dealing constantly with morality as a matter of truth"—for example, in *Veritatis splendor*—while also speaking of Christian humanism. Says Grisez appreciatively: "That's light years away from how it would have been looked at in the old days, and I don't think it's going to go away. If the Church gets itself straightened out . . ." As for his own efforts: "What I'm doing is coming along and getting picked up in a few places." Still, the overall picture is bleak. The renewal of moral theology for which Vatican II called "isn't happening." And: "On the whole, a dissenting moral is prevailing around the world. If I had been thinking about fighting and winning some kind of war, the whole thing would be completely impossible. You just couldn't do it. I don't have the status, I don't have the power. I haven't accomplished that much."

Given the current crisis in the Church, I suggest, the most encouraging aspect of the present situation may be that post-Enlightenment secular humanism is intellectually exhausted and falling apart. Grisez agrees with this, but relates it at once to his own thinking. "The big picture I've got is that Judaeo-Christian faith eliminates all of the other gods and gives human beings a unique sense of their dignity. But it also has this terrible downside, that it makes demands on you. This is particularly tough for the rich, the powerful, the ambitious, the pleasure-loving." Further complicating matters is the neo-Platonist strain of other-worldliness in Christianity against which secular humanism so disastrously rebelled several centuries back. "More and more it's nonbelievers who set the framework, determine the agenda, establish the public culture. . . . If there is no God, you've got to be a consequentialist and do your best. That's not a bad position for somebody who doesn't believe in anything. And an awful lot of people who think they believe in God really don't believe in anything, because it doesn't have any practical effect. Whereas faith is telling you, 'You're cooperating with God but you hardly know what his plan is.' And you've got to do his will without seeing good results—not killing the baby, not contracepting, sticking to a marriage when it seems impossible. It's terribly difficult. . . . If Christianity is going to survive at all, it's going to survive among people who are very tough and very clear-headed, and there don't seem to be many of these around."

Time has run out. "No one will ever accuse us of optimism," I say.

"No," Germain says, "I'm afraid not. I'm not optimistic."

Back at the house, as I prepare to leave, Germain is donning his academic robe for the graduation Mass, at which honorary degrees will be conferred. Jeannette is helping.

"You look like a real professor," I say.

"Don't you wish you could get dressed up like this and be hot and sweaty?"

"I haven't had one of those on in years."

"We'll wear them when we get *our* honorary degrees," he teases, heading for the door.

NOTES

1. Robert P. George, "Moral Theology: Towards Renewal, Not Restoration," *Lay Witness*, vol. 15, no. 2 (October 1993).

2. Russell Shaw, "He Ties Morality to Christ and Scripture," *Columbia*, December, 1983.

3. Vatican Council II, Decree on the Training of Priests, *Optatam Totius*, 16, in Austin Flannery, O.P., gen. ed., *Vatican Council II: The Conciliar and Post Conciliar Documents*, vol. 1 (Collegeville, MN: The Liturgical Press, 1984), 720.

4. *The Way of the Lord Jesus*, vol. 1, *Christian Moral Principles* (Chicago: Franciscan Herald Press, 1983), 141–171, 871–916.

5. Anthony Fisher, O.P., review of *Living a Christian Life, New Blackfriars*, vol. 75, no. 881 (April 1994).

6. John R. Connery, S.J., review of *Christian Moral Principles, Theological Studies*, vol. 45, no. 4 (December 1984).

7. Benedict M. Ashley, O.P., "Review Discussion" of *Christian Moral Principles, The Thomist*, 48, July 1984.

8. *The Way of the Lord Jesus*, vol. 2, *Living a Christian Life* (Quincy, IL: Franciscan Press, 1993), 567–569.

9. Ibid., 590–595.

10. Ibid., 550–552, 771–787.

11. Joseph A. Selling, review of *Living a Christian Life, Louvain Studies*, vol. 18, no. 4 (winter 1993).

12. Shaw, "He Ties Morality to Christ and Scripture."

13. Ibid.

14. John Finnis, Joseph M. Boyle, Jr., Germain Grisez, *Nuclear Deterrence, Morality and Realism* (New York: Oxford University Press, 1987).

15. J.M. Cameron, "Is Nuclear Deterrence Moral?" (review of *Nuclear Deterrence, Morality and Realism*), *The New York Review of Books*, vol. 34, no. 17 (November 5, 1987).

16. *New Catholic Encyclopedia*, vol. 9, 132–138.

17. *Natural Law Forum*, vol. 10 (1965), 168–201; abridged in Anthony Kenny ed., *Modern Studies in Philosophy: Aquinas: A Collection of Critical Essays* (Garden City, NY: Doubleday, 1969, 340–382); reprinted unabridged in John Finnis ed., *The International Library of Essays in Law and Legal Theory: Natural Law*, vol. 1 (Aldershot, England: Dartmouth Publishing Co., 1991), 191–224.

18.   *Contraception and The Natural Law* (Milwaukee: The Bruce Publishing Company, 1964).

19.   *The Modern Schoolman*, vol. 43, no. 4 (May 1966).

20.   *American Ecclesiastical Review* vol. 153, no. 2 (August 1965).

21.   Vatican Council II, Pastoral Constitution on the Church in the Modern World, *Gaudium et Spes*, 51, in Flannery, vol. 1, 955.

22.   In Hugh J. Nolan, ed., *Pastoral Letters of the United States Catholic Bishops*, vol. 3, 1962–1974 (Washington: United States Catholic Conference, 1983), 164–194.

23.   In Austin Flannery, O.P., ed., *Vatican Council II: The Conciliar and Post Conciliar Documents*, vol. 2 (Collegeville, MN: The Liturgical Press, 1984), 420.

24.   *Abortion: The Myths, The Realities, and the Arguments* (New York: Corpus Publications, 1970).

25.   Charles E. Rice, *Notre Dame Lawyer*, vol. 6, no. 4 (summer 1971).

26.   Ronald D. Lawler, O.F.M.Cap., *The Thomist*, vol. 35, no. 2 (April 1971).

27.   Richard A. McCormick, S.J., *America* (April 17, 1971): "But are the basic values he [Grisez] adduces really absolutely incommensurable? . . . the problem is not so much that some calculus is made or has to be. Rather it is establishing the full Christian context within which it is to be made. That is, perhaps the problem is not being a utilitarian but being a bad one."

28.   *Beyond the New Morality* (Notre Dame, IN: University of Notre Dame Press, 1974); 3rd rev. ed. 1988.

29.   *Beyond the New Theism: A Philosophy of Religion* (Notre Dame and London: University of Notre Dame Press, 1975).

30.   Ronald D. Lawler, O.F.M.Cap., Donald W. Wuerl, Thomas Comerford Lawler eds., *The Teaching of Christ: A Catholic Catechism for Adults* (Huntington, IN: Our Sunday Visitor, 1976), 275–354.

31.   *Free Choice: A Self-Referential Argument* (Notre Dame and London: University of Notre Dame Press, 1976).

32.   "Dualism and the New Morality," *Atti del Congresso Internazionale Tommaso d'Aquino nel suo Settimo Centenario (Roma-Napoli, 17–24 aprile 1974)*, vol. 5, *L'Agire Morale* (Naples: Edizioni Domenicane Italiane, 1977), 323–330.

33.   "Contraception and the Infallibility of the Ordinary Magisterium," *Theological Studies*, vol. 39 (1978), 258–312. Reprinted in John C. Ford, S.J., Germain Grisez, Joseph Boyle, John Finnis, William E. May, *The Teaching of 'Humanae Vitae': A Defense* (San Francisco: Ignatius Press, 1988), 117–219. Simply put, the Ford-Grisez thesis is that the doctrine on contraception contained in *Humanae Vitae* had in fact been proposed by the Ordinary Magisterium of the pope and the bishops in union with him in a manner that satisfies the criteria for an infallible exercise of the Ordinary Magisterium as these are set forth in Vatican Council II's Dogmatic Constitution on the Church, *Lumen Gentium*, 25. If this is correct, it has profound implications, not only for the teaching on contraception but also for a great deal more of the Catholic Church's moral teaching.

34.   Germain Grisez and Joseph M. Boyle, Jr., *Life and Death with Liberty and Justice: A Contribution to the Euthanasia Debate* (Notre Dame and London: University of Notre Dame Press, 1979).

35.   Shaw, "He Ties Morality to Christ and Scripture."

36.   In 1991 Grisez and the present writer published a popularization of *Christian Moral Principles* intended to make its central ideas accessible to a larger

audience: *Fulfillment in Christ* (Notre Dame and London: University of Notre Dame Press, 1991).

37. Formulated by Grisez this way: "In voluntarily acting for human goods and avoiding what is opposed to them, one ought to choose and otherwise will those and only those possibilities whose willing is compatible with a will toward integral human fulfillment." *Christian Moral Principles*, 184.

38. *Christian Moral Principles*, 205. The modes of responsibility include such principles as, "one should not be deterred by felt inertia from acting for intelligible goods," "one should not, in response to different feelings toward different persons, willingly proceed with a preference for anyone unless the preference is required by intelligible goods themselves" (the Golden Rule), "one should not be moved by a stronger desire for one instance of an intelligible good to act for it by choosing to destroy, damage, or impede some other instance of an intelligible good."

39. See *Christian Moral Principles*, chapters 19, 34.

40. See especially *Christian Moral Principles*, chapters 22, 30.

41. Ibid., chapter 26.

42. See especially *Christian Moral Principles*, chapters 27, 31; *Living a Christian Life*, chapter 2.

43. *Veritatis splendor*, 16–18.

44. William Ryan, "The Moral Thought of Germain Grisez," *National Catholic Register*, June 24, 1984.

Contributors

WILLIAM E. MAY is Michael J. McGivney Professor of Moral Theology at the John Paul II Institute for Marriage and the Family in Washington, D.C. He is author of many books and articles, including *An Introduction to Moral Theology* (revised edition, 1994).

BENEDICT ASHLEY, O.P., is Professor of Moral Theology at Aquinas Institute of Theology, St. Louis, Missouri, and the author, with Kevin D. O'Rourke of *Ethics of Health Care* (2nd edition, 1994) and *Healthcare Ethics* (4th edition, 1997).

EDWARD C. VACEK, S.J., is Paul McKeever Professor of Moral Theology at St. John's University in Jamaica, New York, and Associate Professor at the Weston School of Theology in Cambridge, Massachusetts. He is author of *Love, Human and Divine: The Heart of Christian Life* (1994).

KEVIN FLANNERY, S.J., is Professor of Philosophy at the Pontifical Gregorian University in Rome. He is author of *Ways into the Logic of Alexander of Aphrodisias* (1995).

RALPH MCINERNY is Grace Professor of Philosophy and Director of the Jacques Maritain Center at the University of Notre Dame, South Bend, Indiana. He is author of many philosophical works, including *Ethica Thomistica* (1982).

PATRICK LEE is Professor of Philosophy at the Franciscan University of Steubenville, Steubenville, Ohio. He is author of *Abortion and Unborn Human Life* (1995).

GERARD V. BRADLEY is Professor of Law at the University of Notre Dame. He is author of *Church-State Relationships in America* (1987), and coauthor (with Robert P. George) of "Marriage and the Liberal Imagination" in the *Georgetown Law Journal* (1995).

JOHN FINNIS is Professor of Law and Legal Philosophy at Oxford University and Biolchini Professor of Law at the University of Notre

Dame. Among his many books are *Natural Law and Natural Rights* (1980) and *Aquinas: Social, Legal and Political Thought* (1998).

GERMAIN GRISEZ is Harry Flynn Professor of Christian Ethics at Mt. St. Mary's College in Emmitsburg, Maryland. He is author of the multivolume work *The Way of the Lord Jesus: Vol. 1, Christian Moral Principles* (1983); *Vol. 2, Living a Christian Life* (1993); and Vol. 3, Difficult Moral Questions (1997).

JOSEPH M. BOYLE, JR., is Principal and Professor of Philosophy at St. Michael's College, University of Toronto, Ontario, Canada. He is author of important articles in journals such as *Ethics* and the *American Journal of Jurisprudence* and coauthor (with Germain Grisez and John Finnis) of *Nuclear Deterrence, Morality, and Realism* (1987).

ROBERT P. GEORGE is Associate Professor of Politics at Princeton University and a presidential appointee to the United States Commission on Civil Rights. He is author of *Making Men Moral: Civil Liberties and Public Morality* (1993) and editor of *Natural Law, Liberalism, and Morality* (1996).

RUSSELL SHAW is a writer and consultant. He has served as Director of Communications for the Knights of Columbus and is coauthor (with Germain Grisez) of *Beyond the New Morality* (Third Edition, 1988).

Index